Acclaim for *Mestizos Come Home!*

✳✳✳

"This visionary book celebrates the social and cultural contributions Latinos and Latinas make as they forge a better future for the United States of America. A thoughtful consideration of major Mexican American artistic and literary accomplishments, it helps explain the importance of mestizo culture in forging a more equitable and inclusive national identity today. *Mestizos Come Home!* evaluates the significance of such major authors as Rudolfo Anaya, Sandra Cisneros, and Denise Chávez. It also discusses the social dimensions of lowrider culture, historical memory in Day of the Dead celebrations, the radical visual art of Alma López, and the racialized portraiture of colonial Mexican Casta paintings. Davis-Undiano's book offers a sweepingly comprehensive vision of mestizo culture vital to the nation at a critical moment."

RAFAEL PÉREZ-TORRES
author of *Mestizaje: Critical Uses
of Race in Chicano Culture*

"*Mestizos Come Home!* is a deeply researched, provocative, and compelling study of the ways Mexican Americans have struggled to belong to the place they come from, and to reclaim their heritage in the United States and throughout the Americas. Davis-Undiano provides us with a deep understanding of the cultural strategies and folk traditions that have sustained Mexican Americans for centuries. A must-read for those who wish to understand the future of the United States."

NEIL FOLEY
author of *Mexicans in the
Making of America*

"In this comprehensive study of Mexican American history and culture from colonial times to the present, Robert Con Davis-Undiano offers a historically grounded analysis that questions the misrepresentations heaped on one of the largest ethnic populations in the United States. *Mestizos Come Home!* joins Mexican American writers and artists who have, as Americans, envisioned their cultural past and present as a journey home and as the promise of renewal, new beginnings, and the enrichment of the American experience. This inspiring and thoroughly researched book perceptively and courageously engages the major ethnic, social, and political issues facing the United States today."

ROBERTO CANTÚ
editor of *The Forked Juniper: Critical Perspectives on Rudolfo Anaya*

"Long a force for the study and dissemination of Chicano/a literature as teacher, scholar, and editor, Robert Con Davis-Undiano brings his erudition and his personal experience as an American of Mexican descent to the subject of Mexicans in America in a book that is at once accessible, scholarly, filled with insight, and wonderfully readable. Encompassing the history and magnitude of the contributions of Mexican people, literature, and culture to the fabric of America, *Mestizos Come Home!* is an important book by an important author, and it couldn't come at a more opportune time."

RILLA ASKEW
author of *Kind of Kin: A Novel*

"*Mestizos Come Home!* is a work of great intellect that shares Eduardo Galeano's vision of a people freed of a 'broken' sense of history. Davis-Undiano provides a map bridging past and present, which is so essential not only to the spiritual and political empowerment of Latinos but also to anyone who wants to take that journey with us. This is a compelling read with an urgent, welcome message."

DEMETRIA MARTÍNEZ
author of *Confessions of a Berlitz-Tape Chicana*

MESTIZOS COME HOME!

CHICANA & CHICANO VISIONS
OF THE AMÉRICAS

MESTIZOS COME HOME!

Making and Claiming Mexican American Identity

ROBERT CON DAVIS-UNDIANO

UNIVERSITY OF OKLAHOMA PRESS ✳ NORMAN

A previous version of chapter 3 was published in Roberto Cantú, ed., *The Forked Juniper: Critical Perspectives on Rudolfo Anaya* (Norman: University of Oklahoma Press, 2016).

Library of Congress Cataloging-in-Publication Data
Names: Davis, Robert Con, 1948– author.
Title: Mestizos come home! : making and claiming Mexican American identity / Robert Con Davis-Undiano.
Description: Norman : University of Oklahoma Press, 2017. | Series: Chicana & Chicano visions of the Américas series ; 19 | Includes bibliographical references and index.
Identifiers: LCCN 2016038508 | ISBN 978-0-8061-5719-1 (hardback : alkaline paper)
Subjects: LCSH: Mexican Americans—Ethnic identity. | Mestizos—United States—Ethnic identity. | Mexican Americans—Social life and customs. | Community life—United States. | Mexican Americans—Intellectual life. | American literature—Mexican American authors—History and criticism. | United States—Ethnic relations. | BISAC: HISTORY / United States / 20th Century. | SOCIAL SCIENCE / Ethnic Studies / Hispanic American Studies.
Classification: LCC E184.M5 D29 2017 | DDC 305.868/72073—dc23
LC record available at https://lccn.loc.gov/2016038508

Mestizos Come Home!: Making and Claiming Mexican American Identity is Volume 19 in the Chicana & Chicano Visions of the Américas series.

The paper in this book meets the guidelines for permanence and durability of the Committee on Production Guidelines for Book Longevity of the Council on Library Resources, Inc. ∞

***

Para mi familia con amor,

Julie M. Davis,

Joshua M. Davis,

Noah M. Davis,

y Risa E. Davis

***

Our system is one of detachment: to keep silenced people from asking questions, to keep the judged from judging, to keep solitary people from joining together, and the soul from putting together its pieces.

EDUARDO GALEANO
"Divorces," *The Book of Embraces*

. . . either I'm nobody, or I'm a nation.

DEREK WALCOTT
The Schooner "Flight"

The future is mestizo.

VIRGILIO ELIZONDO
The Future Is Mestizo

Contents

Illustrations

Preface

My original goal in writing *Mestizos Come Home!* was sharing with non-Latinos what Mexican Americans have accomplished since the 1960s. U.S. mainstream culture does not know what Mexican Americans have done to fit in, maintain important aspects of their culture, and build community. I wanted the national culture to recognize these achievements and understand what Mexican Americans deal with every day. I soon found that any discussion of milestones led to engagement with the issues of race, gender, the representation of the Mexican American community to the larger culture, assimilation, identity, social justice, and underlying assumptions about Mesoamerican and European views of the human body and well-being. In focusing on their successes, in short, I had to confront important questions that go to the heart of life in this hemisphere. The resulting book highlights Mexican Americans productively grappling with the most vexing and important issues of our time, issues relating to who they are in regard to the U.S. mainstream.

Eduardo Galeano describes culture in the Americas as hobbled by "amnesia," a problem expressed most directly as a flawed sense of history. He notes that U.S. mainstream culture remains unable, or unwilling, to acknowledge the impact of colonialism in this hemisphere on mestizos (those of mixed indigenous and Spanish descent) and indigenous people. This denial continues into the present even though the cultural gap it creates hampers everyone with a misleading sense of the Americas' life and history. Like Rudolfo Anaya and Cherríe L. Moraga, Galeano sees the Americas as having a disconnected sense of past and present and an obstructed view of how the history of the Americas is shaping and marginalizing mestizo lives today. He adds the warning that there is a widespread tendency in the region toward "detachment: [designed] to keep silenced people from asking questions, to keep the judged from judging, to keep solitary people from joining together, and the soul from putting together its pieces" (1992a, 123). Many mestizos live with fractured "souls" and disempowered lives, with historical fragmentation and discontinuity becoming virtual defining features of this region's cultures. European victors have not only written the histories of the Americas but have stifled the rise of challenges to colonial accounts of that past.

Some readers will be surprised to discover that the Americas' version of community and culture was taking shape as early as the sixteenth and seventeenth centuries during the Spanish colonial period—a perspective clearly not part of U.S. public awareness. This period's casta system of racial categories, combining Mesoamerican and European standards of physical appearance and differing conceptions of the human body, along with a strict colonial social hierarchy, is still shaping mestizo identities and limiting mestizos' social participation everywhere in the Americas. The current elevation of white over brown bodies and the cultural marginalization of mixed and indigenous people across Latin America and the United States give testimony to this continuing postcolonial impact. Hence *Mestizos Come Home!* takes on a sense of urgency owing to the fact that Mexican American achievements since the 1960s are revealing not only a neglected history but a needed cultural bridge between past and present. These developments are opening a new era in the Americas with an enhanced sense of history and the potential to undo many aspects of colonialism's social and racial damage.

Why focus on bridging the past and present in the Americas? There are ethical and historical implications in such cultural recovery work and in what it can reveal about this region. Even though the influence of the colonial era is still shaping racial and social practices across the hemisphere, public culture in the United States does not register Latin America or the Caribbean as relevant to U.S. cultural interests. Historically preoccupied with England and independence, the dominance of Anglo-Protestant culture, and American exceptionalism, mainstream culture has overlooked the legacy of Spanish colonialism and its social impact for over two hundred years.

The great awakening of Mexican American and Latino culture in the 1960s challenged this amnesia with a new awareness of the Americas as a historical setting with deep ties to the United States. That challenge found expression in the Chicano Renaissance's literature, art, music, history, sociology, and philosophy. I am seeking to advance that challenge to the next level by using this book's chapters to connect in every way possible neglected landmark events of this hemisphere to current Mexican American and U.S. culture. Among the most pressing of such events are the inauguration of race as a category in the Americas, mestizo identity's historical development across the nineteenth and twentieth centuries, the reemergence of indigenous ideas about land, and the conflict between Mesoamerican and European conceptions of the human body. As my sense of the need for historical and cultural connections has grown, so have the chapters. Each of this book's chapters is now a large-scale exploration of Mexican American culture that I pursued with the help of many living writers, artists, and cultural critics but also with the testimony of figures from the past whose stories need telling, too.

Take the example of the people shown in the casta paintings of eighteenth-century New Spain (see chapter 1). These intimate portraits from Spanish colonial America depict los antepasados, the ancestors of current Latinos and Latin Americans—people who lived in slavery and serfdom from the early sixteenth through the eighteenth centuries. Generating new racial identities, their world was already shaping ours, creating strict social hierarchies that became the Spanish legacy to the modern world. Given the sparse historical awareness of the casta people and few attempts at historical recovery, casta women and men are still sending signals across five centuries, still gesturing from the casta paintings to get our attention, still asking us to acknowledge them and note that they lived and are part of us. With such open channels to the past and a sense of history currently arising like a new Atlantis, we can no longer ignore the ancestors, especially since our grasp of their racial and social lives in the eighteenth century is *critical* to understanding racial and social distinctions now. We need to remember those who came before and even see and "hear" them, as the casta paintings and other artifacts make possible. We need to heed what the ancestors can tell us for understanding the Americas' sense of history and culture.

What is true about the Mexican American community is also true of others. Mexican Americans are traveling a cultural journey that began long before their time with the conquest and continues into the present. Other ethnic and racial groups in the Americas—tribal peoples not directly part of the conquest, Asians, Middle Eastern peoples, and others—also have stories to tell and histories that need to be recovered and recognized. For all living in the Americas, assimilation into European culture, as Adrienne Rich notes, has meant giving "up not only your history but your body, to try to adopt an alien appearance because your own is not good enough, [and you must even] . . . fear naming yourself lest [the] name be twisted into [a] label" (1994, 142). Reinforcing a kind of "post-colonial stress disorder," the residual cultural and social effects of the postcolonial era (social isolation, communal fragmentation, personal lack of confidence, suspicion of mainstream cultural intentions, etc.), the ghost of colonialism is still alienating and disenfranchising mestizo communities.[1] Recognizing this hemisphere's collective cultural amnesia and its debilitating effects, all in the Americas will benefit from gaining a truer sense of the region and where it could be heading.

In other words, while this book focuses on the Mexican American community, it is also about the United States and life in the Americas in the broadest sense—everyone in this hemisphere. Fully engaged with creating a more inclusive sense of the past, Mexican Americans are pursuing social justice for those whose sense of belonging to the national culture has been thwarted or lost. Given that this manner of "coming home" can point the way for others, everyone should have a stake in the success of the Mexican American community's journey and quest for social justice.

This book's topics have come together like guests attending a resolana—the traditional town hall gathering in New Mexico where neighbors congregate by a sunny wall to share news and rehash the problems of the day (see chapter 7). That is, this book is an assemblage of topics, writers, historical figures, and artists that previously did not belong together or had no logical reason to be grouped—or were somehow *kept* apart. An occasion for gathering ideas and issues long-overdue for discussion and resolution, like a resolana where unexpected guests can show up at any time, this book is a forum for sorting through topics

that are *in need* of attention. Also, many of the resolaneros (participants) important in this discussion are no longer with us. But as with
the *disappeared* in Latin America, there are many ways that the dead
can give testimony and participate in the life and culture that we
share. Neglected cultural artifacts like the casta paintings, some of the
Americas' earliest literary and social texts, and new, inclusive histories
of the region are part of this book's resolana conversation for exploration of once-forbidden ideas, cultural practices, and values.

Key participants in this book are the Peruvian social critics of the
last century, especially José Carlos Mariátegui and Víctor Raúl Haya de
la Torre, writers dedicated to bringing the Americas' past into conversation with its present. Add the contemporary Peruvian sociologist Aníbal
Quijano—to take just one example—and we find that Peruvian social
critics have a potentially game-changing impact on how we understand
Mexican American and Chicano culture now, the U.S. national culture
now, the border zone intersections of these cultures now, and everything else discussed in this book. The Peruvian critics' groundbreaking
work on race, class, and culture helps us to see how Mexican Americans
are operating on the same historical stage with others from Latin
America with similar historical ties and familiar social barriers to cross
for achieving social justice.

Many of this book's topics are implicated in the competition
between Mesoamerican and European views of the human body and
racial issues embedded in those perspectives, topics demanding the
large canvas of Latin America as a cultural backdrop for clarity. Prior
to *Mestizos Come Home!*, I wanted to advance these broad approaches
when I commissioned volumes of literature and cultural studies that
became the Chicana & Chicano Visions of the Américas series at the
University of Oklahoma Press—the distinguished series publishing
volumes of fiction, drama, poetry, and literary criticism and engaging
topics that otherwise get little recognition in American culture. With
longtime friend Rudolfo Anaya, I carried on a dialogue about the body
and race in his fiction and revisited these topics again when preparing
the Oxford guide to his work.

Recent historical events also prompted this book. Tens of millions
of people in the United States do not know who Mexican Americans

are, especially their history and contributions to the United States. Currently, many non-Latinos and even some aspiring Latino politicians speak of Mexican Americans as interlopers working in the United States illegally, taking from America's cultural and economic wealth while giving nothing in return. For a time, it seemed to me of small consequence that those not involved in the Mexican American experience might know little of our community's history and its contributions to the country. It also appeared unavoidable that non-Latinos would have misconceptions about us and even that some Latino politicians would promote a strict assimilationist agenda and immigration policy arbitrarily dividing "Mexican" from "Mexican American."

Sometime after Barack Obama's first election, as higher levels of discriminatory attitudes and racial violence became common across the United States, I realized that this lack of knowledge created a situation both volatile and dangerous. I noted new directions in public policy in Arizona, where I was born, and across the Southwest and the country that were reshaping communities and suppressing Latino culture and civil rights. Such tendencies were usually based on misleading assumptions about Mexican Americans and values inconsistent with America's highest aspirations, particularly the country's most cherished traditions of democratic inclusion. These alarming historical and cultural shifts prompted a new urgency for the questions that I was already asking in order to write this book.

Discussion of these issues and questions, hastened by social forces, became *Mestizos Come Home!*, an examination of six ways that Mexican Americans have changed the country and their own culture since the 1960s. This book focuses on the casta system and race in Spanish colonial America, mestizo identity in the history of the Americas, ideas about indigenous ties to land, contrasting European and Mesoamerican views of the human body (especially the "brown" body), a revealing style of popular culture, the rise of a "voice" that represents the Mexican American community, and the cultural significance of Chicano literature and Chicano studies in higher education. How do these landmark practices impact Mexican Americans and shape U.S. culture? In what ways are these practices changing lives? These are important questions for which there have been few good answers. Writers and scholars immersed in their work do not always remember, or even intend, to ask such pragmatic and practical questions. But as a Mexican American, I needed to understand a number of fundamental issues regarding my community and its future in the United States. Writing *Mestizos Come Home!* was a way to address those concerns.

One prominent theme of *Mestizos Come Home!* is that inquiry and knowledge must serve the community that produced them, as I discuss in chapter 2 and chapter 7. We must remember that culture and cultural inquiry arise not from the work of scholars and writers but from the community that makes possible all that we do. Those who think and write about cultural and social issues do not always acknowledge this debt, but—given these origins—the pursuit of knowledge arrives with a moral imperative to make life better for others. If those who think and write do not enrich our communities, do not choose to close that loop, what is the point of pursuing new knowledge in the first place?

Classic examples of this perspective at work are the participatory, communal practices of resolana in New Mexico (see chapter 7). As I noted, resolana is a kind of democratic town hall meeting tradition that illustrates in dramatic fashion what is possible when joint endeavors focus on solving problems and advancing the interests of actual people in a local setting. Such ideas about participation and the need to act on the community's behalf are staples of indigenous cultures in the Americas and abiding values of the Mexican American community.

Likewise, I intend for *Mestizos Come Home!* to help repay los antepasados (the ancestors in the United States *and* Latin America) and also the people alive now in every walk of life in the Latino community for making our lives possible. I think of my father and uncles, newly arrived from Mexico, driving delivery trucks for a living in Phoenix, Arizona, and my grandmother and aunts cleaning other peoples' houses, as well as the countless educators, artists, engineers, scientists, and doctors— all Latinos who work hard every day to keep our community vital and advance the interests of our culture to make America *better.* We now need to find effective political representation and improve educational outcomes for Latinos at every level. One of the practical goals of this book is to embolden Latinos to refine and finish the process of acculturation, to make still-needed changes, to no longer feel a need to apologize for their U.S. presence, and to "come home" fully to their American lives.

ACKNOWLEDGMENTS

Writing this book has happened owing to favorable circumstances. A number of good friends in the Latino community—Rudolfo Anaya, Roberto Cantú, Denise Chávez, Arlene Dávila, César G. Ferreira, the late Luis Jiménez, the late E. A. Mares, Demetria Martínez, María Herrera Sobek, and John Undiano, among other writers and artists—had at one time or another urged me to write a book about our community. I also received encouragement to undertake this task from colleagues at the University of Oklahoma—Rilla Askew, Millie C. Audas, Belinda Biscoe, David L. Boren (our university president), Molly Shi Boren (our university first lady), Jeanette Davidson, Kyle Harper (our provost), Kathleen Kelly, David W. Levy, Marta Luce, Nancy Mergler, James Pappas, B. Byron Price, Charles Rankin, Joanna Rapf, Robert A. Rundstrom, Ronald Schleifer, Sue Schofield, Jonathan Stalling, and Alan R. Velie. I also got support and encouragement from supporters of the university, my dear friends Nancy Barcelo, Dolores K. Neustadt, Kathy Neustadt, and Susan Neustadt Schwartz. I regret that my good friend Walter Neustadt Jr. is no longer here to see his name listed as one of this book's champions.

My incredible staff at the *World Literature Today* organization also helped with spot-on research support, and I owe much to Merleyn Bell, Jennifer Blair, Kay Blunck, Marla Johnson, Michelle Johnson, Daniel Simon, Terri Stubblefield (the biggest thanks), and Robert Vollmar. I owe an abrazo fuerte to the many student interns who requested interlibrary loan books, scanned articles, and searched for materials— Madeline Alford, Tyler Allen, Emily Bibens, Michael Bibens, Meredith Boe, Armando Celayo, Marilyse Figueroa, Kayley Gillespie, Victoria Greenwood, Lyda Hartness, Christine Hoagland, and Jessica Mitzner. I am indebted to the Latino student organizations that I sponsor at the University of Oklahoma, Omega Delta Phi and Sigma Lambda Gamma. Their members remind me every day through their impressive achievements that ideas and insights about our community will never do justice to their evolving young lives. A major boost for this project came from home and the moral support that I got from my beautiful wife, Julie M. Davis, my sons, Joshua and Noah, and my daughter, Risa. Julie is a more demanding editor than I am, and her good ideas and prose corrections are scattered throughout this work.

GUIDE TO TERMINOLOGY

With the hope of making this book as useful as possible to all who read it, I here give brief definitions of important terms appearing in the following chapters.

Mexican American: This is the most basic, literal designation of an American whose ancestors, on one or both sides, are from Mexico—like me. A Mexican American can be a recent arrival from Mexico, or someone who grew up in the United States, like my father and his siblings, or third-generation people fully assimilated into American culture and mores. Sometimes this term is written with a hyphen to make it an adjective describing literature, culture, or community. When this is done, following customary practices in English, "Mexican-American" has a kind of contingent, adjunct status. More recently, there is a tendency, which I follow in this book, to drop the hyphen in favor of recognizing Mexican American as a cultural identity in its own right. That is a lot of significance to place on a hyphen, but this change is intended to emphasize being Mexican American as a cultural identity and not merely as an adjective or an added description of something else.

Chicano: This is a term that most people believe was originally derived from the name of some of the ancient peoples of the New World, the predecessors of modern-day Mexicans—the Mexica. During the Spanish colonial period, to be a Mexica was to be a Mexicano, and the Nahuatl (Aztec) pronunciation of that term ("Meshicano") over time was probably shortened to "Chicano"—hence the possible development of Chicano as a nickname for an ancient Mesoamerican community. Whatever its ultimate origins, for most of its history since the conquest,

Chicano has been a largely derogatory reference to a marginalized and persecuted people.

This term came into new prominence and was reframed in the 1960s as the name of the Mexican American civil rights movement—the Chicano movement. The movement's focus on labor relations and working conditions for exploited migrant farm workers quickly morphed into a cultural renaissance with many new developments—literary, artistic, political, social, religious, and economic. In the 1960s, the term "Chicano" identified a Mexican American with a clear cultural and political agenda, someone who promoted communal cohesion and health, including relevant political and economic concerns. A Chicano was someone who valued the development of communal self-determination as a priority above mere assimilation into mainstream American culture.

Currently, some in the Mexican American community, mostly scholars, choose to use this term interchangeably with "Mexican American." This choice suggests a general acceptance of the outcomes of the Chicano movement. The fact remains, however, that not all Mexican Americans, especially outside of the academy, want to be called Chicanos or are even any longer mindful of what that term means. This lack of awareness, or actual resistance to the term, severely limits its currency and usefulness. Hence there remains a strong rationale and commitment to historical accuracy in using "Chicano" to designate the social and cultural movement in the 1960s but also those Mexican Americans currently who embrace that identity and whose values and beliefs match the 1960s criteria for being a Chicano. The deliberate use of this term with a specific historical significance is the practice that I follow in this book.

Mestizo: Used widely in the Americas past and present, "mestizo" began as a term for designating people of mixed indigenous and Spanish heritage. Originating in the Spanish colonial period in the Americas, mestizo was an official racial category of Spanish colonial society and was created as a key part of the Spanish casta system (see chapter 1). The Spanish created a number of such racial categories to monitor and control the many social and cultural identities coming into existence during the sixteenth, seventeenth, and eighteenth centuries. This term is still in use but now is more general in designating a broad range of people with mixed racial origins.

Mestizaje: Also commonly in use across the Americas, "mestizaje" refers to the *process* of racial mixing that produced mestizos during and after the conquest—the historical events that created the nationhood of mixed-race peoples. In present usage, it sometimes also refers to the community of mestizos in a particular country or even mestizos as a single people (a kind of nation) across the Americas.

Hispanic: "Hispanic" came into use during the Nixon administration when it appeared on U.S. census forms. Government bureaucrats coined this term to designate various Latin American or Spanish peoples and their descendants—Mexican Americans, Salvadoran Americans, Cuban Americans, and so on. For some, this term could reference only Spanish-speaking Latin Americans and did not include, for instance, people from Brazil, who speak Portuguese. Currently in wide use as a general reference covering U.S. descendants from Latin America, this term often still carries the negative connotation and taint of being a bureaucratic innovation, a contrived category that the U.S. government imposed on a diverse community as a governmental convenience.

Latino: The popular use of "Latino" came after the introduction of "Hispanic" and in many ways was a reaction to it. For many people of Latin American origin, "Latino" has been the preferred, supposedly nongovernmental term for referencing this complex community in place of "Hispanic." For others, "Latino" is simply a broad designation that references all Spanish- and Portuguese-speaking people in the United States who are of Latin American or Spanish origin. Currently, both in society and in scholarly circles—in this book, for example—"Latino" and "Hispanic" are often used interchangeably as umbrella terms for people in the United States of Latin American, Spanish, or Caribbean origin.

MESTIZOS COME HOME!

INTRODUCTION
Mestizos, Come Home!

Since the 1960s, Mexican Americans have been creating a home for themselves in six areas (among others) of cultural and social change—hence their "coming home." Each area of change has been a part of acculturating to a new life in the United States but has also altered and in most cases improved the national culture, helping it to become a better version of itself. Their success in these huge undertakings, some of them subtle but all of them far reaching, is slowly creating a receptive cultural environment for them and a better future for America.

***

I would like *Mestizos Come Home!* to work for two audiences. A Mexican American and Latino audience should see important parts of themselves in my discussion of their cultural and social achievements since the 1960s. I want them to be inspired and a little proud as they read about how they have overcome the challenges of immigration and acculturation. I also want them to be encouraged to succeed further in their quest to embrace the United States as their home. A second audience, a general one unfamiliar with Mexican American culture, will discover that community's (our) formidable achievements, values, and aspirations in a history that is likely unknown to them. I want this group to be enlightened through this encounter with a vibrant culture and perhaps more understanding about what Mexican Americans are trying to achieve. Finally, this is also a book about the ways that Mexican Americans are influencing the U.S. mainstream to create a better future for the country. I examine how Mexican Americans are helping to reshape American values and attitudes for the current century—making America *better.*

In the late 1990s through the early twenty-first century, there were several voices predicting America's destruction at the hands of Mexican American immigrants, most notably Peter Brimelow in *Alien Nation: Common Sense about America's Immigration Disaster* (1996) and Samuel P. Huntington in *Who Are We? The Challenges of America's National Identity* (2004). They judged Mexican Americans to be unwilling to assimilate, turning their backs on the country's traditional values and culture, preferring their own company and culture to that of the community around them, and ultimately hastening the decline of a once great nation. *Mestizos Come Home!* has the goal of countering those earlier claims and becoming part of a new tide of appreciation for what Mexican Americans are already contributing to American culture. This book could be grouped with Neil Foley's *Mexicans in the Making of America* (2014) and, I hope, with other books that will join us in explaining that Mexican Americans and other Latinos are not recent U.S. invaders, as they are often taken to be, but are already a part of a "thoroughly composite culture of racially blended peoples that defies the notion of some normative or static understanding of what it means to be 'American'" (Foley 2014, 12). The time has come, I argue, to examine and take seriously the cultural and social contributions that Mexican Americans are making to the United States, particularly the extent to which their presence helps American culture to become a better version of itself and to move a little closer to being the multicultural, democratic, egalitarian country that America has always aspired to be.

Mestizos Come Home! advances this argument by focusing on six important changes that have taken place in the Mexican American community since the 1960s—changes celebrating mestizo identity, finding a new relationship to land, making innovations in popular culture, learning to resee the human body, fostering the rise of a Chicano cultural voice, and the development of Chicano literature and Chicano studies in higher education. These changes represent cultural shifts that are altering Mexican Americans' sense of themselves and reinvigorating their community, as well as enhancing traditional and new dimensions of the national culture. Three of these initiatives concern people as individuals—celebrating mestizo identity, refinding a living relationship to land, and promoting a Mesoamerican conception of the human body. The other three, broadly cultural and social in orientation, reference a revealing style of popular culture, the rise of a cultural "voice," and the inauguration of Chicano literature and Chicano studies. The detailed accounts of these initiatives are intended to embolden Mexican Americans to complete this journey "home" by improving education for young people and demanding effective political representation to promote Latino needs and interests. This book should also help non-Latinos to see more deeply into Mexican American culture and to appreciate what the United States is becoming as Latino populations (primarily Mexican Americans) over the next several years grow and help to shape the national experience.

Mestizos Come Home! arises from the belief that the current generation of Mexican Americans is poised to "come home," to make major strides in the process of acculturation, as they reclaim their histories, revitalize their communities, and celebrate who they are as Americans *and* citizens of the Americas. They have arrived at this historical juncture owing to their own perseverance and their understanding that there is some knowledge so important that it changes the people who know it. Mexican Americans have been actively reclaiming that important knowledge about their culture, about fundamental aspects of who they are, about the United States, and about how their values and commitments mesh with the dominant culture's aspirations. Since the 1960s, they have actively acquired a new cultural awareness of what they want and how they fit into America's future, and this effort has strengthened their sense of who they are and what they bring to the American experience.

This account of Mexican Americans "coming home" during the 1960s, 1970s, and 1980s also touches on historical challenges of living in the Americas referenced in Eduardo Galeano's *The Book of Embraces*. Galeano describes the Americas as a region with an unprocessed past, a broken sense of history, one in which past and present remain separate, and in which "the past has nothing to say to the present, [and] history may go on sleeping undisturbed in the closet where the system keeps its old disguises" (1992a, 123). He references the fact that five hundred years ago in the Americas the Spanish colonized and enslaved millions of indigenous and African peoples, and contemporary Latin Americans, Afro-Caribbean people, Latinos, and Mexican Americans are that period's living legacy. Contemporary mestizos live with an unresolved sense of the past and a view of history that needs recovery and recognition. This missing historical piece, if we had it, would tell about the impact of the colonial past and how that past's racial and social residue is still an active force today in mestizo lives across the Americas—the prime example of knowledge so important that it changes the people who know it. The Americas' forgotten past has left mestizos with "souls" that need to be reunited, as they are people still living the effects of racial typing, social marginalization, and the undervaluing of mestizo lives (123). Galeano is right about the Americas' history and the need to understand more about how mestizos and nonmestizos alike fit into that history. This book is an attempt to answer some of these questions.

This book's title also issues a challenge for Mexican Americans to complete what they began in the 1960s, to "come home" by consolidating gains in American culture and society. This is a time to go forward without apology valuing mestizo identity, a Mesoamerican view of the human body, traditional ties to land, and popular culture, all of which reflect beliefs and values that Mexican Americans already hold. Other developments, like the inauguration of a cultural "voice" and Chicano literature and Chicano studies, have created new and exciting cultural avenues to explore. Mexican Americans have come home a little more every year in each of these areas. Never intending merely to "fit in," they have sought to build a vibrant community and to discover for themselves America's promise of a better life. They have met adversity head-on and have reached important goals, even though much more needs to be done to improve primary education, their experience in colleges and universities, and their uneven political representation.

The developments chronicled in these pages tell about Mexican Americans changing themselves, their culture, and their country to become full-participation U.S. citizens. They will "come home" when they can confirm their own culture, getting credit for their contributions to the national community and the economy, and being acknowledged as people of consequence. To gain such acceptance, as much from themselves as others, they have refused to disappear anonymously into the U.S. melting pot, giving up everything that is distinctly theirs in the process. Some who stand in judgment of Mexican Americans have mistaken their clarity of purpose for a refusal to assimilate. That explanation also ignores their cultural and social accomplishments, what they have done already to come home. This book's six initiatives demonstrate that Mexican Americans have taken important steps to institute cultural adjustments difficult for any community to make. Those already living safely inside U.S. culture may too easily forget that assimilation is a painstaking *process*. Mexican Americans are not taking any longer than other groups to assimilate into U.S. culture—to come home in a sorting and effective melding of two cultures.

The history of the Americas and Spanish colonialism's impact on this hemisphere mandate that this process be understood as fully as possible. Mexican Americans share this hemisphere's history with many others, and too much has happened, too many lives have been damaged and lost for this story to be rendered only partially now. Mexican Americans are retelling their story, and as long as key parts remain untold a significant dimension of American history, "our denied [American] history," as Ronald Takaki warns, "bursts with [the need of] telling'" (1993, 428). Until that history is known, historical, cultural, and social realities are excluded from the national narratives about what America is and what it can become. A fragmented account of Mexican American cultural realities serves no one and costs too much in long-term cross-cultural misunderstanding and alienation.

It is my goal in this book to shed light on some of the broken connections between past and present. Studies of Mexican American culture and history seldom address Spanish colonial culture in the sixteenth, seventeenth, or eighteenth centuries, as this book does, and that is one of my points. In Chicano studies, we need a greater recognition of the history and cultural context for understanding race in the Americas. Powerful institutions like racism always have a revealing history and a genealogy, and it is critical to understand the past to change what began and still has its roots there.

A formative part of the Americas' past was the casta system, the cultural order based on skin color and encouraging ethnic identification with the Spanish, which advanced racial identities and predetermined social hierarchies as natural and inevitable. Relying on racial typing and strict social ranking, the casta system in the seventeenth and eighteenth centuries created a brand of racial inequality that still oppresses the United States and all of Latin America. The conquest and Spanish colonialism were devastating for this hemisphere, and without a sense of the connections between race and culture in New Spain, as Galeano and others argue, we can little understand social realities and the current forces shaping mestizo lives. Pushing against these limitations, this book is highlighting the casta system's impact in this hemisphere to right a balance with strategic acts of remembering the racial identities that relatively recently were inaugurated and set adrift in the New World.

Mexican Americans will succeed in "coming home" *not* by forcing themselves to deny who they are but by *remembering* the culture of the Americas and celebrating mestizo identity. In the 1960s, Mexican Americans recognized that they had a role to play in the national culture and that they could contribute constructively to what it means to be an American. Their effort is still a work in progress and replicates an ancient pattern in the Americas that Tomás Rivera references wherein indigenous, European, African, and Asian peoples have unceasingly *searched* across this hemisphere to find their truth as a community, making this hemisphere the land of people in motion, the land of "searchers" (1992a, 285). Indigenous people crossed the Bering Strait to search for better lives. The Mexica searched to found Tenochtitlan in ancient Mexico. The Spanish searched when they came into the American Southwest, and Mexicans have been searchers when they crossed the U.S.-Mexican border looking for work. Mexican Americans were even searchers when they became migrant farm workers in the United States and moved from job to job. In each case, the people of this hemisphere came to find their own truth and a new home, and they have shaped this continent's values and beliefs by searching for and reaching their goals a little more every day. Mexican Americans are rekindling a time-honored promise of renewal for those who come to the United States to find their own truths.

In undertaking this search, Mexican Americans challenge conventional notions of what an American is. Most often, Mexican Americans are English speaking, they are citizens, they are frequently European in appearance, and they know vast amounts about American popular culture, politics, sports, and fast food. Other Mexican Americans are distinctly *not* like the mainstream. Just as often, they are dark skinned, recently arrived from Mexico with accented (or little) English, and an appreciation for indigenous culture and food. Lovers of soccer and Day of the Dead celebrants, they watch telenovellas and listen to Latin American pop singers and Mexican bandas.

Which version is the reality? Mexican Americans are both, identical to those in the mainstream—with jobs, mortgages, children to put through school, and worries about the country's future *and* also unfamiliar and seemingly exotic, like the brother or sister adopted from a faraway place. That dual identity *is* who we are. For historical reasons since 1848, as I reference throughout this book, Mexican Americans project a split identity. Anthropologist Tomás R. Jiménez notes that each year "newcomers from the ethnic homeland continually replenish" the U.S. community as new arrivals, and while immigration has drastically slowed, it is still responsible for creating a split image of Mexican Americans that will not soon disappear (2010, xiii).

There have been several crises in the country's history with Mexican Americans. In 1848, after the Mexican-American War, the Treaty of Guadalupe Hidalgo ceded almost *half* of Mexico's territory to the United States. A major trauma for Mexicans, this loss is still relevant for understanding their response to current immigration issues. During the years after 1848, Mexicans were encouraged to "self deport" and have not been eager to repeat that experience. There is little awareness nationally of what Mexicans gave up *for* America to take its current geographical and cultural shape, an event that has created irrevocable deep ties between the two countries. It is true, as Ronald Takaki comments, that "America has been racially diverse since our very beginning," but the Mexican American experience since 1848 has dramatically shaped historical events that continue to link the two countries with a special bond and closeness (1993, 2).

After 1848, Mexicans were forced into *Mexican American* lives with a hyphenated identity as they discovered how little land they would keep while the American victors gradually commandeered the spoils of war. In the 1930s during the Great Depression, mainstream U.S. culture blamed Mexican Americans for taking poorly paid jobs and reducing employment opportunities. The Bracero Program for guest workers ended in 1964, and from the late 1960s through the present there has been increasing national concern and suspicion over illegal immigration and the inability of the United States to patrol the border and deport violators. Recently, there has also been a national backlash in response to the new prominence of Mexican Americans in the U.S. national culture, including books unfriendly to Mexican Americans (Brimelow 1996 and Huntington 2004b), the passing of English-only laws, and Arizona's 2011 ban on teaching ethnic studies—all gestures intended to limit Mexican American cultural influence. These events coincide with pockets of racial discrimination around the country and acts of violence that are supposed to legitimize the myth of a "pure" American culture that needs protecting.

Mexican Americans stepped further into the national culture in the 2008 and 2012 U.S. presidential elections when they supported Barack Obama. These were landmark events for the Mexican American community, taking political action as a group for the first time. The community in the future will likely impact politics and the national culture far more than it does now. Such changes "in our nation's ethnic composition," as Takaki notes, or even the perception of such changes, will change the way that all Americans "think about [them]selves" (1993, 2).

Some of this book's discussions are filtered through my own family lens. María Atancia Arce de Undiano, my grandmother, left Lerdo (adjacent to Torreón), Mexico, in April 1920 to cross the El Paso Bridge into the United States. Hopeful on this journey, perhaps beyond reason, that she and her four sons were "coming home" to the United States, she had just buried my grandfather before the trip. She and her children—with a fifth child, my aunt Consuelo, on the way—were part of a wave of Mexican immigrants coming north as political refugees after the 1910 Mexican revolution.

María Undiano sought a new home to raise children and a better life in what used to be Mexico during her grandparents' time. This father-less family came to Phoenix, Arizona, where her grown sons eventually ran a trucking business with probably no inclination to think about creating a better future for America. But within two generations, those very thoughts would be a reality for their grandchildren, including the one writing this book. *Mestizos Come Home!*, in other words, is about the world that my grandparents' generation made possible and those who have come after them since the 1960s.

The Mexican American journey "home"—in the process of becoming totally committed to finding a new life in the United States—in an important way commenced on March 23, 1969, in Denver, Colorado, when 1,500 Mexican American young people attended Rodolfo Gonzáles's National Chicano Liberation Youth Conference. Coming from every corner of the United States to find new cultural directions, these "bronze [young] people with a bronze culture" were there to "declare the independence" of the "mestizo nation," their way of seeking to live fuller and more engaged U.S. lives ("El Plan" 1989, 1). Old social boundaries were fading in the era of civil rights and street protests advocating for freedom. These young people sought "those [new] tasks which are justly called for by our house, our land, the sweat of our brows, and by our hearts" to effect large-scale cultural change (1).

As young Chicanos debated the future, a sense of excitement about new possibilities arose during the talks, breakout sessions, and poetry readings. The conference building vibrated with young people dancing, singing, reading poetry aloud, and reconceiving almost every aspect of their hybrid lives. When the conference ended, the organizers issued *El Plan Espiritual de Aztlán (The Spiritual Plan for Aztlán)*, declared the Southwest the Mexican American homeland, and promised their community's renewal. *El Plan* encouraged Mexican Americans to celebrate mestizo identities and to revamp ties to mainstream culture. Acting like a movement for the first time, they demanded full participation in American culture, to live in a just, democratic society, to work at good jobs, and to nurture healthy communities—the traditional U.S. promise of a better life.

By today's standards, this conference proclaimed Mexican American cultural pride in terms overly general. The conference failed to "integrate the subjectivities of Latino men and women" with different sexual orientations and radical political perspectives (Segura 2001, 548). It did not deconstruct being "Mexican American" or "Chicano" as categories and identities, as might be done today. This conference did ask for a rethinking of fundamental values and the steps needed to bolster a poverty-stricken people deprived of civil rights, advancing these notions with a new exuberance and expectation of success. Stories about this conference inspired a generation of activists and encouraged the exploration of mestizo identity, testing the boundaries of community, and innovating new ways to make the United States a home. The Mexican American community responded to the Denver conference with cultural and artistic achievements and community organizing triumphs that became the 1970s Chicano Renaissance.

Mexican Americans began telling the history of mestizo peoples in the Americas, reinvigorating their culture and the arts, and reconfiguring their relationship to the U.S. national culture. Chronicling the changes that *El Plan Espiritual de Aztlán* called for, areas in which Mexican Americans were refocusing and celebrating their culture, *Mestizos Come Home!* is itself a distant product of that period, a kind of delayed postscript, discussing many of the cultural forces that resurfaced in the early 1970s and 1980s.

After the 1848 war between Mexico and the United States, there was a one-hundred-year period of cultural oppression, a time in which Mexican Americans were invisible socially to mainstream culture, lived on the culture's periphery, and were exploited as cheap labor. The 1960s Chicano movement responded to that period by creating an exhilarating era of social protests, strikes, public art, and community organizing— the time of a Latino Great Awakening. Mexican Americans became activists and began working as a social movement, and the Chicano Renaissance from 1970s through the 1980s, or the 1990s, as some claim (in some ways continuing into the present), saw the rise of many cultural, social, and artistic developments. The present moment is yet *another* era, a time when everyone knows that the exploding Latino population will alter the United States in additional, far-reaching ways, but no one can yet see the exact direction that political, social, and cultural changes will go.

Mestizos Come Home! focuses on the Chicano Renaissance and the tail end, up through the present, of one of world history's greatest migrations. In 1850, the U.S. Mexican American population was about 100,000 people. In 1970, it ballooned to 5 million. In 2012, it climbed to 33.7 million. Currently, the arrow still points upward as the Mexican American community has gone over 34 million (Gonzalez-Barrera and Lopez 2013, 1–2). Behind these numbers are courageous people arriving in the U.S. Southwest that used to be Mexico. Crossing over scorching deserts and scrambling along the "devil's highway" through barbed-wire fences to reach el otro lado, the other side, they came in waves hoping for a better life, as my grandmother, father, and uncles did, even if a better life was not always to be found.

This Mexican American great migration created the need for acculturation in the United States on a massive scale. Mexican Americans faced stark cultural differences, like Anglo-Protestant (Puritanical), highly restrictive attitudes regarding the human body, hygiene, sex, and death. (Mainstream American culture is surely more distinct in exhibiting these traits than it can possibly recognize about itself.) Never shying from such challenges, Mexican Americans became activists, through community organizing and development and through the arts and literary achievement. Their acculturation has been a constant effort starting in the 1960s Chicano movement and continuing into the present. The exploration of mestizo identity, developments in popular culture, and the emergence of Chicano literature and Chicano studies were public and apparent for all to see. Other projects, like the exploration of Mesoamerican perspectives on the human body, the promotion of a living relationship to land, and the emergence of a cultural "voice" were new and required more framing and explanation.

These milestones reconnected Mexican American to the American Southwest, which until 1848 still belonged to Mexico. Mainstream America is no longer mindful that in the 1848 Mexican-American War, Mexico lost all of its northernmost territory, roughly *half* of its land total, thus forcing one hundred thousand Mexicans to confront and accept their new *Mexican American* identity, a development Mexicans never sought. In a way that remains difficult for non-Latinos to appreciate, mestizos (in my case, with a father from Lerdo-Torreón, Mexico, and a mother from Oklahoma) continue to regard the American Southwest as a homeland because in historical terms it *used* to be Mexico only a moment ago.

This book's title draws on the traditional "homeland" idea, as Richard L. Nostrand notes, citing "three basic elements: a people, a place, and [an] identity with place" (1972, 214). To be in a homeland, "people must have lived [there] long enough" to have an "impress in the form of a cultural landscape." When they "have developed an identity [in connection] with the land," and when they have created social customs and cultural practices tied to land, "emotional feelings of attachment, desires to possess, even compulsions to defend [their land]" will develop (214).

In contemporary culture, "homeland" has an even broader range of associations established roughly when Mexican Americans were renewing ties to the Southwest. The *Oxford English Dictionary* cites the word "homeland" as appearing first in England in 1627. In the United States, that word was not in *Webster's Collegiate Dictionary* until 1973, when it was inevitably colored by the contemporary association of displaced peoples as victims of political upheaval and strife. Cultural theorist Sara Ahmed and her colleagues see "homeland" not as expressing a simple tie to a place but as a modern "reclaiming and reprocessing of habits, objects, names and histories that have been uprooted [owing to frequent] migration, displacement or colonization" (2003, 9). For them, returning *home* means "*making* [a] home," "*creating* both pasts and futures through inhabiting the grounds of the present" (italics added). Associated with "returning to," "repossessing," and *re-creating* a lost place, even when that claim is mythical and the "loss" historically inaccurate, the "homeland" claim conveys a cultural "regrounding" of people finally arriving at a contested site to build their new lives (9).

The Mexican American assertion of Aztlán as the Aztec homeland is exactly such a historical *and* mythic claim. Many contemporary Mexicans still believe in the idyllic Aztlán that they left when one of their gods instructed them to leave and found Tenochtitlan. In the 1970s, many people claimed that the ancient Aztlán was located somewhere in the American Southwest, and, whether it was or not, this idea had a profound effect on the Mexican American spirit. Most Mesoamerican scholars have not been convinced that there was a "real" Mexican homeland called Aztlán (an issue I discuss in chapter 3), but the Aztlán idea nonetheless emerged during the Chicano Renaissance as expressing a resurgent spirit and hope for the future. If the Aztec homeland *were* located somewhere in the Southwest, then Mexican Americans were not exiles or illegals hiding in the U.S. shadows but a people trying to get back *home*. The place in question—perhaps Santa Fe, New Mexico—actually *was* a part of Mexico before 1848, literally *home*. But the Aztlán assertion was something larger, an encompassing idea, a symbol in the 1960s of *all* prior Mexican American cultural ties to the United States—historical or mythic.

The title of *Mestizos Come Home!* echoes these two associations with a homeland. The first calls for recognizing existing ties, based on the history of the Southwest, that Mexican Americans have with American culture in general. It references a process of migration and transformation since the early twentieth century and says that mestizos are arriving "home" in the place that used to be theirs. The other version, with a comma after "mestizos," implores Mexican Americans to create, transform, and reinvent ties to the Southwest. Losing their cultural voice in the conquest and again after the 1848 Mexican-American War, Mexicans found a new way of belonging in the United States. This second version of the title asks Mexican Americans to finish the cultural work of immigration by *creating* opportunities and taking their rightful place in American culture, as every other U.S. community settling here has done.

Chapter 1, "The Casta Tradition and Mestizos in New Spain," explores the institution of race in the sixteenth-, seventeenth-, and eighteenth-century Spanish colonial Americas, an event that radically redirected life in the hemisphere and created racial designations and divisions such as mestizo, castizo, morisco, mulatto, pardo, and so on. Colonial expansion and the importation of Africans into the Americas as slaves created the conditions for complex communal and cultural mixing. The Spanish created the casta system to monitor and control the new ethnic and cultural diversity that emerged. All who were part of that scheme had a social identity tied to some level of identification with the Spanish. The casta system ranked peopled according to skin color and physical features and still exists in the Americas today as the residue of an imposed system of racial division.

The casta system immortalized these new ethnic categories in collections of paintings that highlighted the new racial identities and communicated a social order. Still key to understanding a cultural and social phenomenon that has advanced a hugely influential racial vision of humanity, these paintings open the door to inspecting the Americas' strong ties to eighteenth-century European ideas about race, what were thought then to be the origins of the human species, the meaning of being a Caucasian, and the significance of having a white or brown body in the Americas. All of these developments need to be brought into the light to frame and inform the discussion of race and its impact on the current social order.

Chapter 2, "In Search of Mestizo Identity across the Americas," explores emerging nineteenth- and twentieth-century definitions of mestizo identity and culture. In the nineteenth century, José de Alencar, a Brazilian colonial apologist, identified many issues pertinent to recognizing mestizo identity. José Martí from Cuba recognized mestizo social inequities and the lack of social justice in mestizo lives. Other leading Latin American thinkers from this period, especially José Vasconcelos, joined this dialogue about mestizo identity that has lasted for 150 years.

Touching on five regions of the Americas—Brazil, the Caribbean, Mexico, Peru, and the United States—we can follow writers and cultural theorists from the nineteenth and twentieth centuries who helped to shape mestizo identity and reframe the meaning of race. In the last fifty years, Tomás Rivera, Rudolfo Anaya, Gloria Anzaldúa, Rodolfo Gonzales, and many others have further adjusted the call for social justice in mestizo lives everywhere in the Americas and have helped to create the context for new understandings of racial identity. They have tried to reveal the residue of colonial traditions from the eighteenth century and the "scientific" theories of human origins and the meaning of race that Mexican American writers, critics, and artists are continuing to challenge and replace.

Chapter 3, "There's No Place Like Aztlán: Land, the Southwest, and Rudolfo Anaya," examines Mexican American relationships to land and the importance of the "homeland" ideal in Aztec and Mexican American culture. Discussing land grants and how the Chicano movement generated an understanding of mestizo culture in relation to land, it shows how Mexicans and Mexican Americans have kept alive the idea of reclaiming the original homeland somewhere in the American Southwest, possibly in Santa Fe, New Mexico, as a gesture toward revitalizing traditional approaches to land as a cultural artifact and historical archive.

The writer who conveys the power of the homeland issue, especially in the novel *Shaman Winter,* is Rudolfo Anaya, who clarifies how the Aztlán homeland idea answers questions that plagued the Mexican American community for well over a century. *Shaman Winter* and many of Anaya's novels, stories, and essays clarify a sense of the homeland's importance and point toward the possibility of a new, revitalized (indigenous) relationship to land and land traditions.

Chapter 4, "Remapping Community: Cinco de Mayo, Lowrider Car Culture, and the Day of the Dead," examines Mexican American attempts through popular culture to narrow the gap between American and Mexican values and render Mexican Americans more connected culturally to their new home. Cinco de Mayo, a relatively new U.S. holiday, addresses the social challenges of living in the United States, and this chapter shows how such cultural inventions as holidays create an index for gauging Mexico's influence on the Mexican American community.

Lowrider car culture (a subculture of car enthusiasts redesigning and rebuilding spectacular luxury cars) and the Day of the Dead demonstrate how popular culture contributes to Mexican American attempts to adjust the relationships among tradition, the claims of tradition on the present, and contemporary social needs. With the Day of the Dead practice, a rich history of the Americas unfolds in relation to attitudes about death, the body, and colonialism, making this holiday a treasure trove of historical conflicts and practices in the Americas.

These contemporary popular-culture practices and the hemispheric perspective that they support suggest a broad, nuanced history of the Americas and an advance over "exceptionalist" views of the United States that ignore cultural and historical forces that indeed have shaped the Americas. Mexican Americans have used the critical perspectives arising from popular-culture practices to create a more encompassing view of the United States as part of the hemisphere.

Chapter 5, "Recovering the Body: Literature, Painting, and Sculpture," this book's most expansive inquiry, examines Mesoamerican and European conceptions of the human body and the influence of those models on writers but especially artists from the Chicano Renaissance, late twentieth-century Chicana fiction, and early twenty-first-century American culture. It examines the culturally revealing presentation of the human body in the work of Sandra Cisneros, Denise Chávez, Demetria Martínez, artist Alma López, and painters John Valadez and Alex Donis. It singles out the work of Chicano sculptor Luis Jiménez and the many writers and artists from this period who draw on assumptions advanced in what Richard Shusterman calls "somaesthetics," or body consciousness, an awareness of the world as understood *through* the human body. Somaesthetics reveals a tie to indigenous culture and a particular focus on the body and culture highlighted in the Chicano Renaissance period. During this time, writers and artists forged what it means for a community's voice to arise through the body-culture dialogue that Mexican American writers and artists have defined as their own channel of experience.

Exploring the body in literature and art shows the practical implications of "reclaiming" the body, a task most notably undertaken in the groundbreaking work of the sculptor Luis Jiménez and other contemporary Mexican American artists and writers. The cumulative impact of this work in art and culture and also the scientific critique of race during this period signal the dramatic end of *race* as a sustainable or desirable approach for understanding the body, human nature, and social behavior.

Chapter 6, "Tomás Rivera and the Chicano Voice," reintroduces a neglected writer who helped to define what it means to be Chicano—Tomás Rivera, the novelist, short-story writer, poet, and cultural critic from Crystal City, Texas. Embodying and shaping his culture, devoting himself to bringing recognition to Mexican American lives, Rivera established a cultural "voice" that contributed in major ways to this period's recognition of the Mexican American community. "Signal" writers like Rivera and Anaya create such "voices" to give form to (as if reinventing) their own cultural heritage—in essence, bringing that heritage and its values fully into public view.

The inauguration of such cultural voices marks a moment of empowerment and potential alliances with U.S. mainstream culture, from engagement with Mexican American art, literature, and culture to contributing to ideas about what it means to be a cultural citizen. The bold initiatives of the early Chicano movement—meditations on mestizo identity, the homeland, popular culture, and the human body—combine to produce the effect of a Mexican American cultural "voice" that could be shared with the national culture and the world through literature and other cultural expressions. This is the same "voice" that continues to grow stronger now as the Mexican American community, achieving many of its early goals, gradually assimilates into American culture and focuses on a future with new challenges.

Chapter 7, "Write Home!: Chicano Literature, Chicano Studies, and Resolana," tracks the rise of Chicano literature and Chicano studies as complex and rich expressions of the "voice" that Rivera and Anaya inaugurated. Chicano literature and Chicano studies create vehicles for exploring their community's causes and issues with readers everywhere, legitimizing interest in Mexican American culture for the U.S. mainstream. With this major cultural innovation, non-Latino readers could explore Mexican American culture through the work of Anaya, Rivera, Ana Castillo, Helena Viramontes, Sandra Cisneros, Lorna Dee Cervantes, among others. They could interact with and explore the Mexican American community through literature's examination of cultural practices, values, and ethics. Mexican Americans could examine their own engagement with the national culture and reevaluate goals on their community's behalf. The rise of Chicano literature and Chicano studies greatly amplified the possibilities for Mexican American cultural dissemination and introspection.

Miguel Montiel, Tomás Atencio, and E. A. Mares present a new direction for Chicano studies and for Mexican American culture with the reframing of the old/new practice of resolana. Describing the New Mexican resolana practice of townspeople meeting to share news, solve daily problems, and make decisions about their community, they describe how resolaneros confer to make decisions in the protected space of communal dialogue traditionally valued in New Mexico villages. The contemporary reframing of this traditional practice envisions a new communal knowing and the dialogic sharing of information that deliberately moves outside of higher education and puts traditional knowledge alongside emerging technology and science.

The conclusion, "A Better Future for America," advances that this book's six initiatives have contributed to a new, long-term, better environment for Mexican Americans and an improved future for U.S. mainstream culture. Exposing the cultural differences separating Mexican Americans from mainstream culture, including the cultural conflicts and overt racism that still persist, the initiatives described in this book are reframing traditional values and creating bridges between two cultures, enhancing many of the values fundamental to America's future. Mexican Americans empower themselves by recognizing their own mestizo identity and history in the Americas. Their work toward those goals highlights the emergence of new and old paradigms for understanding identity and culture as hybrid, inherently diverse constructions. Modern genetics has shown that humanity is as varied as the possibilities of the human genome, and the traditional Mexican American foregrounding of mestizo identity, which long ago foreshadowed the genetic argument for human diversity, is instructing the national culture in how to understand ethnic diversity and different forms of cultural and ethnic identity in ways that impact and undercut racism.

This book's chapters as a whole show that Mexican Americans are grappling with cultural and social issues that, owing to globalization and the reigning economic and social forces of our time, are becoming everyone's issues. The initiatives treated in this book, milestones of the Mexican American journey home, have the potential to strengthen U.S. culture by bolstering traditional American values and cultural practices, even filling in ethical and moral gaps where American culture has remained silent. These six areas of cultural change are not the *totality* of Mexican American influence on the United States since 1960, but they are significant initiatives that are transforming U.S. communities with a broad, cultural transformation recapturing some of the grand scope, determination, and spirit that launched the United States as a country to begin with.

Mexican Americans, like other displaced peoples, have been learning to live in multiple worlds and cultures and have learned to navigate issues that others will face as globalization and cultural crossing become everyone's common reality. They are instructing other

Americans through example concerning the complexities of mixed-race identity, hybrid culture, and the hope of bringing about a world more accepting of ethnic difference and cultural diversity. The full picture of Mexican American history in the United States relates many successes and failures, and *Mestizos Come Home!* is telling the detailed story of what they have accomplished, including the new cultural climate that they are creating around their hybrid identity.

Addressing changes that have been opening cultural doors for Mexican Americans since the 1960s and continuing to create new opportunities for the future, this book's six initiatives narrate what is actually happening in Mexican American culture at different levels of cultural change, changes that tie Mexican Americans to demographic realities connected with a quickly expanding population, new voting trends, and emergent economic power. These six changes also represent the story behind the story by revealing deep shifts in the community's view of itself and the United States that foreshadow cultural and social developments that will reshape the country in the years ahead.

Mestizos Come Home! is sharing the outcome and the still-emerging promise of a journey that Mexican Americans have been traveling together since 1848. This journey is not only changing America but enhancing its sense of itself and the viability of democracy as Mexican American and other mestizos gradually take the reins of cultural, social, economic, and political power over the next fifty years. For Mexican Americans, there may never be an actual resolution, no final or definitive arriving home, even in light of the cultural energy of their initiatives. But if the lasting frontier of the American experience is to live in the open interaction and competition of diverse cultures and communities, then Mexican Americans, who define themselves in terms of diversity and multiple ethnic identities, will be at home in the complex future that is evolving for the United States.

As the mainstream culture looks at what Mexican Americans are going through now, they see what the entire country will be facing in the years to come. The question haunting this book throughout is how mestizos can effectively negotiate the tensions involved in preserving ties to their cultural past while adapting their values to reflect not just the current reality but changes yet to come. Other ethnic and

regional communities have come under the same economic pressures
of globalization and international cultural and market forces, and many
traditional communities and large portions of the U.S. middle class are
losing, or have lost, their cohesiveness owing to the changes needed to
compete culturally and economically on an evolving international stage.

I want *Mestizos Come Home!* to be encouraging to Mexican
Americans, showing them that the country is capable of understanding and appreciating, even admiring, what they have accomplished to
travel this journey. This book should also enlighten American mainstream culture, which has too few ways to know about mestizos coming
home. The questions that Mexican Americans are asking surely relate
to everyone in America. How do communities hold together and adjust
to new challenges in a quickly changing world? How does a culture
maintain ties to the past while adapting to the social and economic
demands of the present and the future? Mexican American answers to
these questions appear in the following pages, and it should become
apparent that all who think about the future have a stake in the success
of the Mexican American community. Mexican Americans are engaged
with rapid change during a period of momentous cultural transition,
and almost everyone else will need to learn from them as they discover
their way home.

* I *
CRITIQUING THE SPANISH COLONIAL LEGACY

CHAPTER 1

The Casta Tradition and Mestizos in New Spain

The Spanish created the casta system of racial classification during their colonial period in the Americas. The fullest expression of that system was a genre of painting called "casta painting," an unusual and powerful art form that articulated racial categories and a strict social hierarchy. The remnants of that system are still having an enormous influence on racial identity and social stratification in the United States and the Americas. While Mexican Americans joined an ongoing Latin American conversation about race, culture, and life in the Americas in the 1960s and after, there is still a need to focus on the original Spanish colonial conception of race and the remnants of that system in contemporary culture.

In 2000, the Peruvian sociologist Aníbal Quijano made the remarkable claim that the modern practice of racism, where an entire community is judged according to its racial identity, originated in the Americas. Racism has taken other forms, but Quijano shows that its modern practice may be a more specialized and *recent* phenomenon than many have thought. He was speaking neither of discriminatory attitudes coming out of U.S. slavery nor of "white" dominance in the modern era but of a development in New Spain from the sixteenth through the eighteenth centuries. This "new" form of racism bears not only on Latin American traditions of racial typing before the modern era but also on Mexican Americans and other mestizos in the present and all whose home is in this hemisphere. He writes that the "idea of race . . . does not have a known history before the colonization of America" and adds that "terms such as Spanish and Portuguese, . . . which until then indicated only geographic origin or country of origin, acquired from then on a racial connotation in reference to the new identities" (2000, 534).

Quijano's specific claim is that the Spanish virtually invented racism as it is now practiced—a new social order for which "race and racial identity" became the "instruments of basic social classification." Prior to these developments, the world knew racism as applied to a nationality, culture, or the inhabitants of a region irrespective of skin color or physical features. The new standards for racism that the Spanish created in New Spain have informed all racial identity and racial practices in the Americas and indeed in the world since that time. The "new historical social identities in America—Indians, blacks, and mestizos"—were "new" in the sense that these labels had not been used before to name a specific community based on race in a systematic approach to the domination of a people—in this case, a people who would become the source of labor for a whole economy (534).

Those new social identities came about when the Spanish, seeking wealth and religious conversions in the New World, colonized indigenous peoples and later brought Africans into the Americas. There is no reason to think that the Spanish anticipated where these actions would lead or the world-changing processes that they had set in motion. Robert J. C. Young comments that in their eagerness to promote empire in the Americas, the Spanish instead "produced [their] own darkest fantasy—the unlimited and ungovernable fertility of 'unnatural' unions" (1995, 98). The huge wave of "'unnatural' unions," a defining event for New Spain and the history of social and political life in the Americas, meant the rise of new racial and cultural identities and the emergence of new communities within the colonial world.

To cope with the reshaping of New Spain's cultural foundations, the Spanish designed el sistema de casta, the casta system, an elaborate plan for social ranking to monitor and control the outcomes of these immense demographic changes. Comprised of racial and social categories and elaborate schemes for assigning people to those categories, el sistema de casta structured social life in the Americas for almost three centuries. The far-reaching effects of this landmark experiment in social engineering are still having an impact on Mexican Americans and all in the Americas in the way that people understand and live the daily reality of race. It is for these various reasons—mainly the connection between Spanish colonial and present-day racial practices—that an understanding of mestizo identity and race in the Americas must reference this racial innovation from the Spanish colonial period.

While New Spain's indigenous population as a whole declined drastically under Spanish rule, reducing the population by almost 25 million people over the seventeenth century alone (Cook and Borah 1979, 1, 100), in 1811 the overall population of Mexico City reached 169,811, a tripling of the population documented in 1689. This increase came through intermarriage with the Spanish, indigenous, and black people (Carrera 2003, 38). With this population increase in the capital city, and with the high rate of intermarriage, the active mixing of cultures during the seventeenth and eighteenth centuries challenged the Spanish to monitor cultural and social changes. The casta system was a way for them to oversee the proliferation of racial identities, the rise of new social classes, and, in effect, keep themselves relevant in terms of actual governance and cultural influence.

Where do we find the beginnings of this important racial history in the Americas? Do we look at Christopher Columbus's governorship of Hispaniola in the 1490s, or the exploits of conquistadors such as Vasco Núñez de Balboa, who created the first permanent European settlement in the Americas in 1510? Do we look at the years 1519–21 and the conquest of Mexico as Hernán Cortés defeated the great Aztec empire, fathered a child with the Nahua interpreter Malintzin, and in 1551 occupied the Yucatán Peninsula? Perhaps we should focus on 1532 as the colonial surge reached its zenith when Francisco Pizarro established the first Spanish settlement in Peru and conquered the Inca Empire.

Any of these venues and time periods would do, as long as we focus on the racial system that Quijano references. We must begin, in other words, with the families created by the mixing in New Spain of indigenous, African, Asian, and European peoples under the harshest of circumstances. With little social precedent and no official support or encouragement, indigenous, European, Asian, and African people formed families, built communities, raised children, resisted oppression, and courageously improvised New World lives in spite of all of the hardships thrust upon them. How might we examine these unions? Where might we find accounts of them individually and as families?

Shortly after Quijano's (2000) comment about the origins of modern racism in the Americas, a veritable archive of Spanish colonial culture became readily available, an archive that referenced a large variety of interracial families and emerging identities in New Spain. The 2003 publication of Magali M. Carrera's *Imagining Identity in New Spain: Race, Lineage, and the Colonial Body in Portraiture and Casta Paintings* and Ilona Katzew's 2004 *Casta Painting* put into general circulation a rich gallery of New Spain's families and their offspring. Featuring the lower classes and working poor, these paintings were historical portraits, not of known people, but of racial types from that era.

The format of these casta paintings was always to depict two parents and one or two children and present families as one might have seen them walking on New Spain's streets, in intimate moments of conversation with friends, with work tools in their shops, in their homes, and as they might have looked strolling into a painter's studio to sit for a portrait. These casta paintings especially foreground children, usually one child, as in every case representing an emergent "new" racial identity. These books were not the first to make this rich material available, but their wide dissemination in English made it newly accessible for a large audience.[1]

The Mexican painters who worked in this genre created casta paintings to reflect the official view of race and show how parents and their children, typically young or middle-aged parents and a child of three to eight years old, fit in the larger social context that the Spanish were creating and tried to monitor. Both the quality of the renderings and their historical relevance make them valuable for understanding the social structure and culture, as well as the racial orientation, of New Spain. Also, with no existing single document or formal statement about the casta system's racial categories and terms and no single decree or treatise explaining how the Spanish categorized racial mixes appearing rapidly in New Spain during this period (at least, none so far), these paintings are still the best record of the casta system and the racial categories that the Spanish invented.

Carrera (2003) and Katzew (2004) provide, in other words, ready and unparalleled access to a rich reserve of Spanish colonial culture—views of people with new racial identities, behaviors, body postures, facial expressions, and varieties of clothing, tools, and furniture. With many reproductions of eighteenth-century casta paintings, and offering vital cultural and social insights about Spanish colonialism and life in New Spain, these two books show roughly two hundred families—about four hundred adults and two hundred children. While in the modern era the people depicted in these abundant and diverse paintings will be called simply "mestizos"—the modern name for the Americas' mixed-race people—the casta paintings focus on the precise details of many official racial categories of that time and offer a level of nuance and clarity that portraits and sets of paintings are especially effective at providing.

Created from a Spanish colonial perspective, these casta paintings interpret the complex world of racial identity and new social orders emerging in colonial New Spain. Many were painted anonymously, but well-known Mexican painters of the period—Miguel Cabrera, Luis de Mena, Luis Berrueco, Juan Patricio Morlete Ruiz, Andrés de Islas, José de Páez, and José Joaquín—created the best and most revealing of them (Katzew 2004, 3). The quality varied, but the painting's immediate goal was always to categorize and rank the new racial identities appearing in the rapidly expanding, New Spain social system.

The casta paintings were popular and plentiful, and many European visitors bought them as souvenirs. While no one knows for sure, the Spanish probably intended the paintings to be tools to enable a serious reconceptualization of race in the Americas consistent with maintaining social control of New Spain (Katzew 2004, 7).[2] The unintended social consequences of broad racial mixing and the Spanish attempts to categorize those "unnatural" unions in New Spain—"the nightmare of [those] ideologies and categories of racism," as Young calls such institutions, the way the Spanish went about defining and implementing a social hierarchy based on race—"continue to repeat upon the living [today]" as racial categories that still define many contemporary social classes (1995, 28). Moreover, the legacy of the casta system is evidenced in the continuing phenomenon of racial discrimination, oppression, and violence in the United States, and it is for these reasons that casta representations of mestizo identity in New Spain need to be a part of any discussion of what it means for modern-day mestizos, the inheritors of that tradition, to understand the social conditions that shaped racial identities in the United States and this hemisphere.

Quijano's observation about the Spanish approach to race in the Americas helpfully emphasizes the *making* of race, exactly as Mexican Americans will do in the late twentieth century (see chapter 2), the *how* of creating mestizo identity and race as social constructs. That focus on process provides insight into the issue of race in the Americas and a basis for understanding its operation. *How* did race happen in the Americas? There are hundreds of casta paintings that can be called upon for an answer. Each one stages a kind of racial "beginning" and creates the specter of race emerging anew with different racial categories constantly appearing in casta paintings every few years. Each painting says, "Here, look at me, and you will see one of the mixed-race families in New Spain and also the results of that mixing in the child who stands before you."

These paintings are the Spanish colonial version of *how* race happened in the Americas, and the paintings also show what the casta process produced as a hierarchical racial system, a complex, racialized culture. In these paintings, we peer at bodies and clothes on display *within* defined aesthetic, economic, and social settings and categories. Like a police lineup with suspects marching through to have their pictures painted, the casta system presents human bodies in a continuum with some people *embodying* Spanish values and others with dark skin and merely hanging on for dear life trying to be relevant on the margins of Spanish colonial culture and society.[3]

After almost five hundred years, this system of racial typing is currently in tatters, except that many of its principles still define racial identities and continue to divide people from each other. When Young comments that "the apparently ineffaceable, proliferating legacies of racialism continue [to this day] to generate the cultures that produced them" in the first place, we can add that the brown bodies in the Americas are still harvesting crops for low wages, still cutting lawns, still washing dishes, cleaning houses, and tending to white children.

Those who employ them are still the privileged class, most frequently with light skin, who are far removed from the reality of low-wage labor—a social scenario disturbingly similar to that of Spanish colonial America (1995, 141).

Quijano's observation also leads to the question of "voice" in the casta paintings. We can try to hear the individual voices of colonial culture in these paintings. What do the voices of the people presented—elites and the lower classes—say about race and social harmony and the potential of social order and disruption in the Americas? We can hear the muted voices of mestizos and other castas in these paintings—"silent" voices that can be heard through channels that the Spanish could not control. Just as the bones and carcasses of the *disappeared* in Latin America in the twenty-first century speak through forensic clues and hidden circumstances, we can hear the people in the casta social classes who, like bodies hidden after a crime, still try to rise up to speak from these paintings to tell their long-delayed story. We must be patient to hear what the casta people say and what their bodies tell us about how they arrived where they are, what they wanted, and who they still want to be.

We need to understand these four issues in relation to the casta paintings because each can help to explain the legacy of the mestizo presence in the Americans and what it will mean later for mestizos to "come home." Those issues are:

1. *How* race happened in the Americas.
2. The social outcomes of el sistema de casta in the Americas.
3. What the casta paintings show about the human body in New Spain.
4. The voices heard in the casta paintings—both those of Spanish colonialism and the lower-class voices not officially permitted to speak.

We also need to query the assumptions that the Spanish brought to their understanding of identity for the underclasses, especially their characterization of indigenous and black people as animalistic, degenerative, and monstrous. Those assumptions, too, are part of the tradition of mestizo identity in the Americas, a key part, particularly making the brown body a convoluted and destructive racial puzzle that has been left for us to understand, unravel, and reimagine.

HOW RACE HAPPENED IN THE AMERICAS

We begin with the casta paintings *as paintings* reflecting what they are as an artistic medium along with the concerns and issues of this period. In spite of their belonging to the casta, formulaic genre, these paintings were often masterful color portraits of New Spain's mixed-race people—craftspeople, merchants, manual laborers, women, men, and children. Usually painted on canvas or copper plates (approximately 80 x 105 centimeters or sometimes smaller), the paintings always came in sets of sixteen (Carrera 2003, 63–65). Like contemporary film storyboards or graphic novels, they were created to be viewed in sequence, starting with the least racially mixed (painting 1) on the top left of a set of sixteen and ending with the most racially mixed figure at the social hierarchy's fringes, the bottom right of that set (painting 16).

The figures in the paintings are a broad sampling of people drawn from Spanish colonial culture, a few of the calidad, or people of the highest social standing, but mainly the working poor for whom the paintings offered guidance and direction for official and proper conduct. The figures also offer a glimpse of how a person's own demeanor and conduct relate to the larger picture of other social classes. No one knows for sure, but in colonial New Spain the paintings appear to have had this didactic function showing appropriate self-presentation and, as much as a painting can demonstrate behavior, how to act. The format for each painting, a family in a private, domestic moment, sometimes in nature but more often indoors, usually shows three people—two parents and a child. The whole family will be posed before a blank wall, or, later in the genre (after 1760), in a drawing room, a kitchen, or on the grounds of the family's house. The parents are always of different races, and in the moment depicted in the painting, the families are immersed in a domestic drama, parents sometimes scolding their child or in an argument or in intimate couple communication. Intended to pinpoint racial identity, the paintings generally have a legend inscribed beneath the image to specify the child's identity and ranking in the social hierarchy.

There are about one hundred complete sets of casta paintings still in existence, along with a few incomplete sets, many in museums and others in private collections (Katzew 2004, 5). Each complete casta set highlights sixteen racial categories, with four racial labels (in addition to Español) commonly repeated in many paintings—usually mestiza, castiza, mulata, and morisca (36–37).[4] Viewing the paintings from left to right, the intended order of viewing, we see that each painting generally moves one step further away from being a "purely" Spanish person, with the final three or four paintings (13, 14, 15, and 16) showing people with complex racial backgrounds, examples of people having little or no social standing to claim (figure 1.1).

Showing a panorama of eighteenth-century young people living in New Spain, these paintings probably depict actual people. At least, we can speculate on that since their appearance is nuanced and often appears with a kind of photographic clarity. Whether showing people who posed for the paintings or were friends that the painters knew, the paintings create a robust sense of life and vitality and as a genre are literally without precedent in Western art. At the same time, the portraits presented in sequence form a rational grid with the graphic display of racial and social types who might appear in a catalog or typology chart. The two-tiered effect of this presentation allows the casta paintings, when seen up close, to be a celebration of the rich drama of human diversity in New Spain with nuanced facial expressions as the people respond to the challenges of domestic life. But when viewed from further back, we see racial types rigidly grouped in sets of sixteen, four rows of four, creating a racial chart accompanied by an explicit set of racial names and judgments. At this greater distance, the faces readily become anonymous "types" with each one occupying a slot in a grid for an ordered, enlightened, and highly rational understanding of race as expressing the social logic of Spanish colonialism.

Whatever the Spanish were intending, the painting sets convey an austere and systematic understanding of "race" in New Spain. The tension between the paintings' close-up vitality and the imposed racial grid runs throughout the casta sets. This is the same tension, by the way, that runs throughout much of Spanish colonial culture as a world ordered by a teeming sense of humanity *and* an ordered grid of racial organization. This same tension runs through broader eighteenth-century racial thought and "scientific" approaches to race in Europe, and these paintings connect with and contribute to that larger conversation, as I will discuss in a moment.

A key feature of the casta paintings is the eighteenth-century assumption that racial features are *naturally* visible on the human body's surface. The assumption is that a person's appearance or body can accurately reveal character and essential identity traits. In other words, the markers of calidad (high social prestige) were thought to be features observable through the body's physical appearance, clothing, social bearing, along with the natural association with fine furniture and comfortable surroundings. The Spanish found a way, in other words, to represent those details visually so that a painter could include all of them in a single casta portrait. The paintings' details (facial features, clothing, tools, and appropriate setting) could then be observed by a Spaniard who, occupying a high social ranking outside of the casta system, could judge others according to how they looked, by their skin tone and racial categories, in effect judging others by how "Spanish" or near-Spanish they might be. In this way, the lower classes could be monitored in light of their appearance to allow for accurate identifications of race and pedigree.

Much about the casta paintings and the reality of race in New Spain involves displaying human bodies as objects and the process of labeling their social value. The Spanish promoted the idea that people with dark skin with certain "phenotype traits [skin color, hair type, facial features, etc.] as well as their cultural features were . . . inferior" and even edged toward the threshold of being inhuman (Quijano 2000, 535). The Spanish painters strove to make every detail of physiognomy visible in the casta paintings—skin, hair, eyes, facial shape—to point *not* toward the possible intricacies of individual character, culture, and circumstance but toward a precise social ranking. This odd connection between physical traits and class membership was powerful but also novel for that time and in its own way went to the heart of the Spanish approach to race. Before this time, one's identity was more likely tied, as Quijano (2000) notes, to a geographical region, and the details of hair and skin color, eye color, and other traits were individual peculiarities and accidents of birth and nationality. For the Spanish in the colonial period, *all* of those characteristics of phenotype were transformed into being arrows, in an enormous act of human reductionism, that point in one direction toward a racial and social category (Quijano 2000, 534).

With race and its privileges for the first time linked directly to physiognomy, a lower-class person in New Spain, and in the world since, wore the signs of race like a badge or a prison uniform that never comes off. This is the legacy of race that belongs to the Americas, where the accidents of physiognomy are cast as precise signifiers of race, social privilege, and power. When the process of imposing such connections gets repeated many times between the sixteenth and eighteenth centuries, complex racial communities take shape with various connections to different levels of social power and privilege—hence New Spain's "modern" approach to identity, race, and social categorizing.

It is remarkable to note that the Spanish went through this process and took such steps to create completely new categories of people. They first brought new ethnic groups into the hemisphere and then, with the unplanned explosion of mixed people, created new racial identities according to their own dictates. They adopted the term "Indian" (after Christopher Columbus's usage) as a class of slave and serf labor referring to native peoples, little concerned with the tens of thousands of cultural and social distinctions pertinent to actual tribes and cultures. They named Africans "blacks," using a label of convenience, a kind of color coding, that had meaning only as a contrast to the "red" community of serfs and slaves with no connection to actual African cultures. Such colonial categorizing and naming reflected Spanish attitudes toward their human possessions and the efficient management of colonial business interests (Quijano 2000, 533).

We can already see that an awareness of race as the cultural inheritance of the casta system is critical for gaining insight into race and racism's deeply entrenched historical, economic, and social complexities in the present. Uncovering racism's deepest roots in New Spain creates an enhanced ability to see what to this day has too often been the invisible but powerful legacy of opportunistic exploitation shrouded in religious or pseudoscientific discourse about divine sanction, racism, and the natural order. With the advantage of historical perspective and seeing the social construction of race for what it is and understanding where it started, we become equipped to productively challenge racism's myriad forms of oppression and violence in the present.

THE SOCIAL OUTCOME OF EL SISTEMA DE CASTA IN THE AMERICAS

We know that the results of the casta system are evident in contemporary culture in the Americas. How do we know that? Anyone who speaks of blacks, whites, Indians, mestizos, and mulattos is referencing casta terminology that was applied to Spanish slaves and serfs between the sixteenth and the late eighteenth centuries. The casta system not only was a system of racial terms but a set of strictures and prohibitions. A Spanish royal decree of 1563 stipulated that lower-class people, former slaves, could live only in approved neighborhoods, and as early as the late sixteenth century the lower classes were "forbidden from employing Indian labor, bearing arms without proper permission, claiming Indian nobility status, working as public notaries, and being ordained priests" (Katzew 2004, 40). The lower classes paid "tributes" and taxes higher than the upper classes, and the Spanish elites found many ways to reward the social classes who did their duty and punished those who strayed, so clearly much hinged on where one fit into the casta system (Cahill 1994, 336; Katzew 2004, 45).

This racial classification system impacted virtually every aspect of social and cultural life in the Americas, and no one alive during the Spanish colonial era could escape its racial typing. This system expressed not only the social reality of New Spain's diversity but also a perspective revealing about the Spanish colonial mindset. Always understanding mixed-race people in relation to themselves as a final cultural reference—what Gilles Deleuze and Félix Guattari call "racism [as] . . . degrees of deviance in relation to the White-Man face"— the Spanish sent a racial message so impactful that even today those of us with indigenous ancestors, but virtually any citizen of the Americas, must peer at the skin of our arms, legs, and faces as seen through the racial filter that the Spanish created (1977, 178).

The elites of the colonial period were the Spanish, the gente de razón, "people of reason," and they were the primary reference for the casta system. The lower classes were the gente sin razón, "people without reason." These were categories fixed by birth and physiognomy, but someone relatively higher up in the casta system on occasion could succeed and claim higher status with documented claims to a better ranking. But the message of each painting was generally that people in every racial category belong in the social slot where "nature" and God placed them in terms of what they looked like, their responsibilities, the social rewards that they could expect, and how they needed to behave.

The behavior of the elite Spaniards in the paintings shows their supposedly superior character, refined demeanor, and display of calidad. This character came out as measured and reasoned responses to everything and a calm and dignified demeanor. The lower classes, by contrast, tended to have bad tempers and showed a lack of compassion and refinement, behaviors shown commonly in the bickering and fighting of parents and in the poor behavior of mixed-race children. These standards of behavior depicted in the paintings convey the cautionary moral principle about the social benefit of accepting one's place in the colonial great chain of being, of striving to be on the better side of one's nature—regardless of how inappropriate or counterintuitive such compliance might have seemed.

The paintings also dramatize that moving away from being purely Spanish through marriage with non-Spaniards was costly and generally not a good idea. A family lowering its social position by marrying into other races, especially Africans, quickly tumbled down the social hierarchy. They would earn negative identity points expressing the community's dismay over their fall and be labeled with terms such as "lobo" ("wolf"). These are frequently shown in the eighth painting in the series ("Tente en el aire" ["He Is Held in the Air"]), the fourteenth painting in the series ("No te entiendo" ["I'm Not Understanding You"]), the fifteenth painting, and the sixteenth painting ("Torna atras" ["A Jump Backward"]). The person named in these categories lost social positioning and could be classified as no longer rational and could possibly be starting to exhibit animal traits, as the labels suggest, all indicating the fate of the fallen.

A discredited family on occasion could raise its limpieza de sangre, its purity of blood—the prototype for modern "blood quantum"—through "blood mending." This option was a lengthy process of inter-marrying with Spaniards (Carrera 2003, 10–14). Classic blood mending occurred when a castizo (the product of mestizo and Spanish parents) married a Spaniard. This was an option suggesting forgiveness and active encouragement for families to return to the correct racial order, and this couple's child would actually be a Spaniard again. The absolute limitation on blood mending concerned black people. In *A Description of the Kingdom of New Spain, 1774,* Pedro Alonso O'Crouley writes that a mulatto "can never leave his condition of mixed blood" because when black people are involved "the Spanish element . . . is lost and absorbed in the condition of [being] a Negro" (1972, 20). Whereas mestizo blood was merely *"diluted,"* with a mix that produced lower social value, black blood was indelible "pollution," and the Spanish allowed no blood mending for the polluted person (Carrera 2003, 12; emphasis added).

Casta paintings produced before 1760 tended to show people posed against a blank or undifferentiated background. After 1760, as racial mixing increased in eighteenth-century New Spain, the Spanish worried about "discerning the different social groups in the colony, owing partly to the fact that clothes were [also] often used to disguise identity" (Katzew 2004, 107–8). In response, painters added real-life work back-grounds and tools to their paintings, specific details that tied lower-class figures to actual jobs with observable social status. This change "articulate[d] the anxieties" of Spanish elites who feared that they could no longer identify race based on the mere observation of skin tone and clothing alone, which meant that they were finding that racial realities, unlike racial systems, were impossible to control or keep from changing and evolving (Katzew 2004, 109, 203; Carrera 2003, 104).

Casta painters after 1760 also showed more upper-class families in stylized portraits foregrounding their superior demeanor. In these paintings, refined figures sit tranquilly, are patient in their contemplation of problems, and express loving regard for their children. By contrast, the conventional wisdom said that the racially mixed often act badly, as is shown in paintings with discord and violence. These paintings pinpoint social problems such as child neglect, marital conflict, bickering, domestic violence, and so on. An example of such family discord is shown in a 1763 painting where a Barsino child (a zoological term meaning "white and spotted" but applied here as a lower-class racial category) cries while her mother brushes her hair. The child is handing money to her father, while her brother offers her food. The viewer and the brother are the only witnesses to the child's tears (Carrera 2003, 79). The painting's judgment concerns the parents' lack of compassion for their daughter. A moment of greater familial conflict is seen in a 1774 painting in which the parents are actually fighting (figure 1.2). In this painting, the Spanish husband fends off his wife's blows, while the black wife swings at him with a kitchen utensil, and their frightened child struggles to hold the parents apart.

The subtleties of demeanor come up frequently in these paintings. In a 1763 painting, a black mother sits in profile and looks straight ahead as if staring through her unhappy child. The little girl before her leans in the other way to her Spanish father, and he comforts her tenderly with a kind face and warm embrace (Katzew 2004, 102). The painting connects compassion as a characteristic consistent with being of the gente de razón but not of the gente sin razón. The painting implicitly cautions against an upper-class person looking to lower-class (mixed-race) people for understanding and deeper feeling.

A famous casta painting from 1763 by the great eighteenth-century painter Miguel Cabrera makes an even stronger statement about the supposed inherent tendencies of the gente sin razón. In this painting, a "coyote" son (the product of mestizo and indigenous parents) sits atop a horse behind his parents. The stern-faced boy raises a stick in an ominous gesture and appears ready to strike his father (figure 1.3). The stick holder is only a child, but the boy's compositional prominence in the painting and the attention given to his raised arm and stick invite speculation that his actions could foreshadow a future of rebellion against authority, social disruption, and violence—in short, a warning to the calidad about the seeds of potential violence present in the casta classes.

There were clearly more racial identities possible in New Spain than the depiction of sixteen shown in the individual casta sets. The one hundred or so existing casta collections show the possibilities for racial mixing to be great indeed.[5] However, depicting sixteen types at a time tended to reenforce Spanish identity, since the sixteen racial categories could be specifically chosen to contrast in a flattering way with Spanish traits such as light skin, a rational approach to the world, a calm demeanor, compassion for others, and so on. The casta painting sets, as Carrera comments, systematically defined by contrast "what elite identity was *not*—that is, not poor, not laboring, not dressed in tatters, and, thus, not debased as were the depicted urban poor" (2003, 104). This set of mutually defining identities, as Robert Young notes, is typical of colonial cultures where the clear aim is to *subordinate* and yet not destroy the lower classes within a colonial social hierarchy. Whereas the casta system officially speaks with the "single voice of colonial authority," that voice constantly reveals a dependence on the lower classes to define the fact of prestige at the upper levels. The continual dialogue going on between racial categories creates this kind of "double-voiced" effect for almost everything conveyed "officially" in these paintings or in colonial culture (Young 1995, 23).

We see this same logic of double voicing at work in the five casta paintings referenced here, particularly in their four most prominent themes: (1) impurity versus purity of blood; (2) disorderly conduct versus self-possession; (3) poverty versus wealth; (4) and manual labor versus mental work. These paintings show that a Spaniard is "white," racially unmixed, has a refined manner, is wealthy, and has a prestigious job, profession, or governmental post. By contrast, a lower-class person is dark skinned, impetuous, violent, poor, and has a job with little or no social prestige. There are degrees of correspondence between upper- and lower-class people, and in this instance each negative feature in the lower-class person generally references a positive one in the upper-class person.

This colonial logic points up the historical irony of the Spanish fostering a view of themselves as an unproblematic and "unified" racial and social reference. A creole cleric from New Spain, Fray Servando Teresa y Mier (1703–1827), writes about Spanish hypocrisy in this regard when he notes that fellow "Spaniards [are] infinitely more 'mixed' than [are] Mexico's natives" (Katzew 2004, 204). In point of fact, Spanish ancestors—Roman, German, Moorish, Celt, Basque, Vandal, Asian, North African, Catalan, Galician, Jewish, and Chinese—were numerous, and the Spanish worked through many complex cultural and identity stages before finally being able to establish a clear sense of being "Spanish," as M. J. Rodriguez-Salgado discusses. By the time of New Spain, the Spanish social identity could be presented as being unproblematic—the light-skinned, self-possessed, wealthy, and naturally refined people from Spain. They were the people who worked with their minds and so naturally could orient all other people and social categories to their own refined nature, a claim possible to make by virtue of being the group in power. Winant comments in *Racial Conditions* that such a racial system for short periods can incorporate "contestation," any sort of challenge to or change in its operation, including new racial categories, as long as there is a consistent, nonproblematic racial reference point in place. The Spanish understood this logic and presented themselves as that point by defining themselves almost completely with the traits and values that they chose to be associated with (1994, 113).

As representatives of modern science and race theory, Michael Omi and Howard Winant point out the obvious in that, contrary to the racial assumptions conveyed in these eighteenth-century paintings, there is no automatic natural, cultural, or racial significance to facial and bodily features beyond being the accidental manifestations of being human (1986; Winant 1994, 2004). Omi and Winant not only caution against backing in to these assumptions about the telling nature of human physiognomy that belong to the eighteenth century but also weigh in against modern folklore and legends still circulating in the twenty-first century that say the exact same thing—that people *can* be known through the details of how they look. Such assumptions are frequently unstated but present even in contemporary popular culture.

The Western history of race—especially since the Spanish conquest in the Americas—includes depressing collections of charts for noses, faces, eye shapes, jaws, and body types, all of which are meant to contrast the supposedly superior from the inferior varieties, and such attempts at racial typing have always been doomed to failure. The modern, more enlightened arguments are simply that human features do not naturally reveal social life, human destiny, a person's worth or potential. Human physiognomy, in fact, is the great blank screen on which people have always projected character strengths, personal shortcomings, and various indicators of calidad. Such projections of value have always failed, and will always fail, to solve the mystery of why one person looks and acts differently from another (Omi and Winant 1986; Winant 1994, 2004).

Omi and Winant also remark that detailed aspects of human physiognomy, in fact, take on cultural and "racial" meaning only when someone *assigns* meaning to them. The casta painters, for example, present the details of how people look to indicate the relevant racial categories that Spanish colonial elites assigned to people as fundamental to how the casta system worked. Such racial labeling reflects the influence of whatever social and ideological forces, some benevolent and some pernicious, some reflective of eighteen-century politics and ideology and some more ephemeral expressions of eighteenth-century taste, that were in motion in New Spain when racial assignments were made.

However they occur, assignments of racial status create a system of racial types with predetermined social value. Such constructions of meaning may at times be difficult to detect because when racial categories come into existence, they are usually presented as if to *seem* natural, preexisting, God given, or unalterable. There is a tradition of regimes and elite groups constructing racial hierarchies disguised as reflections of the natural order or God's will. Most people in any period would probably not accept the extremes of social coercion or widespread tyranny indexed to racial categories without an imposed or supernatural rationale justifying the oppression.

Omi and Winant add a last crucial point, which is that the social construction of race never completely succeeds. Social identity and socioeconomic placement operate not as simple assignments of one-to-one meaning, given once and with no modicum of meaning left over, but as multipronged "processes" always generating more meaning and significance than a racial category can generally encompass at any one moment. Winant explains in *The New Politics of Race* that racial identity constantly evolves as new racial types appear and as old ones change. Social evolution and history, changing significance, will always frustrate attempts to direct or control a culture's racial identities. This is true since racial categories are dynamic and susceptible to change at every moment as they react to ongoing "sociopolitical conflicts and interests in reference to different types of human bodies" (2004, x).

Those "sociopolitical conflicts and interests" alter the conditions in which racial categories are constantly re-formed as the "social, economic, and political forces determin[ing] the content and importance of racial categories" invariably change over time (Omi and Winant 1986, 61). The effect of time and history on racial categories will always unsettle cultures and societies, as happened in New Spain, where for hundreds of years race was officially viewed as a fixed and unalterable system of racial references even while it was rapidly evolving.

The end result of racial formation, as Omi and Winant call racial development, will always be framed by that culture as "natural," as if God at some point separated people into different social groups and gave each a credit account for future goods and services based on racial assignment. We can see that the Spanish themselves doled out the racial assignments of the casta social order, set in motion the appropriate reward system, and then attributed those assignments to nature and God. They did all of this and sorted indigenous peoples, Africans, and others to consolidate and expand their own social, economic, and political influence as colonialists and social engineers.

It is notoriously difficult for people to critique their own cultural categories, their own ideological investments, especially when race enters the picture. The process of assigning categories is most successful when the construction of race happens in someone else's culture in a historical period remote from one's own. In the case of the casta system, where we arrive on the scene almost five hundred years after the fact, we clearly have the advantage of distance and perspective sufficient to analyze Spanish colonial culture to another level and discover some of the values expressed in the casta system's display of bodies and social rankings that connect this system to other racial practices in the seventeenth and eighteenth centuries.

WHAT THE CASTA PAINTINGS SHOW ABOUT THE HUMAN BODY IN NEW SPAIN

While the casta paintings are unique as a genre of Western art, they also echo other practices during this period and after that associate lower-class people with dark skin and bad behavior. We can look at the period between the American Revolution and the Civil War, for example, and discover the fairly common practice of publishing "descriptions and pictorial representations of whites coupling with blacks. . . . Novelists, short-story writers, poets, journalists, and political cartoonists . . . devoted a vast amount of energy to depicting blacks and whites dancing, flirting, kissing, and marrying one another. Invariably, the blacks are portrayed as ugly, animal-like, and foul-smelling. This makes them easily distinguishable from the whites, who are usually portrayed as physically attractive" (Lemire 2002, 1). These pre–Civil War depictions of racial mixing promoted the idea of bad behavior as natural to people with dark skin and suggested that animalistic attributes and human malformation proliferate in such circles, even on occasion among white people in those social groups, owing to the association with black people in a degraded environment.

Such depictions of black and white comingling reference a number of racial assumptions that circulated throughout the eighteenth and nineteenth centuries within, but also well beyond, the Americas. Eighteenth-century "scientific" race theorists in Europe, for example, tended to rely upon implied or expressed taxonomies for different kinds of people conveying the judgments that Elise Lemire describes as a basis for racial "rankings." In other words, underlying this description of racist art and literature, where pre–Civil War artists and writers associated dark skin and white lower class people with the debased human body and a low order of humanity, is the belief that being closely associated with the human body, especially in connection with the lower classes, signals an actual loss of humanity. Many eighteenth-century race theorists, in fact, believed in an animalistic and monstrous potential generally evident, but perhaps not always expressed, in lower-class people and associated with their close connection to the human body. These were assumptions about the degrading effects of the human body expressed even in "scientific" approaches to race, attitudes about the human body with a lineage going back to Plato.

Richard Shusterman comments that Western culture historically has shown a consistent reserve and at times deep suspicion about the human body that was evident in eighteenth-century religion, art, and gender relations. In these scenarios, the Western body consistently gets cast as a debasement to human dignity and a strike against the higher aspirations of being human, associations tied to manual labor and those performing activities defined almost solely as physical and the work of bodies. The body frequently even appears in Western culture as a dank "prison" that encloses the human soul, a sad burden of being human, fostering "fallen" and even tragic dimensions of being alive. In many Western societies, the body is also at times a kind of living contagion that prompts the need for rites of purification and rituals of ascesis and self-flagellation intended to address the basic overwhelming impurity of having a material body along with everything that can go wrong with it (Shusterman 2008, 5).

As part of the Western acculturation that comes with belonging to a high social class or station, upper-class people in many cultures simply learn to tolerate their bodies but also to actively resist the body's degrading influence in whatever ways possible. The traditional wisdom here says that to fulfill humanity's greatest potential, people must elevate their human identity above the bodily realm so that its material, corrupt nature will not restrain them. There is a long tradition in the West of so-called cultured people viewing the body with great disdain and seeing it as a threat to a superior mental and spiritual life, the body being a material obstacle to the supposed transcendent beauty and perfection of human potential, "the life of the mind" (Shusterman 2008, 5).

Richard Sennett notes in *Flesh and Stone: The Body and the City in Western Civilization* that a traditional response to the supposedly impure body is to institute an ideal form of it, an elevated and transformed version, as a defense against the decay and death normally associated with it. The result is a version of the body seemingly immune, or resistant, to destructive, material processes. This strategy is evident in Christianity and Eastern religions where there is an emphasis on a "risen," transformed body that can defeat death. Its way of defeating death is held up for imitation by others. When a community or a religion establishes such an ideal, elevated body, or a class of such bodies, or "when a society or political order speaks generically about 'the body,'" or about the body's transcendent potential, as Sennett comments, "it can [also] deny the needs of bodies which do not fit the master plan" (1994, 23). In proclaiming the transformed version of the body to be transcending the corporeal level of normal bodies, a community's "master plan" triumphs over the real body's base, physical nature, which often means creating a lowly status for the bodies left behind for common people and the lower classes.

This scenario is precisely the case in New Spain as the gente de razón, the upper classes, defined the otherworldly side of being human and themselves as belonging to the calidad that represents the refined world. Superior beings in this world belong to a rarefied social class, the gente de razón, and have wisdom, calm demeanors, social prestige, and little direct identification with the human body. All of this is true especially since their refined temperament lifts them into a cultured world that appears not to depend on the body for any definition whatsoever. The gente de razón assign normal bodily life and its functions to the fallen, material bodies of the underclasses that serve them, projecting onto the gente sin razón, in other words, the life of base appetites, gross bodily functions, and social responsibilities anchored in the body and physical labor. When the casta system degenerated and ended in the late eighteenth century, mestizos accordingly had to begin the long process of recovering their lost, taboo bodies, a process that they are still engaged in doing to the present day.

We can find parallels to the casta system in race theories in Europe from the same time period. In the work of naturalists Carl Linnaeus (1707–78), Johann Blumenbach (1752–1840), and Christoph Meiners (1747–1810), we find the familiar preoccupations of the casta system concerning race, skin color, body types, social class, and the tension between a recognition of human diversity and rational schemes categorizing and ranking varieties of bodies. In the early eighteenth century in Europe, there was an emerging wave of interest in the new physical anthropology and the measurement and comparison of human skulls, skeletons, skin types, noses, hair, beards, genitalia, and every dimension of the body with human and nonhuman specimens sampled from around the world. The excitement of science during this period came from knowledge produced by this new perspective and comparative techniques that allowed naturalists to extract human metrics (the measurement of skulls, pelvises, arm height, and so on) and place them, as Londa Schiebinger describes, among the "natural qualities of plants, animals, and [other] humans." This comparison reveals "a continuous natural order that stretched seamlessly from nature to culture and back again." This was a heady time in which naturalists discovered taxonomic comparison as a productive engine for driving science and peering into the natural world where the objects of science were supposedly "stripped clean of history and culture." During this period, there was excitement about the knowledge produced through the discovery of the rich animal and human order rife with diversity, generating new and potentially challenging forms of scientific information (Schiebinger 2004, xii).

At the same time, as naturalists peered into this great diversity of life forms for investigation, they were also imposing over these discoveries typology charts, schemes, categorical "slots," and racial hierarchies to give order to the diversity and richness that was opening before them. The most prominent of these imposed rational schemes is the famous race theory from *Systema Naturae* (1758), in which Carl Linnaeus divides all of humanity into four races or types, which he designates as white European, red American, brown Asian, and black African. He offers these racial categories as distinctions based on observable human attributes (skull size, skin color, etc.) and behavior gathered from around the globe. In reality, this scheme purportedly showing separate human races is one that Linnaeus modeled, as Stephen Jay Gould comments, using the four geographic continents readily available from any world map of the day (1981, 404). Also, as Schiebinger notes, Linnaeus modeled his supposedly scientific racial categories on the medieval four elements (air, earth, fire, and water) so that each "race" is closely associated with an element (2004, 119). Linnaeus's theorizing of the separate races of humanity allows for eventually ranking and judging races in some divisive ways, culminating in the nineteenth century with huge debates over whether there is a single version of humanity with a "monogenesism," single-species origin, or several versions with a "polygenesis," multi-species origin (Young 1995, 9).

In *On the Natural Variations of Mankind,* Johann Blumenbach— the father of modern physical anthropology, who is known for naming white people "Caucasians"—proposes a revision of Linnaeus's system creating five types of human beings instead of only four. In this strategic move, he names his categories Caucasian, Mongolian, Malayan, Ethiopian, and American. He then designates Caucasians, which include people from Europe, northern Africa, southwestern Asia, and India, as the original and *first* humans and the source of all other human racial strands (1969, 269). This claim makes Caucasians a separate category elevated over the rest of humanity and seemed to close down additional questions about human origins before they could be asked.

Blumenbach's proposal was that Caucasians came first as a kind of prime stock that all humans thereafter derived from. Creating this category had the effect not only of making Caucasians humanity's original people, but it designated them as the embodiment of its highest aspirations, in that Caucasians started out at a level of human attainment that no subsequent people could ever hope to match. Young notes that Blumenbach's elevation of Caucasians to the status of original super people was accompanied by a similar elevation of European culture as also sitting "at the top of a scale against which all other societies, or groups within society, were judged" (1995, 94). Caucasians and their culture together were placed at the "top" of the human hierarchy, certainly at the top of the evolutionary scale, owing to Caucasian physical and mental superiority. In such circular, self-aggrandizing thinking, eighteenth-century scientists were "uncovering differences," as Schiebinger adds, "imagined as natural to societies based on natural law." These differences made Caucasians and everything associated with them superior to everyone and everything else (2004, 9).

For naturalists and racial theorists who came later, the notion of Caucasian superiority takes ever more sinister turns with increasingly value-loaded claims for the elevated physical and mental superiority of being white. Blumenbach's colleague Christoph Meiners, for example, used the five-race scheme to posit that the "ancient Germans" were the white people, the Caucasians, vastly superior to everyone else on the planet, and so those descended from them are superior to other humans as well. He took the notion of Caucasian as prime stock, in other words, and made it absolute. In *The History of White People*, Nell Irvin Painter comments that Meiners saw the "ancient Germans" (the original Caucasians) as having reached human perfection with their Germanic bodies "strong like oak-trees," their physical features "beautiful" beyond all others, and their vastly superior intellects—in effect, a "superior, master race." Painter notes that in the twentieth century Meiners "became the Nazis' favorite intellectual ancestor," since the they based their theories of Aryan and German superiority on his assertions about ancient Germans as having reached a human pinnacle never to be reached again by subsequent and progressively degraded humans, especially by those in different lines of development (2010, 90).

Blumenbach's promotion of a Caucasian race, as a matter of science, as Painter notes, never gets beyond being "mythical" in that he presented no proof or actual evidence for any of his claims (2010, 84). But in advancing the notion that Caucasians are superior and "beautiful," he succeeded in doing one important thing. He avoided the loss of human stature that may come with viewing humanity amid a collection of diverse bodily metrics and comparisons with other plants, animals, and various species, a claim that potentially rescues humanity from dignity-deflating comparisons with other living things. Blumenbach's special focus on Caucasian "beauty," which never made, or even tried to make, scientific sense, was a way of promoting and also *protecting* human uniqueness by creating a category impenetrable by science because it was *not* scientific. Since Caucasians were the standard for all other human beings to be measured by, no other human being, or anything alive, could be used as a standard to judge them.

This ranking of races also allowed naturalists to continue striving toward the neoclassical aspirations for humanity (identifying with the mind, valuing neoclassical culture, and rejecting the body) as captured in the definition of being Caucasian. This approach allowed for a body-oriented explanation for humanity amid the lower classes, since they belonged to the other racial categories ranked below Caucasians. That is, since humanity supposedly existed in several separate strains with different origins, a Caucasian could be a beautiful person with a superior mind and a perfect body in one strain while a dark-skinned person who works with his or her body could exist as an imperfect person in another. As long as these orders are in place as *separate* strands, there is no need to resolve the tension between mind and body and perfection and imperfection.

The elevation of Caucasians declared whites generally superior without offering that theory for scientific challenge. Creating the Caucasian category also gives credence to the dubious notion that "race" is a verifiable and scientifically based distinction. In the nineteenth and twentieth centuries, the idea of *race* as a gauge and predictor of human potential and intrinsic worth led to numerous unsavory and dangerous theories of identity and social order. In "the latter half of [the twentieth] century," race as a supposedly scientific category gets "largely discredited," as John Willinsky notes. After that time, however, racial theories continue to promote race as a scientific category but without being able to claim scientific legitimacy or advance an actual argument. Those racial gestures later in the twentieth century tended to retrace steps taken earlier in the historically pertinent and scientifically faulty work of Linnaeus, Blumenbach, and Meiners as they developed race-based theories of humanity's origins (2000, 162).

Among eighteenth-century race theorists and scientists, Linnaeus was the most explicit in imposing a rigid interpretive scheme over the teeming diversity of bodies in the animal kingdom that eighteen-century science was discovering. Linnaeus at one point divided humanity into the categories of *Homo sapiens* and *Homo monstrous*—*Homo sapiens* being people in the neoclassical mold who, like the calidad, are self-aware, rational, and have a sense of their own culture and history. *Homo monstrous* are those people closely associated, for various reasons, with the human body. Because of their unusual size, physical demeanor, skin color, or bodily malformation, they are subsequently defined as existing outside of accepted eighteenth-century norms of rational proportion and beauty. Deviant people could be monstrous when their bodies were in any obvious way unique. Such far-reaching judgments were not generally accepted in the eighteenth century, but they still contributed, as Willinsky comments, "to an increasingly elaborate mixture of scientific and moral distinctions" that often worked to confuse the status of race theory, especially for nonscientists (2000, 162).

While Blumenbach explicitly rejected the idea of *Homo monstrous* as a poorly conceived category, he went on in an equally revealing gesture to create his own version of this monstrous type. He defined the Mongoloid and African races as "degenerations" far removed from an original Caucasian version of humanity. In his version, the idea of a lower human order survived in a more palatable and plausible form since "monstrous" people in the East and in Africa, far from Europe and less familiar, were easier to put into large categories (they were not around enough to resist). They were degenerations that became, in effect, a version of *monstrosity*.

With such racial schemes, eighteenth-century naturalists developed categories for being human that recognized a base, physical human nature, a kind of basic, default person, and an elevated humanity capable of advanced mental and spiritual aspiration. "Scientific" taxonomies, in other words, were opening up a world of rational classification and comparison that generated exciting, new but sometimes deeply flawed knowledge. At the same time, such accomplishments were potentially challenging traditional and neoclassic conceptions that supposedly recognized people as unique in the animal kingdom. Naturalists could argue that human beings have a nature reflected in their bodies, *become* their bodies, and in this way humanity is brought back to the reality of having a body to be compared with other species—the very association avoided by neoclassical thinkers.

The classical tradition (since Plato) promoted something very different, the idea that humanity is always degraded through close association with the body. Citing Plato whenever they wished, Blumenbach and Linnaeus could argue from different angles that superior, rational people could exist in one strain of humanity and that inferior, unreasoning people could exist in another. This multitiered system made it possible to avoid defining humanity entirely in terms of bodily measurements and comparisons with other mammals.

The world of eighteenth-century scientific theories of race in many ways dovetails with the assumptions and conclusions of the casta system. The earliest casta paintings preceded Linnaeus's and Blumenbach's theorizing about race and the body by more than two decades, but it is evident that the casta system and the practitioners of racial science shared important concerns and beliefs (Katzew 2004, 7). The casta system has its parallel to enlightened *Homo sapiens* in the category of the gente de razón, the people of reason, who are also models of neoclassical humanity in their belief in rational order, gentile behavior, and culture's uplifting power. *Homo sapiens* and the gente de razón are thus both models of an elite humanity.

The counterpart to *Homo monstrous* in the casta system is the designation of gente sin razón, people without mental ability or reasoning who live close to the body and material reality. This colonial judgment put the gente sin razón in the harshest possible light as human beings who, without the guidance of reason, are not *completely* human. Living close to the body, like the *Homo monstrous,* the gente sin razón failed to participate in the classic aspirations of cultural attainment, transcending bodily limitations, and attaining Plato's dream for an elevated, aspirational humanity with exclusively spiritual and mental goals.

In these names for the upper and lower classes, terms that previously may have seemed gratuitously severe in their reference, there is a recurrent association of dark skin with being lower class and inferior. Schiebinger comments, for example, that among eighteenth-century race theorists "blackness . . . was seen as the [common] characteristic of lower-class peoples," much as, in the same vein, the casta system associates dark skin with the lower classes (2004, 7). In both systems, there is the assumption that the lower classes have close ties to the body and of the body's possible return (like the return of a monster in gothic horror) as a defining feature of being human. If Linnaeus, Blumenbach, and Meiners did not know the casta terminology of gente de razón and gente sin razón, and they probably did not, they would nonetheless have been familiar with the honorific *and* derogatory judgments behind those terms, especially the associations with the mind and the condemnation of the body. Gente de razón and gente sin razón as terms, in other words, voice the same judgments about the body and being human that are already incorporated into eighteenth-century "scientific" notions of superior and inferior races.

The gente sin razón represented a severely constrained potential of bodily life in New Spain in that, as people on the margins of Spanish social and racial norms, they are defined not by their positive attributes but by their systematic violation of the canons of calidad. This judgment is inherent to the casta system and Spanish colonial culture owing to the mutually defining nature of these categories—the logic of being Spanish as a primary reference in that system. The lower casta people *appear* similar to the calidad from a distance as a gentleman or painter might view them, but up close they have different skin color and differently shaped, even "monstrous," bodies. On even closer inspection, the lower casta people lack self-control, mental ability, good judgment, compassion, and the refined proportions of Caucasian "beauty" expressed in face and body. Lacking virtually *all* of the strengths and qualities that distinguish and define the calidad and *Homo sapiens,* the extreme lower classes carry the immense burden of having bodies and of being bodies, in effect, simultaneously enabling the gente de razón to be elevated beings while situating themselves at the level of animals. Young calls this phenomenon the colonial gestures of "inscribing and expelling" (rewarding the higher ups and punishing the lower downs) all at the same time (Young 1995; 39).

From the Spanish perspective, the lower classes are people whose bodily nature conflicts with being human as judged by the calidad standard, but they are also a defining feature of the system that makes that standard possible for those with higher placement. The monstrous potential of the gente sin razón cannot be removed from the casta system, and this potential is seen in the casta paintings as the threat associated with the body and physical violence. That is, without refined judgment and higher sentience, the lower classes are forced to live close to the body and undirected emotions—hence the potential for disorder and violence, providing a contrast and rebuttal (as well as support) for everything that the calidad stands for. Living *in* the bodily realm, the night world of being human, they are (supposedly) prepared to strike against the gente de razón at any moment. The threat that they pose makes it clear that the monster to be contained and feared among the casta people is none other than the recalcitrant *body* itself.

The threat of monsters lurking in New Spain parallels the crisis over the physical body's emerging preeminence in eighteenth-century race theory. The growing recognition and threat of each is that the human body's return could disrupt and even destroy the classical model of being human by compromising its status as a predominantly mental and spiritual being. Both the casta system and the eighteenth-century science of racial classification try to turn away from the body, or the implications of having a body, denying it whenever possible. It follows that haunting both ordering systems is the threat that the recovered body might at some point assimilate and somehow cancel the elevated claims about being human and the life of the mind that Plato and many since have pronounced as critical to human aspiration and goodness. As a result, the body gets pushed away into the realm of non-Western peoples of color, especially the casta lower classes, Mongols, and Africans, who are themselves banished to the social fringes and hidden corners of the worldwide colonial experience.

In the racial and cultural legacy that Spanish colonial culture bequeathed to the Americas, the mestizo brown body, to this day, is still in need of *recovery*. Further, examining the casta legacy also points up the gender bias of the debased body and the particular threat that gender poses. Nonwhite female bodies create a special challenge for New Spain's culture, and this is evident by going back to the casta paintings. If we take the paintings shown in the Carrera and Katzew volumes as large random samples drawn from all known casta paintings and focus on the ones where we can accurately decipher the racial legends beneath the paintings (which is most of them), we find a total of 184 paintings to consider. If we note in each painting if it is the male or female adult figure who has the higher casta status (a lower number or occupying a higher position on the chart of sixteen categories), three out of five times (107 versus 77), women in these paintings are classified as a group with lower social status. Since the lower casta status always means living closer to the body and being closely associated with bodily functions, as opposed to being calidad and associated with elevated human (largely mental) goals, in this sample of casta paintings 60 percent of the time women are more closely associated with the body and its base degradation than are men.

If there are monsters lurking in the casta system who threaten the life of the mind and the upper classes, that monster is the female body. This observation is consistent with the long-standing Western tradition of associating women, as philosopher Susan Bordo comments, with the body's ephemeral and potentially corrupt nature. She points out that in Western culture there is a close association of women and bodies, of women as "the negative term" in the human gender equation. She notes that in Western culture women consistently carry the burden of having a body and of *being* a body, exactly as we have been discussing, while men are associated with the mind's otherworldly, spiritual aspirations much like those of the calidad. She comments that "the cost of such projections to women is obvious." "If, whatever the specific historical contents of the duality," she goes on, "*the body* is the negative term, and if woman *is* the body, then women *are* that negativity, whatever it may be" (2003, 5).

Women in the casta system, certainly a majority of the time, threaten the world of the calidad in being the representatives of bodily life and all activity that is associated with bodies and manual labor. In New Spain, women are bodies and men are minds, and these tensions and grotesque distortions relate to how the body and mind are given a particular relationship through Spanish colonial influence. By contrast, as I will discuss in chapter 5, the Mesoamerican, indigenous valorization and foregrounding of the body, the body as central and valuable to everything human, contrasts dramatically to the Western focus on the mind and the body's rejection. The Mesoamerican perspective on the body, which is an embrace of the body as a world unto itself, and its relationship to the Spanish denial of the body, create a contrast and tension that is revealing both about Mesoamerican values and attitudes toward the body and Western associations of degradation and the body. This tension and contrast between two views of the human body are also a defining theme of culture in the Americas.

THE VOICES HEARD IN THE CASTA PAINTINGS

We started this discussion with Quijano's comment that there were "new historical social identities in [the] America[s]—Indians, blacks, and mestizos." We can now add that the casta system created not only those identities and class distinctions but a legacy for mestizo identity that touched every aspect of life, every person, and gender in the Americas. The Spanish colonial legacy created an innovative approach to "race" by associating human phenotype—bodies and their dimensions—directly and permanently with placement in a social class. This legacy created a racial and social hierarchy that dismissed and punished people who are not white and designated them as an inferior order of humanity.

Being a mestizo in New Spain meant being of an "indigenous and European" racial mix, one category in the casta system. Being mestizo also has since become the complex label of a people carrying the historical, racial, cultural baggage related to the human body's suppression and class privilege in the Americas. The bodies on display in the casta paintings speak to us across five hundred years about race, about placement in a brutal colonial caste system, about genocide, about severely limited marriage choices among casta classes, about jobs and professions, and about the uncertain prospects for staying alive in the Americas.

If we listen carefully to the voices of the casta paintings, taking into account what we know of the period and the culture, we hear an official voice from the gente de razón that tells about the Spanish superior and refined nature and the European destiny to bring civilization, Western religion, and economic prosperity to New Spain. Those voices of calidad describe the hardships and burdens of promoting empire in New Spain and the indignities of attempting to have a faux, "uncivilized" social life with Indians, blacks, mulattos, and mestizos. They tell of their own sacrifices and hard lives while trying to serve the homeland and build a meaningful life in New Spain, all the while attempting to bring the gente sin razón out of cultural and spiritual darkness.

We may also hear the gente sin razón speak of the difficulty of living amid New Spain's changing social rules and the severe limitations placed on casta lives. They speak to us about working impossible hours and receiving little or nothing for their efforts. They describe fulfilling the capricious demands of the gente de razón and of friends and relatives who died when those demands could not be fulfilled. They express the fear that the same will happen to them. They speak of celebrating indigenous and African culture in their homes and of keeping such practices secret for fear of evoking the wrath of the gente de razón. They worry about their families and confess, in whispered tones, their dread of being beaten and killed and of needing to speak Spanish well enough to protect their families and find a better life.

We also hear the women of the gente sin razón telling about working day and night and of having no time for their families. They speak of caring for Spanish children and about neglecting their own. They speak of being raped and of finding no recourse for injustice and abuse. They express fear for their families and want their children to live safely and eventually to escape New Spain. They want recognition for who they are, for the ethnic identities that they celebrate but must hide, and for the hard work that they perform endlessly.

In chapters to come, we can listen to these voices further as we follow the rise of mestizo identity across the Americas. That rise includes Mexican American artists and writers attempting to recover the human body, especially the female body, from a tradition of cultural amnesia, denial, and repression. It includes Mexican American communities defining an indigenous relationship to land and place and looking for strategies to maintain ties to land. In contemporary healing practices, literature, and art, it includes the fate of persecuted bodies and the specter of disposable people. It will become clearer what it means to have a mestizo, brown body in the Americas in the present—to have a such a body in a culture of white privilege and a class system based on race.

The casta paintings identify a mestizo voice that will be foundational to recognizing being Mexican American and having a hybrid identity with a distinct history in the Americas. A key focus going forward concerns an evolving sense of what it means to be an heir of the New World's ancient peoples and how the mestizo voice is central to shaping the Americas' future, as many modern theorists of race comment. The prominence, rise, and recognition of mestizo identity, or what José Vasconcelos calls the "cosmic race," will be achievements that will be signature events of the modern era.

Interrogating the casta system brings much to light about Mexican American culture as a mestizo phenomenon. As an emergent set of social and cultural practices and beliefs, mestizo culture may yet again appear monstrous in different guises as it explores new initiatives and ways of knowing itself and the world in the Americas. In the twentieth and twenty-first centuries, mestizo culture will not look like mainstream culture but will break those barriers to discover alternative ways of living and, in so doing, establish its own cultural direction and expectations of being educated and cultured.

Knowledge of the casta system is information so valuable that it changes the people who know it, and that knowledge will encourage hemispheric perspectives and new ways of viewing the Americas. The coordinates for framing mestizo identity are not those of British and Dutch culture on the Eastern Seaboard but the north-south references that come with seeing the Americas as the grand stage for life and culture in this hemisphere. This perspective includes Spanish, Dutch, and British settlements on the Eastern Seaboard, but it is also a broad view that focuses on life in the Americas from the time of the New World's ancient peoples—the Inca, Toltec, Mayan, and Aztec Empires—the conquest, and the mestizaje that define the Americas in the present.

María E. Montoya comments that Chicano studies has historically sidestepped discussions of the conquest and Spanish colonial culture and has provided few bridges between the colonial period and present-day Mexican American struggles and social life (2000, 186). This chapter's engagement with the casta system shows the shortsightedness and impossibility of maintaining this pervasive separation that Galeano describes when he references the needs of mestizos to gather the pieces of their souls through the histories that they re-create. Focusing on the casta system and racial typing in New Spain yields foundational insights for understanding the Americas and the racial and social issues of our time.

One of the insights to come from the Spanish colonial experience and the casta system is the need for community to act on its own behalf (and the tragedy of being unable to do that) to advance the economic, political, and cultural aims of a people. The mandate arising from knowledge of the casta system and the multiple dimensions of the Spanish colonial world should be to take responsibility for community and to bring together and heal the mestizo world still coming together in the Americas. Being a mestizo is more than an ethnic label, a perspective, an attitude, or even a way of living. It is also an awareness of the ancient peoples of the New World and the casta peoples of New Spain as los antepasados, the ancestors. In the chapters to come, that crucial knowledge will emerge further to help guide Mexican Americans and show how the Americas are the mestizo homeland and the mestizo the Americas' cultural citizen.

CHAPTER 2

In Search of Mestizo Identity
across the Americas

The formal discussion of mestizo identity in the Americas—how it came about and what it means—begins in Latin America in the late nineteenth and early twentieth centuries. Major contributors are Brazilian novelist José de Alencar, Cuban political activist José Martí, and Peruvian social theorists José Carlos Mariátegui and Víctor Raúl Haya de la Torre. Most prominent in this grouping, José Vasconcelos is the Mexican politician, educator, and philosopher who establishes the dominant approach for understanding mestizo identity. All of these writers focus on what it means to create, live, and claim an identity in the postcolonial Americas. In the 1960s, the Chicano movement explores these definitions in relation to Mexican Americans, and in the twenty-first century, Chicano historians and political scientists, such as Julie A. Dowling and Natalia Molina, evaluate attempts in modern U.S. history to define mestizo identity in response to changing perspectives on race and political expediency.

In the Chicano epic poem "I Am Joaquin" (1967), Rodolfo Gonzales describes the coexistence of "Aztec Prince" and "Christian Christ" in the same body, the traditional definition of a mestizo (ll. 539–41). As the casta system originally defined it, a mestizo is someone with indigenous and Spanish ancestry, and yet Gonzales's poem takes over five hundred lines to describe Mexican Americans struggling to gain recognition for who they are. He shows their history to be fraught with obstacles and amnesia about their achievements. A central document of the Mexican American experience, this poem depicts a community marginalized and forgotten by the national culture.

As *Mestizos Come Home!* documents, there have been few issues across the Americas so pervasive in their impact and yet so little recognized as mestizo identity—a fact reflected in the twentieth-century cultural and social marginalization of Mexican Americans and Latinos. Like a secret hidden from public view or a family scandal never fully aired, what it means to be a mestizo historically commands too little attention in the United States. There are notable exceptions, and everyone can name important books, films, TV specials in Spanish, and the rise of a small number of Latino politicians. The fact remains that in the United States there is little public awareness of mestizos as a people with a unique history in the Americas. It follows that the reality of mestizo life in the United States remains shadowed and urgently in need of public recognition and understanding.

Mestizos came into existence during the colonial era as the Spanish mixed with indigenous, African, and other enslaved peoples. That mixing created beleaguered communities that only now in the twentieth and twenty-first centuries have overcome formidable challenges to emerge intact and prosper. Mestizos in the modern era in the United States are often succeeding culturally, socially, and economically in ways that few could have predicted, and that fact encompasses much of what I am detailing about mestizo communities and their struggle to survive.

The casta paintings of the Spanish colonial era are the earliest substantial record of mestizos in the hemisphere, and they still convey much of what the ancestors have to tell us—who mestizos are and what they must overcome to find better lives in the future. In casta painting sets, for example, there is always one painting labeled "mestizo" that evokes many of these concerns. Depicting a Spanish man, an indigenous woman, and a mestiza child, this painting typically shows the Spanish father leaning toward his child to comfort and reassure her. The indigenous mother will likely be more distant and may be glancing in the viewer's direction or away from her family. The details of this scenario vary, but beneath this painting will always be a legend pinpointing what the painting is supposed to show—"Español con india sale Mestiza" ("A Spanish Man and an Indigenous Woman Produce a Mestiza").

History tells us that this iconic scene has far-reaching implications. In the sixteenth century, this encounter led indigenous peoples into slavery and serfdom and changed the Americas forever. During the seventeenth century, this painting's domestic scene was a step taken toward enacting mestizaje, the process of producing mixed peoples and culture, which (adding Africans, Asians, and others) reshaped the hemisphere's families and communities. In the eighteenth century, this scene's historic encounter led to the rise of mestizo, hybrid cultures scattered across Latin America, distinctly different Latin American cultures still in evidence today. In the modern era, history tells us that beneath this tranquil "mestiza" family scenario was the violent, brutal reality of colonial New Spain. This picture and all that flows from it mount a challenge to the modern era, a challenge that mestizos have been trying to answer since the conquest. In this mestizo scenario is a message that has been left for us, the distant heirs of that period, to understand and to unravel.

The evidence of "I Am Joaquin" and other Mexican American texts is that the modern recognition of mestizo identity has progressed slowly and with great difficulty—and not because people with indigenous and European ancestry are difficult to find. Counted conservatively through self-identification and census results, mestizos are now the majority in at least seven Latin American countries with a combined population of over 300 million people (Lizcano Fernández 218). Estimated more broadly, by including those who likely have indigenous and European ancestors but neglect to make the claim, that number could exceed 600 million. And where there are no specific numbers for the United States, there are likely another 200 million mestizos there. The problem is that the recognition of mestizo identity, a focus running against the Western value placed on supposedly "pure" ethnicities and blood lines, has been shackled with a bias that has marginalized a vast community. Almost five hundred years have passed since the conquest, but that colonial perspective still renders mestizos invisible as they do manual labor jobs, help to maintain an exploitative economy, and render white lives manageable and secure.

In the modern era, the term "mestizo," when used at all, has a general meaning different from the traditional one. It is now a catch-all term to reference mixed-race peoples in the Americas of every type. Whether saying "mestizo" points toward being Mexican American, Brazilian, Cuban, Mexican, Peruvian (the nationalities referenced in this chapter), or many other designations with mixed ethnic, racial, and national origins, mestizo identity and the fact of multiple heritages are constant reminders of the realities of life and history in this hemisphere.

In what follows, I will discuss four dimensions of being mestizo that Mexican Americans live every day, topic categories that Latin Americans have also used to frame their own sense of history and hemispheric realities. These four topics are: (1) mestizo (individual) identity, (2) the hybrid nature of mestizo culture, (3) mestizo culture's hemispheric dimensions, and (4) mestizos acting to advance their communities. Naming specific realities of life in the Americas, these topics suggest a relationship to U.S. mainstream culture, the hemispheric context for understanding Mexican American culture, the persistence of the mestizo community's indigenous roots, and a current preoccupation with *race* as a concept whose foundations are quickly crumbling.

MESTIZO INDIVIDUAL IDENTITY

The Gonzales epic poem "I Am Joaquin" makes a plea for the recognition of mestizo identity as it maps mestizo history over the last five hundred years. This mural-size poem breaks new ground in the 1960s when it foregrounds these social and cultural issues in regard to the recognition of mestizo culture, the possibility of self-governance, cultural marginalization, and social justice denied. In the 1960s in the United States, these were new and challenging topics to apply to the Mexican American community, and they were also the issues that Latin American writers and social critics had been referencing since the 1920s. In the case of Victor Raúl Haya de la Torre in Peru, he even found ways, innovative for their time, to encourage mestizo participation in governmental, civic, and cultural life. There are extensive connections, in other words, between Latin American and Mexican American thinkers that are seldom noted or discussed. These connections show that

Mexican American writers in the 1960s joined a productive, ongoing conversation that did not have to be reinvented.

The Mexican American exploration of mestizo identity during the Chicano Renaissance (1970–80s) builds on the work of Latin American writers, none of them U.S. household names, but all of them well-known and revered in Latin America. Especially notable were José Vasconcelos (Mexico), Victor Raúl Haya de la Torre (Peru), and José Carlos Mariátegui (Peru); these writers were focused—much as the Mexican American writers would be—on reassembling their pasts, their "souls," as Galeano would say, to understand the history of the Americas. They were trying to find the truth of where they came from, who they are, and who they could be in the future.

Contemporary Mexican American writers joined this conversation while they were creating new businesses, building communities, supporting traditional relationships to land, reclaiming colonized bodies, creating innovative popular culture, and finding their own cultural voice. These are Chicano Renaissance cultural and social initiatives that had the potential to transform life and culture in the United States and the hemisphere. This recovery of mestizo identity on several fronts, starting in the early twentieth century and continuing through the twenty-first, is an instance of Mexican Americans relearning from Latin American writers *how* to be mestizos as they joined the hemisphere's mestizo communities. Reflecting Mexican Americans "coming home" to the United States in the 1960s and after, these developments reveal a large debt to the earlier writers. This debt historically has been downplayed, even though such an oversight distorts the important understanding of what mestizos, as a community stretching across the Americas, have achieved in the modern era.

Mexican American writers not only build on Latin American ideas and traditions but succeed in creating literary and artistic works that revitalize their culture in similar ways. They draw on Latin American traditions when they infuse their communities with knowledge of the hemisphere's history, a history that Latin American writers have done much to retain and protect. They rely on those traditions when they identify the political and cultural forces that shaped the past and continue to shape culture in the present. And they connect with a Latin American tradition of racial critique by challenging U.S. conceptions of race and "whiteness" as can still be found in present U.S. culture.

Three landmark Latin American writers mark the beginnings of this tradition—Brazilian novelist José de Alencar (1829–77), Cuban revolutionary José Martí (1853–95), and Mexican essayist and philosopher José Vasconcelos (1882–1959). Especially Vasconcelos is a towering figure who offers the perspective that others will follow as he redefines mestizo identity and its potential for having a social impact in the Americas. Based in Brazil, Cuba, and Mexico, these writers demonstrate that the exploration of mestizo identity in the Americas has been most insightful where colonialism has left the deepest scars—in Brazil (colonized by the Portuguese), in the Caribbean (Cuba, Haiti, and the Dominican Republic), in Mexico, and in Peru—all countries providing extensive postcolonial critiques and a new hemispheric awareness. Most pressing for our discussion are their different definitions for what "mestizo" means and how it is to be regarded in historical and cultural settings.

José de Alencar's *Iracema* (1865), a work written in praise of European colonialism, gives a rare glimpse into the nineteenth-century colonial mindset about mixed-race peoples. Set in early colonial Brazil, this novel tells the story of a Portuguese soldier (Martim), a female, indigenous tribal leader (Iracema), and their mestizo child (Moacir). Martim is part of Brazil's early colonial business presence, and the novel traces the ills befalling the parents of Brazil's first mestizo. Most notable about this work is its celebration of colonialism as "saving" indigenous peoples in Brazil from their own degraded civilization. *Iracema* creates a colonial perspective on mestizo culture's initiation, identifying the beginnings of social attitudes and cultural practices that Aníbal Quijano calls "the coloniality of power," colonialism's launch of practices that will have a continuing, residual impact on the hemisphere (2000, 533).

The book's plot revolves around Iracema and Martim becoming romantically involved while taking a drug used in a tribal religious ceremony. Under the drug's effects, Iracema seduces Martim, and the subsequent news of their union quickly brings tribal condemnation from all sides.[1] Also, the fact that *she* seduces *him* suggests a procolonial gesture in this novel, a way of deflecting blame from the colonial figure (Martim), who otherwise will dominate the culture. Even at this early point in the nineteenth century, the colonial man who marries an indigenous woman is a stock figure, usually signaling the scenario of a European man conquering indigenous people and then marrying an indigenous woman to signal the complete colonial appropriation of land, resources, and cultural dominance. By 1865, this was already a conventional story line reflected in the narratives about Hernán Cortés and Malintzin in Mexico and Pocahontas and John Rolfe in the British colonies. With Iracema's seduction of Martim, Alencar attempts to show Europeans dominating Brazil and judging indigenous people while, at the same time, avoiding the colonial (often gendered) symbolism of doing so.

The novel's plot complication is that Martim is allied with the Pitiguaras, the long-standing tribal enemies of the Tabararas—Iracema's tribe. By marrying Iracema, a Tabararas priestess, Martim complicates Brazil's social and political situation. The couple tries but fails to weather a judgmental frontier environment, and the novel gradually points toward Iracema as the culprit mainly responsible for the social upheaval overtaking the couple. Juan E. De Castro comments that "Iracema [was] expected to remain celibate," and violating "religious taboos [by using the drug jurema as an aphrodisiac]" and entering into a forbidden relationship with Martim, or any man, depict her as a reckless person. The novel's conclusion is that she is the representative of an inferior, indigenous culture and cannot help but invite trouble and mishap into her life (2002, 45).

With such judgments, this novel views indigenous people much as they were regarded in the casta system, culturally unaware and in need of Western guidance. The essence of the Iracema and Martim story could even be reframed as an eighteenth-century Miguel Cabrera painting in which Martim would be sitting in an upholstered chair, his hand resting on his son Moacir's shoulder. Martim's body language would convey his patient, relaxed, and sophisticated demeanor. Iracema would be standing apart from the other two, her hands on her hips, gazing into the distance. Her stiff body would express the response expected from a member of the gente sin razón (irrational people). The casta legend underneath this painting would read, "A Portuguese Man and an Indian Woman Produce a Mestizo," but its implied message would be that European culture here stands at the center of a new colonial enterprise.

Reading "Iracema" as an anagram for "America" (referencing the Americas), as Alencar apparently intended, also shows this novel to be creating a cultural frame that will influence the hemisphere far into the future. Who is a mestizo? *Iracema* references Moacir's birth and Europe's exploitative dominance over indigenous people as historical thresholds that, once crossed, forever alter the direction of life in Brazil and across the Americas. This novel implicitly informs those who come after the conquest to see colonialism and mestizo identity as shaping every aspect of the hemisphere's culture.[2] In the book's conclusion, there is the broad perspective indicating not only that Martim chooses to live in Brazil to prolong his melancholic remembrance of the dying Iracema but that the colonial practices inaugurated in this work are creating the new outlines of an emerging colonial reality. Iracema's death and Martim's continuing occupation of Brazil foreshadow colonialism's dominance and impact far beyond Brazil and the time of the conquest.

Cuban revolutionary and essayist José Martí focuses on the outlines of this same colonial mindset but tries to frame it with late nineteenth-century progressive thought. In his discussion of anthropologist Daniel Garrison Brinton's *The American Race* (1891), Martí asserts that "if we [in the New World] are not to fail from the lack of a living spirit, or the pursuit of false values," we must be "strengthened and animated by the spirit of men of all races who spring from [the earth's] soil and return to it" (1982, 202). He cautions that Europeans must be inspired by the indigenous people whom they have conquered. On behalf of a more sophisticated perspective, Martí here strives to *appreciate* mestizo peoples and calls for all to recognize and elevate the awareness of native people's plight. His attitude is consistent with the indigenismo movement from this period that principally advocates for a new awareness of native peoples and culture.

Indigenismo is also a view that was often dependent upon an unacknowledged colonial perspective. For those in power to maintain a sense of integrity, Martí argues, Europeans must have an accurate sense of their *own* history, how they came to the New World, what they sought through colonialism, and how that history informs the present moment for those in the dominant culture. Proposing to recognize mestizos as a way of expressing Western benevolence, Martí is responding to the fact that during the conquest in Cuba and the Dominican Republic the Spanish destroyed indigenous nations as a people—*everyone*. Shocked by the outcomes of genocide on a vast regional scale, he judges the subsequent marginalizing of indigenous people as a gesture destined to diminish and impoverish the European spirit. He asks rhetorically, "Is it not yet apparent that the blow that paralyzed the Indian, [also] paralyzed America?" He warns that "until the Indian [nation of the Americas] marches again" America and the other dominant cultures of the New World "will limp" and fail to achieve greatness as world powers (1982, 202).

Walter D. Mignolo notes the limitations of such *appreciation* of mestizos from a European elevated distance "rather than [choosing to enter a dialogue with] . . . the indigenous population of his time" (2012, 140–41.) Martí was a criollo observer (a Spaniard born in the Americas) venturing to recognize and value mestizos, however limited those gestures were, at a time when few others did. Martí may be unable to question his own "benevolent" and ultimately self-serving attitude, but the significant difference between Martí's and Alencar's perspective is that Martí promotes historical awareness of the conquest whereas Alencar is overtly propagandistic on behalf of Brazil's colonization. José David Saldívar finds a fair perspective to assess Martí's "sophisticated" appreciation of mestizos that was still "bold enough to document [. . .] the reality of empire" in this hemisphere (1991, 7).[3]

Martí's and Alencar's benevolent colonial perspectives are more durable and persistent than they might seem. Alencar's colonial scenario in his novel is roughly the same as Joaquin's in "I Am Joaquin," where a monolithic U.S. culture looms over a vulnerable Mexican American community. In that poem, mainstream culture is on the verge of absorbing a small, emerging community, and Gonzales gives a somber appraisal of the prospects in the late 1960s for Mexican Americans to rebel and achieve social justice. He shows Mexican Americans living

under the pressure to assimilate into American culture, almost sur-
rendering to U.S. mainstream society. Joaquin barely rallies at the last
moment to avoid the "American social neurosis / sterilization of the
soul / and a full stomach," a situation only slightly improved over what
Alencar and Martí show.

Thus, the colonial scenario set in the sixteenth century is not clearly
different from that of Gonzales's scenario in the twentieth century.
During the conquest, Europeans were steadily assimilating tribal peoples, the historical reality of which in Brazil was far more violent and
brutal than Alencar dares to depict. In Gonzales's twentieth-century
version of the same scenario, the United States looms as a forbidding
force, "never [a] home, only a menace," as Rafael Pérez-Torres comments.
Gonzales's poem shows the impending threat of unwelcome assimilation
"from which 'Joaquin [justly] recoils'" (1995; 74). Joaquin's rebellion and
breakthrough at poem's end are moments of forestalled doom, a fleeting
moment of turning room, before being forced to adapt to American culture. Joaquin heroically resists assimilation against great odds, but the
win-lose, us-them colonial scenario depicted in this poem is roughly the
same as that shown in Alencar's and Martí's perspectives and does not
bode well for the Mexican American community's prospects.

A decisive departure from this early perspective with its win-
lose colonial logic comes in the early twentieth century when José
Vasconcelos takes a completely different approach to understanding
mestizos and their place in the Americas. Part of a circle of writers
exploring Mexican nation building in the 1920s,[4] Vasconcelos reap-
proaches the issue of mestizo identity and mestizos as a central and
defining reference destined to shape the Americas' future. Refusing
merely to appropriate mestizos into mainstream society or *appreciate*
them from a distance, as Martí does, Vasconcelos notes that at one
time people in Mexican history could legitimately speak of a conflict
in the Americas *between* indigenous peoples and the Spanish. By the
1920s, however, that time had passed. The original racial communities
in Mexico had mixed beyond reversal and had produced a thoroughly
mestizo community across the country. He argues that history ran
ahead of ideas about race and had left many racial concepts potentially
irrelevant.

What did Vasconcelos do with this insight? In *La Raza Cósmica: Misión de la raza iberoamericana* and *Aspects of Mexican Civilization,* Vasconcelos looks out across Mexico and Latin America and sees the fragmentation of culture and humanity often attributed to industrialization and modernization. He particularly sees inequities based on the separation of classes along racial lines and a consistent denial of the reality of racial mixing, as if communities were not already mixed in *every* Mexican social class, which they were. He concludes that after centuries of mestizaje, and after doing little to reconcile classes or races, Mexico was disastrously fragmented and had created a culture of national alienation for all Mexicans (the ideas, of course, that inform Octavio Paz's *The Labyrinth of Solitude*). That fragmentation, however, was not caused by actual racial division. Instead, he argues for a new focus on how mestizo identity should be defined, an important undertaking especially in that, as he argues, large mestizo populations will play an even bigger role in the Americas in the years to come.

In an entirely new approach to race, Vasconcelos henceforth redefines being mestizo in a way that cancels the colonial logic of domination. If everyone in the Americas is a product of mixed-race communities, then everyone is technically a mestizo. This innovative perspective makes mestizos the defining reference of the Americas, a move that puts familiar facts within a new and startling context so that mestizos are no longer outliers to Mexico's national culture. He makes mestizos a cultural prime focus and harbingers of a new reality that they embody and that potentially would reorder social life in the Americas and beyond. Ahead of his time, he argues that the phenomenon of mixed-race peoples was then, as now, a demographic fact the world over, dramatically evident in the complex mixing of ethnic strains and cultures in Mexico.

Possibly too obvious to be noted by others as a prime clue by which to view and interpret life in the Americas, Vasconcelos's insight says that something other than race must be separating people and causing alienation across the Americas. After all, Vasconcelos and collaborators such as Manuel Gamio were working in an environment shaped by the French historiographer Hippolyte Taine, who often asserted the existence of *essential* traits of ethnicity and national character the world over based on the combined influence of race, milieu, and historical moment. In *History of English Literature* and *On Intelligence* Taine gives voice to the near-universal consensus at the time, and probably still the dominant popular view today in the United States and elsewhere—basically, that racial identity once in place shapes cultural differences and generally does not change.

Taine's view placed a high premium on the concept of separate ethnic lines (Asian, African, etc.) and the implicit possibility of restoring "purity" to those lines after they are weakened through "miscegenation," like the process of "blood mending" in the casta tradition. Foreshadowing twentieth- and twenty-first-century views regarding the mixed state of all blood lines the world over, Vasconcelos projects "la creación de una raza hecha con el tesoro de todas las anteriores, la raza final, la raza cósmica" ("the creation of a race composed of all of the treasures of the past, the final race, the cosmic race"), basically a mestizo-centric view of the entire world (1926, 63). In saying this, he took the revolutionary step of advancing the idea of mixed races and a mixed heritage *as* the human condition.

It may be difficult to see, owing to Vasconcelos's pervasive influence, that the resulting definition of mestizo identity could ever have been otherwise, but then we are Vasconcelos's heirs. He writes in *Aspects of Mexican Civilization* that "humanity is going back to Babel[,] and by this I mean that the day of the isolated civilization [and person] is over." Whereas in the past the myths of a racially compartmentalized humanity "transformed Babel into a curse," the world in the present and future will be able to elevate and honor the idea of mestizaje and "change our methods in order to make the new period of Babel a prosperous one" (1926, 99). The world of Babel, a world with people united by their common mestizo condition, is to be the new reality. The inability to recognize that reality is what may separate people from each other. The ubiquity of mestizo identity, in short, puts mixed-race people on *both* sides of any class or ethnic divide. As the world goes forward from that moment of recognition, the racial lines separating cultures must be located *within* people instead of existing as a line dividing them from each other—a modern, far-reaching, highly influential discovery.

In this revised definition of being mestizo, mixed-race people make up *all* of the communities across the Americas, and "race" and racial mixing, as a consequence, cease to be distinctive features that can legitimately be thought to separate or distinguish one community from another. Effectively destroying the natural foundation of race as a social category, he also creates an opportunity to scrutinize anew the basis and coherence of race as a concept. With lines of division within people and not between them, such thinking effectively decouples the concept of race as the basis of culture, overturning the colonial definition of mestizo that we started with.

Vasconcelos's prediction for the future is that mestizos will be the "cosmic" and "final" race once racial mixing is recognized as the universal reality of being human. This will happen once strategies for maintaining separate racial lines and protecting the purity of genealogies have been discredited and the results are evident to everyone. That will happen when the idea of *race* as a natural order is exposed as a sham, and then there will there be a new, brighter cultural and social future, one shorn of racial discrimination and tensions—a virtual next step in the evolution of human consciousness. Vasconcelos projects this scenario for the future saying that, optimistically, it will be recognized that *everyone* is a mestizo, and race will no longer be a point of social discord.[5]

The boldest part of Vasconcelos's work is this view of race. Since the conquest, there have been various changing definitions of race reflected in different views of mestizaje, many that reflect a pre-Vasconcelos perspective. Most recently there are the "full blood," "half breed," or "mixed blood" concepts critiqued in the work of Sherman Alexie, Louise Erdrich, and native critics such as Craig Womack. These definitions raise issues that also get discussed in border theory.[6] Vasconcelos's approach, in short, was a fundamental rethinking of what race is—largely cloaked in a new definition of what mestizo means. After Vasconcelos, the idea of *race* in the old sense as a category based in nature will be discarded as a fiction only held in place artificially by those seeking to impose social hierarchies for their own or their community's benefit.[7]

Twentieth-century race critics such as Gloria Anzaldúa, Michael Omi, Howard Winant, Aníbal Quijano, and Ramón Grosfuguel tend to view race as Vasconcelos did, as a dynamic site of continual renegotiation. Less like a point on a map and more like a storm hovering over a region, race for them, as it was for Vasconcelos, is the product of historical and ideological forces constantly generating new configurations. Largely confirming Vasconcelos's vision, current race theorists and modern genetic science advance that there is, in fact, greater diversity *within* ethnic groups than there is any real genetic difference separating them. Again placing differences within people instead of dividing them, this insight puts "the last nail in the coffin of the biological validity of race" (Wade et al. 2014, 507). Locating lines of racial diversity mainly *within* people, as Peruvian philosopher José Carlos Mariátegui, a follower of Vasconcelos, also endorsed, suggests the irrelevance and falsity of all racial hierarchies that in the past have been used to buttress social hierarchies and inequities.

But while Vasconcelos *believed* that this new perspective on race would usher in a new age, that revolution has not happened, at least not in the way that he predicted. "The demise of biological racism by no means spells the end of racism," as Alan Knight warns, "which is likely to survive, irrespective of shifts in official ideology" (1990, 101)—an unfortunate reality and not a view that Vasconcelos ever endorsed. Mariátegui argues, too, that a "cosmic race" will not come into being automatically, without struggle, without taking the long road that must be traveled slowly, probably a law and a policy at a time.

WHAT IS MESTIZO CULTURE?

Mexican American writers and artists inherit these Latin American approaches to mestizo identity, and in the 1960s and 1970s they begin to promote the insights of the earlier writers and critics, especially Vasconcelos, when they describe mestizo *culture* as a hybrid reflection of this view of identity. Mexican American writers believed that they could build on these new ideas and explain mestizo culture's distinctive features. They sought to frame mestizo culture as a hybrid configuration of several cultures and advance it through plans for broader social participation, economic prosperity, and the promotion of social justice. That is, the marginalizing of mestizos in the Americas had gone on for too long, had been too devastating, and the current willingness to question race and take action against racial discrimination, emboldened by the influence of the Latin American writers, suggested that a window of opportunity was finally opening. Vasconcelos's ideas seemed to bring forward all of the right questions to clarify mestizo culture, and events of the 1960s and the Mexican American openness to innovation suggested that the time could be right for real social change.

In the 1960s, the Chicano focus on social and cultural issues surprised those in mainstream America who thought Mexican American culture was associated primarily with Spain and the Spanish language (even though upwards of 9 percent of Mexicans, over 5 million, speak an indigenous language, and many of those do not speak Spanish [Lastra 1992, 35]). Spanish colonization had deeply imprinted social mores, customs, food, and architectural styles in the U.S. Southwest and Southeast, and for some it was shocking in 1967 to read Gonzales's "I Am Joaquin," a Chicano version of Walt Whitman's "Song of Myself," or in 1972 Rudolfo Anaya's novel *Bless Me, Ultima,* virtually a Mexican American *Huckleberry Finn,* or later in 1987 Anzaldúa's *Borderlands,* a Chicana version of Virginia Woolf's *A Room of One's Own,* and see the new emphasis on mestizo culture and identity.

Many such Chicano literary and social texts from this period promoted mestizo culture over European or even Spanish culture—thus reversing the colonial orientation favoring European culture originally seen in *Iracema.* These writers were not trying to erase completely the effects of colonialism and ignore realities of the postcolonial era, which would be impossible to achieve, but to reanimate voices that were silenced in New Spain's colonial practices. The Chicano message asserted that mestizo culture was at the heart of the New World and was a culture that mattered, or needed to matter, socially and politically. Distancing themselves from almost everything "Spanish" (except the language, and there was even a Chicano version of that), Chicanos in this period elevated mestizo culture, a hybrid, mixed culture with strong ties to indigenous origins, as the central reference for being Chicano and for what should matter in the Mexican American future.

This stance gradually legitimized Mexican American culture for Latinos both regionally and nationally and bolstered recognition of the mestizo presence everywhere. Gloria Anzaldúa, for example, in her much-cited essay "*La conciencia de la mestiza:* Towards a New Consciousness," explains that the "raza cósmica" (again, Vasconcelos's term) is "la primera raza síntesis del globo" ("the first racial synthesis in the world"). Identifying herself as a product of cultural synthesis, a state characterized by "nepantilism," "an Aztec word meaning torn between ways" (1987, 78), she proposes a double vision of mestizo identity as defined by the perspective of an emerging "'alien' consciousness," one "presently in the making," a newly recognized hybrid view of identity and the world (77).

She sees this consciousness a la Vasconcelos as having a spectacular "tolerance for contradictions," simultaneously embracing the culture of the conquered and the conqueror, uniting and rejoicing in multiple identities encompassed in one person. Consistent also with Vasconcelos's and Mariátegui's ideas, she positions a line of cultural division *within* people instead of *between* them (1987, 79). The contrasts and contradictions between European and indigenous cultures are inside the mestiza and not *in themselves* separating people from one another. Those who participate in the breakdown of European modes of thought and the recognition of a New World perspective will need such internal flexibility to straddle two or more cultures—in Anzaldúa's case, as a lesbian, three cultures.

This approach to seeing the replication of mestizo identity in Chicano culture moved her to proclaim optimistically that a better future "will belong to the mestiza," an attitude coming from her appreciation of contradictions, hybrid forms, and deviations from proscribed cultural norms. Those deviations will be a match, a perfect fit, for the moment nearly at hand when "the future depends on the breaking down of paradigms" (1987, 80). The popularity in the United States of El Dia de los Muertos, the Day of the Dead, gives U.S. culture a glimpse of this non-Western cultural frame for basic values and cultural references. In her understanding of the relationship of these and other mooring points of traditional Mexican American culture, she argues that these forces intertwine like a double helix, giving more prominence to death than is allowed in Western culture. These combined life-death structures inform cultural references in Chicano and Chicana novels, poems, paintings, songs, and visual art and continually reproduce new forms of Mexican American culture.

Many Mexican American writers and critics in this period used the concept of "hybrid" influences as a general reference for mestizo culture, usually accompanied by the conviction that mestizos must act as a community to advance their *own* fortunes and establish cultural hybridity as their defining mode. This stance retraced the ground covered by the earlier Peruvians Mariátegui and Haya de la Torre, even though the Peruvian call for self-reliance went far beyond national borders to empower mestizos across the Americas to take collective action.[8]

This activist approach to mestizos helping themselves is at the core of "I Am Joaquin" when it asks who Joaquin, a Mexican American Every Person, could be in light of economic and cultural conflicts distorting his Mexican American identity. Caught between Mexican and American cultures in the 1960s, Joaquin must choose between embracing Mexican culture and starving (literally) with no participation in U.S. mainstream society, or assimilating into U.S. culture, succeeding economically, and losing cultural pride and a sense of himself—thereafter "starving" in an ethical and cultural sense. This is the dilemma more recently of Rudolfo Anaya's novel *Randy Lopez Goes Home* (2011), where Randy, caught between cultures, goes on a spiritual search in a dream world where life and death reconnect with the cultural identity that he left behind. He sees that he has been successful as a U.S. writer, but that success leaves his spirit starving for Mexican American cultural connectedness.

Anaya's *Bless Me, Ultima* gives a vivid example of cultural hybridity in religious terms. Ultima the curandera comes to live with Antonio's family on the llano in eastern New Mexico during her "final days" and teaches young Antonio about many possibilities in religion and culture—balance, justice, and personal responsibility across different religious faiths. This perspective opens the way for him to appreciate the sacred in *this* world as embedded in the cultures that have actually influenced him. Several religious traditions open for Antonio through Ultima's instruction connected to Aztec spirituality, Catholicism, and local indigenous beliefs, suggesting a personal culture with multiple traditions. Antonio embraces this heterogeneous vision of spirituality and the paradoxes and contradictions accompanying it. As a child, he seems to represent a slowly maturing sense of the possibilities for mestizo culture in the United States, and the novel gives ample evidence to show that Antonio is affirming the religious experiences that have converged in him and that shape his identity and that of others as mestizos in the Americas.

Anaya also showcases the hybrid nature of Mexican American culture across his essays, short fiction, plays, and poetry. As a New Mexico native, he thinks and lives hybrid culture, ranging from writing in Spanish and English to commentary on curanderismo (indigenous and Spanish healing practices) and Western medicine, his use of mestizo cultural hybridity such as the image of the Virgin of Guadalupe (one of the most hybrid and complex of religious images), and his exploration of faith in various Western and Latin American traditions. He asks in regard to the early Chicano Renaissance if it is possible to save Mexican American history and community within Anglo-American culture by reincorporating traditional storytelling and indigenous perspectives. His large body of work answers in the affirmative and honors the Mexican American embrace of multiple cultures. His dedication to the metaphor of healing in his fiction and his commitment to exploring healing in broadly indigenous terms with curanderismo and Western medicine point in the direction of honoring cultural hybridity.

Anzaldúa, Gonzales, and Anaya use terms such as "Chicano" and "mestiza" to designate cultural authority that is neither wholly Spanish nor wholly indigenous and challenge the existing formidable traces of Spanish colonial culture. Not only outgrowths of the Spanish legacy but its cultural nemesis, hybrid culture will become foundational for the Chicano movement and Chicano Renaissance as a springboard for further critiques of the colonial social and racial legacy.[9] They solve the dilemma of living in two cultures in the best way possible by claiming *both* sides of their mestizo, hybrid identity. As citizens of the Americas, they adopt the terms "Chicano" and "mestizo," the hybrid identities that bridge Mexican and European cultures and add a dimension of political commitment. They embrace hybrid culture and accept themselves as "Aztec Prince" *and* "Christian Christ" and are prepared to advance their culture's values.[10]

Richard Rodriguez is seldom identified with these writers or the Chicano Renaissance, particularly since in the 1970s he chose not to participate or endorse the Chicano Renaissance while it was taking shape. His work nonetheless relies on Vasconcelos to characterize Mexican American culture. A productive thinker about race, especially in *Brown: The Last Discovery of America*, he highlights the "brown body" as an iconic and culturally significant reference in the Americas— not to race or class, the traditional referents—but as a cultural symbol of communal cohesion. He writes that "brown" "marks a reunion of peoples" (2002, xiii) and here plays on the ambiguities of using a color to designate a human body when no one, in any simple way, can ever be perfectly aligned with or reduced to being a color. No one is exactly *brown*. He describes people in the Americas as variations on a theme wherein "brown" can be understood to signify a range of mixed genetic and racial characteristics of all humanity, an infinite spectrum of human possibilities. With this approach, he draws upon the "cosmic race," the revelations of modern genetics, and the evident inappropriateness of ascribing a color and a single dimension of identity to a person. Like Vasconcelos, Rodriguez is trying to unmask the arbitrariness of racial designations when in reality *everyone* is the product of a mixed heritage and not reducible to a single dimension of anything.

With such comments, Rodriguez tries to cancel the last vestiges of colonial influence by opening a space between bodily features (skin, hair, etc.) and specific social placement, negating any natural connection between skin color and social class. He reminds his readers that traditional views of people as brown and white are ideologically driven and are what is left of a fading colonial legacy. Brown people will not always be poor and marginalized, just as they will not always be "brown," as certainly as "white" people will not always be "white," or privileged.[11]

The attention that Mexican American writers give to these formulations is a reminder of culture's importance as the workshop of development, the place where ideas and values are tested, explored, and possibly accepted. Mexican Americans say that "la cultura cura" ("culture heals"), and in this instance the circulation and impact of mestizo culture are the primary ways that the United States encounters mestizos and learns who they are so that the large gap between mainstream culture and the Mexican American community can be closed and, in effect, "healed." *Culture* carries this burden on behalf of the Mexican American community and has such potentially "healing" properties. In other words, in addition to being a workshop for discovering *and* generating self-knowledge and strategies for social survival, Mexican American culture has had this critical function of representing their community to the national culture.

MESTIZO CULTURE'S HEMISPHERIC DIMENSION

The third dimension of mestizo identity is a widening of references to include the whole of the Americas. Like Anaya, Ana Castillo, Demetria Martínez, Sandra Cisneros, Alfredo Véa Jr., and many other writers with an international perspective, Tomás Rivera saw that the focus on mestizo culture limited within national boundaries can only distort the Americas' past, rendering Latin American history fragmented and incomplete. An early writer of the Chicano Renaissance in 1971, Rivera helps to forge a voice and direction for understanding mestizo identity in broad hemispheric terms. He sees the cultural context of the ancient peoples of the New World as distributed across trade and migration routes in the Americas and asserts that only this hemispheric perspective can reveal the social and political reality that has shaped mestizo identity and culture.

An aspect of that vision is Rivera's sense of the Americas as a place of continual movement and migration—the Americas as a land of "searchers." In a 1980 interview, referencing this tradition of continual movement of peoples throughout the Americas, Rivera describes "an important [guiding] metaphor"—indigenous communities as continually *searching* the Americas for better lives. They first crossed into the Americas over the Bering Strait and traveled the hemisphere's length to found new communities. They also crossed other expanses to look for the "truths" of community and culture that they could find nowhere else. This view of the Americas as a place defined by crossing and searching extends to the late twentieth century and "the migrant workers [who] still have that role." Migrant farm workers are searchers who are looking for better lives than what they left behind—searching, too, to find their own cultural truths (Bruce-Novoa 1980, 151).

Rivera's idea of a hemispheric stage for mestizo identity inevitably raises questions about practicality and effectiveness. Can there be true hemispheric communities? Can mestizos be brought together across national barriers for the common good? These questions get answered in the work of the major proponent of the hemispheric view prior to Rivera, the founder of modern Peru's most important political party— Víctor Raúl Haya de la Torre (1895–1979).[12] A mestizo and towering political figure of Latin American politics, Haya de la Torre has too often been ignored in U.S. discussions of mestizaje, especially in that much of what the Chicano movement attempted Haya de la Torre accomplished in his impressive career in Peru. In the early twentieth century, he moved modern Peru and much of Latin America from the mere recognition of mestizaje as a cultural and social fact into pro-grams to promote fair wages, gain respect for mestizo culture, and find social justice for neglected communities. Like Rivera, he believed that only a view of life situated in the hemisphere can accurately encompass the reality of postcolonial mestizo communities who share a common region of the world and history. His success in bringing recognition to mestizos in Peru and his further influence on Bolivia's Revolutionary National Movement and Costa Rica's National Liberation Party sug-gest that his broad view has already been effective in the promotion of regional alliances and communities—that is, communities that extend across the hemisphere.

Chicana feminists have been among the most receptive to this pro-posal for situating culture and cultural inquiry within a hemispheric context. Debra Castillo argues that there is in existence already a trans–Latin American feminist discourse that includes Mexicans, Chicanas, and other Latin American women (1992). Literary critics Sonia Saldívar-Hull (2000) and Anna Marie Sandoval (2008) agree and see the pertinence of Mexican American women's lives and culture in relation to hemispheric issues and questions, as does Juanita Heredia (2009). They argue that the hemispheric community is a hidden source of strength leading to "political commitment and community connection," benefits that necessarily will come from building community on a regional scale (Sandoval 2008, xvi). Kathryn Quinn-Sánchez (2015) moves across borders in her thinking to define a growing communal identity among women in the Americas. However, it is Heredia who speaks for all of these literary and cultural critics when she comments that we are seeing "the emergence of a critical trend in transnational feminist studies that [will provide] analytical tools to examine narratives by ethnic women writers, including Latinas, in a comparative context across national borders" (2009, 1). Such critics are continuing in Haya de la Torre's path in saying that sovereignty cannot be achieved *for* a community but must be the products *of* a community's own struggle positioned on the stage of the Americas.

ACTION ON BEHALF OF THE MESTIZO COMMUNITY

Chicano Renaissance writers take ownership of the information and cultural distinctions generated by the Latin American writers and thinkers who influenced them, but they also demonstrate an ethical commitment to promote the high moral status of *action* taken on the mestizo community's behalf. Like Haya de la Torre, they define a commitment to activism, a fundamental conviction saying that knowledge gained from the community must be used to advance that community's fortunes. This approach encourages local responsibility for actions that can achieve communal goals, a commitment highly visible when social protests were a large part of the counterculture in the 1970s in the United States and Europe, especially the Chicano movement's activism in the 1970s. It is revealing that little changed for Mexican American activism, for example, when most other groups retreated from such intervention in the middle and late 1980s.

The Chicano movement (1960–80) and the Chicano Renaissance (1971–90s) had a cultural and social basis, but they were primarily social-action initiatives for improving the lives and future prospects of Mexican Americans, an approach that included theorizing social change while emphasizing practical implementation based on that knowledge. This orientation was grounded in indigenous cultural commitments and the idea of action's sacred importance, what Mexican philosopher Ortiz de Montellano notes as the regional mandate to "maintain the equilibrium and the existence of the universe through . . . *actions*" (1989, 191; italics added), actions here meaning the advancement of social values and goals. Taking action on behalf of the community is a sacred trust, in other words, and this perspective has little tolerance for completely detached observation and knowledge without implementation. The sacred dimension of taking action to advance the community among cultures throughout the Americas is a thread of engagement present throughout the region. That thread marks a desire to make connections between ideas and actions in every facet of Mexican American culture's development. Chicano studies even distinguishes itself from many other academic programs in higher education through this commitment to take action on the community's behalf.

The Chicano rubric for exploring and promoting mestizo identity reflects the four categories I have been discussing: (1) mestizo (individual) identity, (2) mestizo culture, (3) hemispheric staging, and (4) social activism. To a remarkable degree, Chicano writers and activists coordinated these values and goals and the passion of "viva la raza!," "viva la causa!," and Chicano social critiques of American culture were not individual political moments of insight so much as parts of a larger, well-articulated vision of a movement. The documents presenting these plans for change, "I Am Joaquin" (Gonzales 1997 [1967]), "El Plan Espiritual de Aztlán" (1991 [1969]), and *El Plan de Santa Barbara* (Chicano Coordinating Council 1969) reference the Mexican American history that was not taught in schools and the action-oriented values that were suppressed in the region's culture and history. With these documents and the new projects that they made possible, writers and planners were trying to counter mainstream culture's idea of a sleeping Mexican with a sombrero over his face and foreground instead Joaquin the community builder.

"I Am Joaquin" and "El Plan Espiritual de Aztlán," for example, served as primers for planning and taking ethical action, blueprints for social movements. Each also cautioned against assimilation into what Gonzales called consumerist society's "social neurosis" (Gonzales 1997 [1967], 20). "El Plan Espiritual de Aztlán" asserted that only by avoiding the destructive promptings of social neurosis and consumerist society could Mexican Americans chart their own viable and sustainable course for the future. This document projected a vision of Mexican American aspirations with a recasting of relationships to land, the creation of jobs, instituting a new cultural voice to communicate Chicano identity and sense of purpose—many issues that *Mestizos Come Home!* identifies and tracks.

The Chicano Coordinating Council on Higher Education (1969) went a practical step further with their *El Plan de Santa Barbara* and advocacy for starting actual Chicano studies programs in colleges and universities—the accent being placed on taking constructive *action*. Its authors sought to develop a body of knowledge by "decolonizing" Mexican American communities through college courses on the history of mestizos, Aztec culture, Chicano literature, hemispheric history, and other Mexican American topics. They stressed that such knowledge should *serve* the community that produced it, and they wanted higher education to be a step forward toward making the national culture more receptive to their community, placing emphasis on what it means to be Mexican American and "American." To this day, their focus on how thought must lead to action—how academic study translates into practical application—remains a key feature of Chicano studies in American higher education.[13]

"El Plan" called for such programs to empower people to make education relevant to the community and to prepare young people for good jobs and careers. Its writers sought to understand cultural, social, and economic transformation, and in the vein of Mariátegui, Haya de la Torre, Alurista, and Gonzales they worked efficiently to reach such goals. Their strategy was to produce guides for creating Chicano studies programs that were so detailed and savvy that they would minimize resistance to the actual launching of those programs—the goal being to advance cultural identity and economic welfare through education. "Chicanismo draws its faith and strength," they proclaimed, "from two main sources: from the just struggle of our people and from an objective analysis of our community's strategic needs." They saw Chicano studies as part of a "common social praxis" to address those strategic needs and improve the quality of life for Mexican Americans (Chicano Coordinating Council on Higher Education 1969, 9). This document quotes José Vasconcelos as saying: "'We do not come to work for the university, but to demand [through the action that we take] that the university work for our people'" (11).

There was irony in their quoting Vasconcelos. While his perspective on mestizaje was revolutionary, Mariátegui had criticized him earlier for promoting a landmark vision of being mestizo but failing to understand the *process* and the practical steps of bringing about actual cultural and social change. The Chicano studies planners were determined not to fall into that trap, and the fact that many Chicano studies programs came into existence through the 1970s and 1980s, and are still operating as programs today, confirms that "El Plan" succeeded in establishing plans for *action.*

Further, "El Plan" writers were often retracing Mariátegui's steps in believing that, as De Castro argues, it was "necessary to [formally] reject the colonial . . . social and cultural heritage" common in the Americas and reconceptualize mestizo culture in relation to current needs and values (2002, 75). The writers took this idea to heart and sought not just to offer new courses but indigenous approaches to teaching, learning, and sharing knowledge. They drew upon tribal values and experimented with different learning styles and curricula, including nonhierarchical classrooms and learning communities, at times seeming to be creating alternative, experimental (Montessori-like) schools and learning environments. Proclaiming that "the point is not to have a college with a program, but rather a Chicano program at that college" (Chicano Coordinating Council 1969, 13), creating the *right* approach was everything.

The writers of this plan were also drawing from a belief that the recognition of mestizaje's existence was an important step but not one that could automatically change how people lived. Mariátegui saw that lifting the burden of colonialism at one cultural site—in education, for example—may lower the barriers of race and class division and can open a new direction for social development.[14] But to change a community significantly over time, the process of change must be nurtured toward democratic goals across various sites and institutions. "El Plan" met many of these criteria, and the fact that MEChA (Movimiento Estudiantil Chicana de Aztlán) adopted "El Plan" as their vision statement and handbook in the 1970s indicates their success in trying to be practical. Even now, MEChA is the oldest, largest organization of politically active Chicano young people in existence, and "El Plan" is still their handbook.

In the 1970s, Chicanos took similar approaches with detailed plans for supporting indigenous attitudes toward how they regarded community and how they saw the future. A detailed tour through this historical period would reveal many commitments to activism with few plans left untried.[15] The Mexican American community took action in community centers, making public art, forming political action groups, starting job programs, organizing unions, founding daycare centers, and in launching the Chicano movement, the Chicano Renaissance, and even the aftermath of these movements in the Chicano community in the present.

Since the late 1960s and the institution of Chicano studies programs, Mexican American writers, critics, and historians are still addressing the four categories discussed here (individual identity, cultural hybridity, hemispheric scope, and the call to action), categories that continue to be relevant for illuminating mestizo identity and community. At certain moments, as conditions warrant, one or more of these categories will come forward to bring greater scrutiny to current cultural and social developments. From 1989 through 2001, for example, there was a focus among Mexican American historians on the impact of social institutions and historical forces as shapers of Mexican American culture and identity, particularly in San Antonio and Los Angeles.[16] This work inspired many historical studies that followed. In 2001, Martha Menchaca published an influential study on land ownership's effect on the formation of mestizo identity in the American Southwest and argued that previous studies had shown the intersection of art, land ownership, and culture but had excluded the contributions of African American racial history. Menchaca's work has helped to bring about a revolution in the *intersectional* way that mestizo identity and race are understood in the United States.[17]

By the 2000s, the emphasis switched again as work on mestizo identity and race prepared for a next generation of approaches to mestizo culture. Julie A. Dowling in *Mexican Americans and the Question of Race* addresses the phenomenon of Mexican Americans choosing to report their identification as "white" on U.S. census forms. When they make such reports, embracing whiteness as "an identity that both historically and currently confers power and property rights" (2014, 133), they create a "disconnect between 'white' [in] Mexican Americans' lived experiences [of racial discrimination] and what they write on the [official] form" (134).

In that the United States has frequently altered racial standards and definitions, whiteness has often been a completely "relational" term, reflecting national politics and social values more than genetics or ethnicity. This situation has caused Mexican Americans on occasion to claim one racial identity while living the reality of another as they search for new strategies to advance their communities. Mexican Americans continue to search for strategies to deal with social marginalization, even as past attempts to claim "whiteness" have been on occasion counterproductive and ultimately are "detrimental [to] efforts to organize against racial injustice" (Dowling 2014, 134).

A similar productive approach to race and mestizo identity is Natalia Molina's *How Race Is Made in America: Immigration, Citizenship, and the Historical Power of Racial Scripts*. Molina cites what she calls "immigration regimes," U.S. government programs and regulations that in 1897 defined Mexicans unequivocally as white, as Julie A. Dowling also notes (Molina 2014, 6). In 1930, the United States began designating Mexican Americans as belonging to their own, unique race (a kind of off white category) and no longer were classified as truly white (6). Such on-again, off-again government definitions of "whiteness" have contributed to a skewed and often confused picture of race in the United States. As a result, "immigration laws [have] fundamentally shaped the parameters of race in America" in arbitrary and often unfair ways (2).[18]

Who decides who is white and who is not? Such decisions are influenced by "racial scripts," that is, "the ways in which the lives of racialized groups are linked across time and space and thereby affect one another, even when they do not directly cross paths" (Molina 2014, 6). Being born in the United States in the 1930s and claiming U.S. citizenship "was far from an uncontested right for Mexicans," a question that is also being raised again in current American politics focused on the undocumented and the birthright provision of the fourteenth amendment. Federal legislation in the 1930s specifically limited "birthright citizenship for African Americans and Chinese immigrants, dating back to the Dred Scot case." Such policies created a political climate that "made birthright citizenship for Mexicans [even] following the 1924 Immigration Act anything but certain" (7). Such evolving racial definitions for whiteness have impacted in irrational ways how people position themselves in the culture and what they are willing to claim about who they are. Federal policy about race has affected not only implementation of the law and the action of the courts but also the psychology of making claims based on the actions of others with similar claims, even if the claims were made many years apart.

In this chapter, the extent of each writer's commitment to the four dimensions of mestizo identity (individual, cultural, hemispheric, and action oriented) helps to explain what constitutes a writer as a major figure writing about mestizaje. Many of the writers and critics discussed here focus on mestizo identity in *all four* dimensions of inquiry, committing themselves to understanding mestizo identity in every way possible. We can also see the continuing central importance of Vasconcelos's perspective, an approach that profoundly influences Latin American writers, Anzaldúa, Rodriguez, and almost everyone that they influenced. *After* Vasconcelos, most approaches to discussing mestizaje *must* respond to and often feel compelled to adopt his perspective on race, especially his challenge to "pure" genetic lines in support of elite social classes. Vasconcelos's perspective also opens the door for seeing what *should* have been apparent earlier in his time and ours—the fact of the Americas being populated by mestizo majorities, a fact that remains part of the untold (or unrecognized) story of mestizos in the Americas.

This discussion about mestizo identity in the hemisphere moves from 1865 and Alencar's certitude about fixed racial categories to Molina's explanation (2014) and Quinn-Sánchez's (2015) of how race is made and unmade along political lines in the United States and the Americas. The search for mestizo identity in each case raises questions that have been avoided for too long. This search suggests the inadequacy of the "racial" approach to understanding human behavior and the differences between people. This search reveals, too, the neglect and marginalization of mestizo culture and its positioning for the future to be a central, defining force in the Americas. The search for mestizo identity shows the Americas as the staging ground for culture necessary for understanding mestizo identity in the United States. The search for mestizo identity also reveals mestizo activism and the need to implement new approaches to social justice as a sacred trust and commitment to the community.

The challenge of these issues connected to mestizo identity is becoming apparent for everyone to see. The search for mestizo identity across 150 years consistently returns to the interplay of nation, social class, and race. In this sweep of ideas and culture, the references for nation and social class change dramatically and often, and the understanding of "race" gets completely reframed in the aftermath of Vasconcelos's influence. The genealogy of mestizo identity mapped on this journey shows a growing recognition of who and what mestizos are and their role in the Americas' future, particularly as they develop as a community and advocate for themselves.

In the United States there is also a rising awareness and even sense of alarm that the Mexican American community could in time shape U.S. culture in significant but not always comfortable ways for the white majority. Peter Brimelow's *Alien Nation: Common Sense about America's Immigration Disaster* and Samuel P. Huntington's *Who Are We? The Challenges of America's National Identity* indict Mexican Americans for the destructive future *potential* of their social and cultural impact as mestizos. The timing of this criticism, especially Huntington's harsh views of Mexican Americans and their political and cultural influence on the United States, is ironic in occurring at a moment when the reign of race is rapidly being eclipsed. Race is falling as a defensible rubric for understanding different kinds of people, an issue that I will take up again in the conclusion.

It was Vasconcelos's contention that closing the cultural and social divide between European and indigenous people happened sometime after the Spanish colonial era but before the twentieth century. The subsequent rise of mestizo communities everywhere was not an event that he projected for the future but a reality check from the past that he was only trying to give a name. His recognition included the fact that mestizos are still the poorest of the poor, a people outside of the cycles of Western economic reproduction and wealth, the people whom history at times has forgotten. Like most of the writers discussed here, he saw that the marginalization of mestizo culture has gone on for too long. His celebration of mestizo identity then follows a wave of Latin American indigenismo, a set of attitudes intended to counter long-standing trends that overlooked mestizo lives.

As the writers discussed in this chapter warrant, mestizos are now advancing to the cultural fore as the living embodiment of an argument against the Western perspective on racial purity and social hierarchies traditionally buttressed by racial divisions. Many of the writers discussed here harbor the suspicion that the moment may be at hand when mestizos can no longer be dismissed or relegated to the cultural periphery of the United States or any country. History is propelling mestizos into this century as the New World's primary reference for citizenship. The fact of mestizos existing in great numbers speaks loudly about cultural trends, a future that was glimpsed with the impact of the Latino vote in the 2008 and 2012 U.S. presidential elections. In the early twenty-first century in the United States, we have arrived at that moment when mestizos are helping to redefine what it means to be "American."

Since the 1960s, Mexican American writers have contributed to the discussion of mestizo identity by offering a nuanced account of the personal and cultural forces that comprise it. We will see in chapters to come that Mexican American critics, artists, and historians continue to create a hybrid space within which mestizo identity mediates between what is left of the Spanish colonial legacy and indigenous culture and calls into question all racial categories and distinctions. The Mexican American decision to speak from the stage of the Americas conveys this commitment to social change, moving forward to advance the community's values, demonstrating what people in the Americas have known for some time about what they can achieve when they are aware of the cultural and social struggles that they share.

The Chicano movement and other social and cultural developments since the 1960s provide a valuable glimpse of this potential to work for change. Choosing "to come home" to become a part of this larger conversation about race and social justice, Mexican Americans are working to reframe their social and cultural lives. They have joined a larger conversation about racial justice and are gaining momentum to assert who they are as a community charting their own way. One of their goals is to go home as they choose, in the sense of committing to a place where they cannot be excluded because they already belong there, a move in the direction of personal and social liberation too-long denied.

Examining Mexican American questions about race in light of these goals creates conditions for change. As Mariátegui often asserts, intellectual work, literary texts, social documents, popular culture, and art do not automatically make racial biases and years of social oppression and bitterness disappear. But la cultura begins to heal the rifts in social life when it creates new awarenesses, fresh approaches, and renewed inspiration. The humanities and the arts bring about the conditions for change in their own way by creating conditions for different perceptions, experiences, and realities, forces that daily alter minds and beliefs.

The fundamental optimism for which Mexican American writers and artists are famous suggests that culture indeed can heal, the function that José Antonio Burciaga claims for mestizo culture when he urges Mexican Americans to *Drink Cultura*—that is, involve themselves deeply and become fully engaged to help culture and history do their work as effectively and thoroughly as possible. Mexican American writers are dealing with realities pervasive in the Americas, as their participation in Latin American traditions discussing race and mestizo identity makes clear. The Mexican American voices discussed in this chapter give an alternative sense of the history of the Americas and encourage the final wearing down and lifting away of a colonial legacy as Mexican Americans continue on their way home while defining who they are as a mestizo community.

* II *
REMAPPING THE MESTIZO COMMUNITY

CHAPTER 3

There's No Place Like Aztlán

LAND, THE SOUTHWEST, AND RUDOLFO ANAYA

The relationship to land and land traditions is a defining topic for under-standing Mexican American and Chicano culture. Land ownership and land use policy in the American Southwest evoke a cluster of cultural issues defining twenty-first-century American culture. The question of land ownership evokes the past and the loss of traditional lands after the Mexican-American War of 1848. The loss of land is connected to the disenfranchisement of mestizo culture in the United States up through the present. The modern acquisition of land by commercial interests is part of the ongoing erosion of the working class in cities and rural communities. From formulations of Aztlán, the fabled, ancient Mexican homeland, to the land and place themes of Rudolfo Anaya's novel Shaman Winter, *these issues reveal important dimensions of Mexican American and American culture connected with the traditions that land embodies.*

In *The Revolt of the Cockroach People,* Oscar Zeta Acosta captures the spirit of the 1970s Chicano Renaissance in regard to land use. In this novel's court scene, a Mexican American lawyer argues that northern New Mexico was the actual site of the famous Aztlán—the legendary homeland of the ancient Aztecs from a time that predates México's founding. He claims that Mexican Americans, heirs to the Aztecs on their Mexican side, live in Aztlán by virtue of living in the U.S. Southwest. "We are not Mexicans," he asserts. "We are Chicanos from Aztlán. We have never left our land. Our fathers never engaged in bloody sacrifices. We are farmers and hunters and we live with the buffalo" (1973, 161). Taking the American Southwest to be the original homeland of the "cockroach people"—Mexican Americans socially and economically marginalized—is presented as comic. And yet this scene from Acosta's novel expresses the Mexican American belief, dating from the late 1960s, which says that the American Southwest belonged not only to México as recently as 1848 but was the traditional homeland of the ancient Aztecs and their heirs—modern-day Mexican Americans.

Acosta also believes that communities "belong" to their homeland and derive their identity and culture from such ties to place. These beliefs are not always evident in twentieth-century America, where land is often stripped of all cultural associations and reduced to being a commodity sold and traded on international markets. As part of the Aztlán claim, Acosta is promoting land, as Mexican Americans did throughout the 1960s and 1970s, as a sacred repository of traditional cultural relationships. In the twentieth century, the tie to land, as Rudolfo Anaya comments, often gets subverted in "the hands of world markets and politics" (2009, 90). Anaya comments that land remains a part, whether always recognized as such or not, of what makes culture work—one of the "healing power[s]" in the world that "the epiphany of place provides" (2009, 145). In the promotion of Aztlán in the 1960s and 1970s, Mexican Americans were probing such beliefs and trying to refind their own ties to place in the national landscape.

According to legend, the Aztec homeland was located north of Tenochtitlan (the early site of Mexico City), possibly as far north as Santa Fe, New Mexico. As the story goes, the Mexica god-of-war Huitzilopochli told his people to leave Aztlán and search for Tenochtitlan. When found, Tenochtitlan became their new homeland, but the Aztecs always wanted to return to their original place. As part of the 1960s Chicano movement, Mexican Americans capitalized on the importance of this traditional homeland idea and saw themselves as fulfilling a historical destiny by living in the Southwest, which they took to be that home. The Aztlán idea told Mexican Americans that by choosing to live in the Southwest, even if they were immigrants, and even if they were undocumented, they were a people claiming rights to an ancient ancestral inheritance.

As Richard L. Nostrand notes, the traditional homeland relationship has "three basic elements: a people, a place, and identity with place. . . . People must have lived [in a homeland] long enough" to make "their impress in the form of a cultural landscape. . . . Having developed an identity [in connection] with the land," they will have developed social customs and cultural practices uniquely tied to land. They will also have developed "emotional feelings of attachment, desires to possess, even compulsions to defend [their land]" (1972, 214).

The contemporary conception of a "homeland" is even more complex than such traditional practices can describe. The contemporary idea of a homeland is often paradoxical, involving a "reclaiming and reprocessing of habits, objects, names and histories that have been uprooted [owing to frequent] migration, displacement or colonization." There is much movement around the globe in the twenty-first century, and the homeland may not be a place where one's community actually lived in the past but could be a claim based on *"making* [a] home . . . about *creating* both pasts and futures through inhabiting the grounds of the present" (Ahmed 2003, 9; italics added). The "homeland" is now as much a cultural construction as an actual place. The contemporary sense of a homeland is as likely, as Anaya comments, the product of the interaction of "place, imagination, and memory" (2009, 142).

The promotion of Aztlán as the Mexican American homeland is precisely such a complex claim, with Mexican Americans having a cultural relationship to a place that may or may not have existed. There are mythic elements of the Aztlán concept and only a few indications of its historical validity. But if Aztlán *were* in the U.S. Southwest, even as a mythical reference, then Mexican Americans are not exiles or illegals hiding in the U.S. shadows, not interlopers trying to gain property and social advantages that are not theirs. They are a people claiming their *own* home. Supporting this idea in the 1960s became an expression of Mexican American hope for the future. The Southwest actually *was* a part of Mexico until 1848, making the homeland claim in an important sense literally true, but the Aztlán idea became a broader reference to *all* prior Mexican American cultural ties to the United States.

How do Mexican Americans focus on traditional ties to land contribute to Mexican American and U.S. national culture? Valuing land for its cultural associations instead of its commercial value reinvigorates communities and helps to counter the loss of traditions, a case that Mexican American writers and land activists often make about land

and land use. During the 1960s, no other activity of the Chicano movement, asserts Anaya, was as "important" as the cultural relationship to
the American Southwest of a Mexican American homeland (1991, 232).
"El Plan Espiritual de Aztlán," originally published in 1969, promoted
such a relationship, which countered the modern debasement of land
and supported land activists striving to protect traditional lands that
had cultural and historical significance. As Chicano sociologist Devon
G. Peña comments, this battle was over cultural "paradigms." Anaya,
Reyes López Tijerina, María Varela, and other land activists opposed
the "bureaucratic model of state and capitalist control of nature as a
commodity" and preferred, as Peña explains, "the indigenous model of
sustainable local stewardship of the homeland" (1998, 274).

Land activists from this period were joining forces with American
cultural geographers. Carl O. Sauer, the godfather of U.S. cultural geography, weighed in strongly against the nineteenth- and twentieth-century
U.S. shift away from a communal model centered on ties to land "where
different ways and ends of life went on side by side" (1962, 47). He
opposed treating land like a commodity recognized only for its market
value. In other words, Mexican American writers and American cultural
geographers joined forces in believing that national social ills tied to
the loss of shared communal values were intensified through the commodification of traditional lands. Hence American geographer James J.
Parsons, sounding like Rudolfo Anaya, advocates protecting "geographic
and cultural diversity, the sacredness of the Earth, and the responsibilities of local communities to it," calling for a broad reassessment of how
the recognition of cultural attachments to land can hold communities
together (1985, 4). Only when we honor social and cultural land ties,
as current ecofeminist Vandana Shiva also argues, can we "resist the
culture of economic organization that destroys both cultural diversity
and biodiversity by promoting and nurturing monocultures and monop-
olies.." Only when communities commit to sustaining cultural and social
ties to land, as Shiva concludes, do they sustain relationships such as
"gender, class, ethnicity and other constructions of difference, identity
politics, and the environmental movement" (1998, viii).

Chicana philosopher Laura Pulido amplifies Shiva's comment
in saying that "social injustice, growing inequality, and a looming

environmental crisis," problems appearing in the wake of losing traditional ties to land, are "the greatest threats facing the global community as we enter the twenty-first century" (1996, 210). Although they have received too little credit for this alliance, Mexican American writers have actively promoted these debates and have consistently argued for maintaining traditional land ties to support communities.

The Chicano movement's Aztlán declaration in the 1970s was basically a vehicle for advancing all of these separate issues. When the Aztlán claim was first made in the 1960s, there were few archaeological or historical arguments for locating Aztlán in New Mexico, or any real support, other than folklore, for making this claim. Even so, for Mexican Americans, the effect of claiming that the homeland was in the American Southwest was catalytic, another step toward turning the United States into a "home," in this case a place where Mexican Americans felt they belonged and could stay no matter what. The claim was even better in that it asserted historical priority from a time before the colonial interlopers took what was originally theirs, a claim stoking a Mexican American sense of pride in ancestral roots and a newfound Mexican American identity.

Once the assertion was made, Mexican Americans were a "first people" with their own land claims. After the Aztlán declaration circulated in literature, social texts, and the arts, many Mexican Americans no longer thought of themselves as marginal, as Mexican exiles. They were now a separate "nation" uniquely tied to a place. Especially for a community that intensely seeks ethical and religious guidance from los antepasados, the ancestors, there was a special significance, a sacredness, in "knowing" that they were living in their ancestral homeland.

The homeland idea has a mixed history, some of it ironic. Several sixteenth-century texts reference the Aztec migration to Mexico from their original home, the earliest being Fray Diego Durán's *Historia de las Indias de Nueva-España y Islas de Tierra Firme*, first published in 1581. The claim for Aztlán as the *original* Mexican homeland came from Fray Bernardino de Sahagún (1499–1590), the Franciscan friar whose work is recognized today as a forerunner of modern-day anthropology. In 1582 he recorded in *Historia General de las Cosas de Nueva España* that the Aztecs relocated from Aztlán to Tenochtitlan, which became the capital of the Aztec empire. These intriguing references to a historical, and yet likely still mythical, Aztlán lay dormant as a concept not to be refound until the modern era.

Assertion of the Aztlán claim in modern times came amid a climate of conflict and debate about land in the New Mexico Territory. Before New Mexico became a U.S. territory in 1850, both Spain and México had awarded many large tracts of land—"grants"—across the Southwest to individuals and groups to encourage the rapid establishment of ranches and villages. By 1850, after having lived under Spanish and Mexican rule, New Mexico was a patchwork quilt of complicated land grants, with names like Tierra Amarilla, Taos Pueblo, Sangre de Cristo, Río Chama, Atrisco, among many others. Subsequent land issues of every sort in New Mexico were played out in relation to these grants, with litigation lasting decades, even centuries, with legal disputes, some of them extending into the present, over water and land rights connected with old grants.

At the heart of the legal problems is that land in New Mexico was awarded under two legal systems, Spanish and Mexican, and they often conflicted with each other. To make matters worse, after 1848, land policies and litigation fell under a third legal system, U.S. law, with a completely different approach for establishing and protecting ownership. We can add to this state of general confusion the fact that New Mexico's fragile ecology, with many arid regions and little available water, made the just distribution of land and water ever more pressing and difficult. Also, during the years of territorial status (1850–1912), before statehood in 1912, commercial developers bought many New Mexico mineral and agricultural lands in hopes of making huge profits as New Mexico assimilated into the U.S. national economy, the commercial capturing of land bringing even greater complexity and regional conflict.

The result was that the history of land-grant disputes in New Mexico has at times been a sordid "legacy of bitterness" (Briggs and Van Ness 1987, 4), a chaotic situation caused by what Sylvia Rodríguez calls a "collective trauma of massive land loss" (1987, 382). Pueblo peoples, mestizos, and Hispanics had owned land titles in some cases for centuries, and since 1848 many of those lands have been lost through fraud, vigilante action, and aggressive corporations litigating in U.S courts to acquire as much land as possible. Over the last 150 years, a major historical development in New Mexico has been the transfer of traditional lands to corporations and commercial interests who have little or no concern for New Mexico culture and traditions, with the exception of "the [strategic] marketing of ethnicity" in New Mexico as a commodity often connected with the promotion of Taos, Santa Fe, and Albuquerque (Rodríguez 1987, 387).[1]

Land issues in New Mexico have often focused on the ejidos, or communal lands, owned by families and groups (Acuña 2000, 369). Common to Spanish and Mexican law, the ejido referenced lands held in trust by the community as a whole, "common lands . . . owned by the community" that "could not be sold" (Ebright 1987, 24). The stricture against selling ejidos was protected by Spanish and Mexican law, but not by U.S. courts after 1850. Under U.S. jurisdiction, "community grants," more common in the nineteenth century, never fared well in the twentieth century and have all but disappeared (23).

This was the land environment in New Mexico that gave rise to the Aztlán idea on two different occasions. The first resurfacing of Aztlán as a concept happened in the nineteenth century through William G. Ritch's slim volume entitled *Aztlán: The History, Resources and Attractions of New Mexico*. This was a promotional tract designed to highlight the "territory's mineral wealth" and its readiness for outside investors to promote ranching and land development. The book pitched New Mexico as the historical Aztlán and described it as an exotic locale that could attract investors for the "superb profits" that could be theirs. "This beautiful country," the book boasted, was "destined to be known as the true El Dorado" (1885, 137).[2] It promoted New Mexico as the perfect real-estate deal and highlighted Santa Fe especially as the original site of the Aztlán capital in the "land of enchantment," creating an exotic aura with commercial attractions that still persist in the popular media today—what Sylvia Rodríguez calls in New Mexico the practice of "ethnophilia" (1987, 386). There was, of course, some distant reason for believing the Aztlán claim, but the goal in Ritch's book was commercial development, a public relations campaign depicting New Mexico as a new, exotic site for investment.

With this new identity, the New Mexico Territory was open for business with an attraction calculated to work for outside investors. In effect, New Mexico took on the identity of fertile primitivism, dark and malleable—a desirable place ready to be shaped by new commercial interests. As Ritch promised all who came, an enterprising "white" person in New Mexico could easily be situated *"on top of the ladder"* of economic and commercial success (1885, 117).

Ramón Gutiérrez has shown how investors in New Mexico promoted the territory as the land of kindly, noble savages, whose presence demonstrated an evolutionary theory then current in the late nineteenth century attributable to Lewis Henry Morgan's book *Ancient Society* (1964). Morgan's book framed New Mexico with Eurocentric standards of culture and society but with the added exotic appeal of a foreignism—essentially, the traditional recipe for tourism. The book held that ancient societies moved through predictable stages to reach the pinnacle of "modern" development, and New Mexico displayed all of the developmental stages simultaneously. A primitive phase happened during "settlement of the country by the Pueblo Indians' ancestral kin" (Gutiérrez 1989, 178). Another period of modern progress began when Francisco Vásquez de Coronado explored the region, and the Spanish and the Mexicans brought in new levels of development and robust economic growth. The last "epoch of history," the fully "civilized" phase, came under the United States, with the "hallmarks of liberal progress," that is, fresh opportunities for venture capital investment (180). The enhanced cultural legitimacy granted at each stage of development matched the incremental movement of culture in the state away from the land's indigenous community.

While the territory's promoters wanted new investors, they were not looking for more Hispanics. In 1850, the territory was sparsely populated with only sixty thousand people. Toward century's end, all knew that New Mexico would soon become a state, and as more people came into the territory, the Hispanic populace would possibly outnumber whites, and a majority of Hispanics could end up governing New Mexico. They would oversee the agricultural and industrial bases of investment that Ritch and others had worked so hard to achieve. On the other hand, an influx of white investors could ensure economic profitability and continued commercial development, and Gutiérrez argues that encouragement of "white" investors into the state was intended to keep the mestizo community from ever governing.[3]

The Aztlán idea surfaced again in the 1960s in the U.S. Southwest. The Chicano Youth Conference in March 1969, in Denver, Colorado, affirmed that Mexican Americans in the Southwest were, in fact, living in Aztlán. These young people critiqued the civil and economic injustices Mexican Americans had faced since 1848, the year of the Treaty of Guadalupe Hidalgo, and called for land reform to begin solving landgrant disputes in New Mexico.

This focus on land was owing to the influence of reclaim-the-land guru and maverick community organizer Reyes López Tijerina, who understood "the resentment that village-dwelling farmers [in New Mexico] held towards those who usurped their lands." Addressing a range of land-grant issues, Tijerina advocated recapturing Mexican American land and reasserting land rights, which the Guadalupe Hidalgo Treaty was never adequate to protect (Rosales 1996, 157–58). Tijerina's organization, La alianza federal de Mercedes, with the motto "tierra y libertad!" ("land and liberty"), argued that vigilante violence and the U.S. courts had taken traditional lands in New Mexico from their rightful owners (Acuña 2000, 370). The Alianza and "El Plan Espiritual" jointly argued for returning lands to traditional people in the Southwest and reasserted that justice should guide the reclaiming of a long-forgotten homeland (Anaya and Lomelí 1991, 1).[4]

Most important in these calls was the promotion of land-based nationalism. "El Plan Espiritual" said that "*we*, the Chicano inhabitants and civilizers of the northern land of Aztlán from whence came our forefathers, reclaiming the land of their birth and consecrating the determination of our people of the sun, *declare* that the call of our blood is our power, our responsibility, and our inevitable destiny." This call to action concluded that "we are a bronze people with a bronze culture. Before the world, before all of North America, before all our brothers in the bronze continent, we are a *nation*, we are a union of free pueblos, we are *Aztlán*" (Anaya and Lomelí 1991, 1). This link between land and identity addressed the underlying struggle for social justice, which had land, economic, and cultural dimensions.[5]

To keep this momentum, the Chicano movement pushed for changes in Mexican American strategies of self-determination by creating new businesses and jobs. The net effect in 1969 was that Mexican American unemployment hovered somewhere between 6 and 8 percent, but Mexican Americans were still entering the professions behind whites by a deficit of 60 percent (Acuña 2000, 384). The Chicano movement wanted to reposition the Mexican American community by reforming schools so that students could compete successfully for jobs. Rodolfo Acuña notes that while Mexican Americans "made some gains during the period of 1968–74, after this point they slipped backward" with a return to high dropout rates when the first phase of exuberance for the Chicano movement waned (2000, 413).

The movement's intense triple focus on protecting civil rights for individuals, enhancing the business atmosphere for communities, and reclaiming land explains much about its success as a cultural and social phenomenon—all despite huge areas of Chicano life changing little at all. Even so, claiming a "homeland" in the American Southwest signaled a new direction on many fronts for a community that was rethinking its place in the United States. Rafael Pérez-Torres comments in *Mestizaje* that "in many ways, land lies at the heart of the Chicano movement" (2006, 115). "The coalescence of land and body [was] part of a new visioning of identity and subjectivity" for Mexican Americans (124). He adds that "a profound sense of dislocation was at the dark heart of Chicano identity" (197). The homeland idea redefined and deepened such recognition of the relationship between land and identity, and this was a huge step forward.

A few Chicano and Chicana writers during this time continued to assert that the southwestern United States was once the literal and actual Aztlán, the "innocent" place, in the face of considerable evidence to the contrary. Most, however, like Mexican American poet Alurista, were beginning to see "Aztlán as borderless and belonging to those who work, who toil for the wealth that, presently, others who own the means of production enjoy" (Alurista 1991, 227). Along the same line, Genaro M. Padilla analyzes the Aztlán phenomenon in light of Franz Fanon's *The Wretched of the Earth* to discuss how a group goes about mending a "threatened or even shattered cultural psyche." He argues that for subjugated cultures to triumph over adversity, they must "reject the colonial structures that distort, devalue and seek to destroy their history." The homeland claim worked as such a strategy for cohesively bringing together the damaged traditions of the past and projecting a favorable future as Mexican Americans' destiny (1991, 113). The homeland idea was a powerful instrument for repairing a "shattered cultural psyche" and was important to Mexican Americans trying to alleviate the cultural and social residue of racism and lack of participation in mainstream American culture.

The Chicano movement worked through various land perspectives in its early history in the 1960s and 1970s. The 1969 *El Plan Espiritua de Aztlán,* focusing on the loss of land grants and the injustices perpetrated after the signing of the Treaty of Guadalupe Hidalgo, calls for lost lands to be reclaimed, as Tijerina had urged. This declaration was typical of 1960s radicalism in calling for the complete transformation of relations between the local community and the larger culture to establish "social, economic, cultural and political independence" for Mexican Americans ("El Plan" 1991, 2). The Mexican American need for Aztlán to exist, and the recognition that the claim received, signaled a momentum that carried forward into the Chicano Renaissance, as Luis Valdez, Rudolfo Anaya, Tomás Rivera, Rodolfo Gonzáles, Rolando Hinojosa, Estela Portillo Trambley, Ester Hernández, and Lorna Dee Cervantes, among others, began developing a distinct Chicano and Chicana voice and identity that referenced the homeland concept as a basis for seeking economic and social reform.

Twenty years later, Rudolfo Anaya's important essay "Aztlán: A Homeland without Boundaries" (1991) signaled a new Mexican American approach to land as the next step in this evolving story. Anaya valued Aztlán as a concept but wanted to create something new, what he adopted in his own terms as the "New World," an approach referencing confiscated lands across the Americas as well as racial and cultural issues connected with the conquest. In some ways supplanting the homeland idea, this new, expansive notion contextualized the cultural agenda that Mexican American writers, artists, and cultural critics had been moving toward since the middle 1980s.

In this new approach, Anaya refers to Aztlán as a useful fiction and acknowledges recent scholarship from the early 1980s that undercut the notion of a historical Aztlán in the U.S. Southwest. The historian John R. Chávez had analyzed sixteenth-century Spanish colonial codices that referenced Aztec and Spanish attempts to find Aztlán, texts from that period arguing that the homeland was but a short four hundred miles northeast of Mexico City, in Nayarit (1989, 51)—or, more likely, as came out later, in the Mexican states of Guanajuato, Jalisco, and Michoacán (Matos Moctezuma 1988).

With a basis for displacing Aztlán as a concept that was direct and pragmatic, Anaya writes that after the Chicano movement the Mexican American community was still in great jeopardy, as it was being assimilated into "mainstream American culture" at an alarming rate. This process, owing to melting-pot pressures, "was occurring so quickly that unless we re-established the covenants of our ancestors[,] our culture was threatened with extinction." The Aztlán ideal—specific, elegant, and plausible, a direct link to the past—worked instantly to crystallize the social and cultural goals that Mexican Americans were beginning to imagine for themselves. But if Aztlán were not an actual place in the Southwest, then Mexican Americans might need a larger, more sophisticated frame for contextualizing land and the residue of colonialism, which was still having repercussions in the Americas (1991, 236).

Anaya's New World script—not a single place but a network of cultural and historical connections—could reframe and contextualize the geographically grounded Aztlán. Even those who did not adopt the New World terminology were nonetheless moving in this direction of depending less on a literal Aztlán in the Southwest. As the Chicano Renaissance succeeded on several fronts in the 1980s, especially economically and culturally—with, for example, the winning of labor contracts from grape and lettuce growers in California—the Chicano movement's ongoing critique needed to match the wide expanse of how Mexican Americans were viewing their lives, so the focus on the New World concept was far sighted and constructive.

Anaya addresses how colonization of the Americas had caused amnesia about the ancient peoples of the New World in relation to mestizo identity, so that the Americas' ancient cultures were covered over by the devastation of the Spanish conquest, even though their "soul" was still connected to the land. Aligned with the thinking of Victor

Raul Haya de la Torre, José Martí, José Vasconcelos, Gloria Anzaldúa, and Aníbal Quijano, Anaya saw indigenous identity and land as threads present in the "substratum of [all] my writings" and as voicing part of "the indigenous American perspective, or New World view" that focused on Native cultural origins in the Americas. He adds that "we must know more of the synthesis of our Spanish and Indian nature, and know more of the multiple heritages of the Americas" (1991, 358).

This "multicultural perspective" (1991, 363) and "the New World view" needed to be "syncretic and encompassing" (364), since the New World concept, as Aztlán had before it, turned away from the Spanish tradition—not to oppose it as European but to embrace the New World's hybrid complexity. With this distinction, he was referencing the Americas' ancient history, the conquest, and the contemporary cultural and political reality of living in the United States. Mestizos needed a land-based culture, but that land did not have to be Aztlán. All of this created a different direction for the mestizo recognition of a homeland. Anaya remarks that the mestizo is "a person that is not known in this country" and that this "unique person" needs a sustainable New World context within which to affirm relations among land, culture, and mestizo identity—all of which restates the urgent need for the Chicano movement to begin with (Jussawalla and Dasenbrock 1992, 255).

The Chicano movement's various land claims were helpful, and the movement's remarkable success since the 1960s has yet to be fully recognized—in part because of its complex social and cultural dimensions but also because the Chicano Renaissance and its aftermath are still being felt. The designations "Chicano" and "Chicana" point with dramatic force socially, economically, and aesthetically not only to a Mexican American association with native lands but to an evolving culture that did not exist in any practical sense before the middle 1960s. There is still a need for Mexican Americans to consolidate the gains that they have made since the 1960s and make greater strides in the areas of education, jobs, and political representation. As they and other Latinos gain more confidence about mestizo culture and their place in it, especially as they become America's majority community no later than 2050, they will make progress in the process of coming home that began with reclaiming their homeland.

Anaya brings together and focuses these homeland and land issues in the novel *Shaman Winter* (1999). Much of his work makes the case for elevating land's importance apart from commercial value, an act of resistance against exploitation and economic, cultural, and racial oppression—a powerful articulation for claiming mestizo cultural and historical legitimacy. Probably owing to this commitment to save traditional lands in New Mexico from commercial development, *Shaman Winter* and many of his other novels, stories, poems, and essays focus on land's importance and point toward the possibility of a new, revitalized relationship to land in the American Southwest and in the Americas as a whole.

Shaman Winter reflects a new awareness of the New World hemispheric staging of the Americas. In what amounts to a second large-scale proposal in Anaya's work (the first being the embrace of indigenous beliefs and cultural patterns in *Bless Me, Ultima*), Anaya focuses on land, the homeland, and the significance of a New World perspective. *Shaman Winter* acknowledges the new framing of the homeland idea that had emerged over the previous forty years with a north-south orientation that connects the United States with the whole of the Americas, in place of the east-west orientation that foregrounds the British in the narrow view of North America's colonization.

Much of *Shaman Winter's* power and appeal come from a focus on the specifics of why Mexican American culture *needs* a homeland and should promote a broad, hemispheric view of mestizo life in the Américas. Like *Zia Summer, Rio Grande Fall,* and *Jemez Spring,* the detective novels in this series, *Shaman Winter* unfolds with detective Sonny Baca's struggle with his archrival Raven—the sorcerer villain whom Sonny faces in epic combat to protect the lands of the Americas throughout this sequence of books.

An ex-schoolteacher who has become a private detective, Sonny Baca is, in many ways, unremarkable. He is a regular guy, footloose in Albuquerque, except that his ancestor and alter ego is Capt. Andrés Vaca, a soldier in the Spanish army of Juan Pérez de Oñate y Salazar (1550–1626), the Spanish conquistador who in 1598 conquered New Mexico. In dramatic fashion, this novel opens with Sonny Baca awakening one morning after traveling back through a dream channel, which

Raven had opened for him, to 1598 and the Spanish entrada into New Mexico.

The novel follows the present action in Albuquerque through Sonny's eyes, and when the text switches to the 1598 historical drama in New Mexico, we see the story through the eyes of Sonny as Andrés Vaca. Sonny is both people—himself when he is awake, and his ancestor Andrés when he is asleep and dreaming. As Sonny's awareness of his double consciousness increases, the reader moves rapidly back and forth between Andrés in the sixteenth century and Sonny in the twentieth, with a split-screen perspective and narrative.

The situation in 1598 is that Oñate's army is preparing to travel from Santa Barbara (Nueva España) to what will become Albuquerque and Santa Fe in El Nuevo México. Anaya builds dramatic tension when the Spanish army crosses into New Mexico to embark on this late phase of the conquest and the probable closing of the northern colonial frontier. Like Keats's Hernán Cortéz in "On First Looking into Chapman's Homer," who contemplates his entrance into the Americas with a moment of pomp, Oñate's army in Anaya's novel contemplates its own "vision of the vast land to the north" and the "throbbing" of a "new time being born" as soon as their feet touch the northern lands (1999b, 14). Their journey will transform Nuevo Mexico, and as they move forward an already convoluted world in the Americas will become ever more complicated as the Spanish colonize Pueblo peoples.

Anaya does two things to frame this 1598 historical moment. Preparing for the entrance into New Mexico, he foregrounds the subplot of Andrés Vaca's marriage to an indigenous woman, Owl Woman, on the eve of the entrada. Their story provides a human-scale contrast to the epic drama taking place in the conquest. Whereas the New Mexico conquest is part of the Spanish invasion and empire building, Andrés and Owl Woman's union represents a counterhistory of peaceful coexistence, which at one time may have seemed possible but ultimately was not meant to be.

Second is that Owl Woman is the bearer of the Calendar of Dreams, a bowl on which Toltec priests etched the history *and* the future of the Americas (a focus that I will return to later). The bowl's calendar tells about the Americas' ancient peoples and how the conquest unfolds, the fated meeting of Andrés and Owl Woman, and even Sonny's exploits in Albuquerque in the twentieth century. The couple brings the Calendar of Dreams to New Mexico to provide a macroperspective on these fateful events, hoping to inspire peaceful coexistence, a potential modeled on their union, instead of the conquest's violent and bloody scenario.

It is clear from *Zia Summer*, the first of the Sonny Baca novels, that the villain Raven does not cause the impasses in Sonny's personal life, especially his tendency to be directionless. Distracted by modern life and culture, and with only a weak sense of his New Mexico heritage, Sonny has been a used-car salesman, a schoolteacher, and a detective, otherwise floating through his life and culture, trying to stay clear of commitments and live in the vato loco (footloose and fancy-free) style.

Zia Summer, Rio Grande Fall, Shaman Winter, and *Jemez Spring* progress along the same path as the United States in constructing important cultural milestones of identity. This series references the melting pot ideal from the past, a notion that loosely reflects Walt Whitman's idea of a composite "American" moving down an "open road" that is the wide expanse of America. This sequence also includes the multicultural phase in the present and the emergence of an as-yet-little-examined era of ethnic identification, which we can call the "see through your own eyes" perspective. This last view suggests Anaya's understanding of other perspectives from a vantage point grounded in ties to land, a sense of place, cultural identity, and personal commitment.

In *Zia Summer* and *Rio Grande Fall*, there are Mexican American versions of these three ways that America has thought about cultural identity in relation to land. In *Zia Summer*, Frank Dominic exemplifies the melting-pot version of American identity. He is a candidate for mayor with a plan to develop Albuquerque as the Venice of the Southwest with an extensive canal system and various expensive tourist attractions. This familiar American type has lost all traces of ethnic identity and ties to land and is motivated primarily by economic pragmatism and greed. Implicit in Frank Dominic's identity is the assumption that America is the neutral meeting ground for people who have shed their ethnicity, especially in their ties to land, to become new, composite "Americans"—everyone and no one in particular. Frank Dominic is an anonymous citizen-investor, a creature of both the modern cityscape and America's large-scale urbanizing and corporatizing of culture.

In *Zia Summer* and *Rio Grande Fall*, Anaya projects contemporary multiculturalism, characterized by an appreciation of the "interesting" differences that make up the "mosaic" of America's many cultures, but with no personal perspective. Sonny's own perspective at this point exemplifies the multicultural movement. This perspective is evident when Sonny has no sense of his past or his own culture. With no standards by which to judge anything, he encounters indigenous cultures and mainstream cultural infatuations in his detective work in Albuquerque, and his inability to judge critically or to discriminate is the weakness that his enemy Raven exploits.

Reacting against the loss of an ethnic orientation in the melting-pot space, the multicultural movement that Sonny exemplifies promotes leaving no ethnicity behind and regarding all ethnic identities as equal in a kind of democratic vision of cultural parity. For a communal or individual identity to be viable, however, one must take ownership of the distinctions and traditions from the past that shape the present. The multicultural approach postulates no preference for any particular ethnic perspective but encourages a "democratic" appreciation of everything existing simultaneously in the cultural mosaic.[6] This appreciation is supposed to establish a universal viewpoint from which to regard all ethnic identity equally.[7] The flaw in this conception is the attempt to view approaches to ethnicities, traditions, and cultures without weighing their merits. Everyone alive has an ethnic history and a social station that color and shape a specific worldview, and the view from nowhere, the completely nonbiased view, is not possible or even desirable.

Anaya satirizes the view from nowhere in the Sonny Baca series as a New Age enthusiasm for supposedly exotic cultures, as seen with Tamara in *Zia Summer*, a white woman passionate about indigenous culture but personally ungrounded in her appreciation of anything. She belongs everywhere but can claim nothing of her own. Sonny himself moves through all three phases: melting-pot person (as a used-car salesman), multiculturalist (when he teaches high school), and then person embracing his past to discover his own destiny (as a detective).

In *Shaman Winter*, melting-pot contradictions and multiculturalism give way to a new space of ethnicity, one that is personal and connects to land and the world. As Sonny and Raven struggle, Anaya describes these two ancient souls battling over a stolen nuclear reactor core and fighting for the spirit of modern culture and the world's very existence. In Sonny's struggle with Raven, to be able to fight at all, Sonny needs to understand Raven's and his own historical ties to the Americas, his own attempts to recover the past and Raven's efforts to erase it. Without that knowledge, Sonny is defenseless. To gain that knowledge he must immerse himself ever more deeply in New Mexican and the Americas' history, both sixteenth-century New Mexico during the Spanish entrada and contemporary urban society in Albuquerque in his Sonny-as-Sonny and Sonny-as-Andrés perspectives—all knowledge connected with land.

Sonny learns about his past by imaginatively traveling there but also by doing archival and historical research. He begins to understand ancient and contemporary ties to land and culture in the Americas. Only when he can see the past in its present manifestation, the pres-entness of the past, as it collides with his conception of cultural space in his contemporary, fragmented life, can he find out who he is. Only by reconciling his Andrés and Sonny worlds can he avoid the modern chaos of personal and cultural amnesia that Raven encourages in the Americas as a cultural plague (Raven's name can be seen as an anagram for "never" as in the radical canceling of history, memory, and identity). Sonny's strength to fight Raven depends directly on the connections he can make between land, culture, and identity—the mestizo tradition in relation to a homeland legacy that he is heir to.

As a *cultural* detective, in other words, Sonny saves the world by learning about his own and the Americas' past, and he demonstrates how that knowledge about the Americas as a historically complex and multilayered place is essential for confronting present urban land-use issues and environmental challenges. Only an exploration of history in relation to a specific place provides the keys to understanding how the present came to be and how it can be changed. Even more clearly than in the previous two novels, Sonny—a combination of bumbling detective and the Mexican matinee idol Pedro Infante, socially awkward but savvy—can be effective as a detective only when he learns to view his life as existing against the backdrop of the complex cultural history that is the Americas. Only the retrieval of the past and a reconnection with land and place in the present can save him and the world.

Sonny learns that a viable approach to affirming ethnic identity begins with a preference *for* a particular place, an ethnic perspective tied to land—also, a preference *for* one's own history with an ancestral and cultural past, however conceived. This approach is suggested not only in the knowledge that Sonny Baca gains about being a Mexican American but in his subsequent commitment to embracing the paradoxes of identity and in what don Eliseo, his curandero and teacher, teaches him about taking an active role in directing his dreams and his life.

In *Zia Summer,* don Eliseo is a minor character with little effect on Sonny Baca, but in *Shaman Winter,* when Sonny has evolved and is capable of moving to the next level of knowledge, don Eliseo is revealed to be a major source of information about the Americas' cultures, an authority on curanderismo, and knowledgeable about historical change in relation to land traditions. In touch with the knowledge that Sonny needs, don Eliseo encourages Sonny to embrace his own ethnic and cultural identity and avoid the "view from nowhere," the forgetting of the past that is the downfall of modern culture.

Don Eliseo explains that the critical time and place for being a mestizo in the Americas is *now.* Legacies from the past carry the promise of helping "the human dream" to be "born again," but people must participate most fully in the human adventure by claiming a personal legacy and living as robustly as possible in the present moment (Anaya 1999b, 130). This approach says that other cultural perspectives can be known through the lens of one's own heritage, but one must first assert ownership of that heritage, based in history and ties to a place of origin, as completely as possible. This perspective involves coming to terms with one's past and developing a critical sense of the present and one's tie to the land and culture native to a place. This deep sense of identity comes with actively using knowledge of the past to participate in shaping the present and the future. The personal perspective, seeing through your own eyes, limited as it may seem initially, is the only valid viewpoint from which to explore other perspectives.

A strong image for the cultural space that this book projects is that of Sonny living in modern-day Albuquerque and (through the open dream channel) exploring the Americas' history, the traces of which, once they are identified, are evident everywhere around him. The message says that the Americas and their cultures have created the cultural underpinning and space of Mexican American life and community. Only with an adequate acknowledgment of history and one's complex "home" space and land can the Mexican American community sustain itself into the future.

Shaman Winter details Sonny's movement between the past and the present as he tries to understand the modern world of Albuquerque as revealing the inheritance of the Americas' colonizing *and* colonized cultures. The many reflections of the New World as a double cultural space in *Shaman Winter*, especially the split-screen perspective of Sonny/Andrés, suggest the ways in which Mexican American culture can be innovative and continually responsive to change. The particular achievement of *Shaman Winter* is its formal acknowledgment of the multiple perspectives required to focus on the Americas' important cultural traditions. Anaya's perspective in this novel is what Gloria Anzaldúa was beginning to describe as "mestiza consciousness," with a strong indigenous appreciation of paradox (nepantla) and nonoppositional scenarios (1987, 235). This was also Rodolfo Gonzáles's concept of "Chicano" as a hybrid term of identity in "I Am Joaquin." *Shaman Winter* creates the split-screen view of Sonny/Andrés and explores strategies for bringing their worlds into a single hybrid perspective with a renewed sense of culture.

An important document, this novel offers a perspective on the legacy of the Chicano movement's achievement, especially with its blended past and present perspectives, which reveal Anaya's version of being a mestizo in the Americas. The Mexican American concept of a homeland, which *Shaman Winter* clarifies in some detail, points to characteristics of the homeland idea that are gradually enriching the American national experience in the twenty-first century. *Shaman Winter* vividly reflects a Chicano realignment of culture following a tremendous shift toward recognizing the Americas as a single staging for culture in this hemisphere. In so doing, this novel projects the possibility of realizing a potential for community in the Americas that has scarcely been glimpsed. In its affirmation of mestizo history and identity, it signals that Mexican American culture since the 1960s has been looking ahead to an ethnically diverse and expanding world that will outlast the legacy of colonialism.

Shaman Winter also shows that the role of the New World person is to be not only a product of Western colonialism but also an active explorer of the Americas as a homeland. At the leading edge of a development defined by Martí, Haya de la Torre, Vasconcelos, Quijano, and Anzaldúa, Mexican American writers and artists are chronicling, as Shaman Winter does, the cultural changes that are affecting the cultures of the Americas in the twenty-first century. What Mexican Americans are creating in the New World as they make a home for themselves has the potential to challenge the reigning ideologies of the postcolonial Americas. Shaman Winter's argument is that establishing a mestizo homeland will further drive back and reduce the colonial legacy's effects. Those involved in reclaiming the homeland will continue to foster an emerging reality of the Americas, as can be seen in the early decades of the twenty-first century, when many aspects of Anaya's vision are coming forward to embolden those making the Americas their home.

Shaman Winter still has more to reveal, and we can go a step further to examine the persistence of colonial influence in Mexican American culture by exploring the relationship between public and private spaces in this novel. Henri Lefebvre's monumental The Production of Space provides a perspective for examining how public and private life in the Americas intersect. This pioneering analysis of cultural space in cultural theory and critical geography argues that the relations between public and private spheres of culture can reveal much about a community's orientation and its manner of distributing power. For example, the mestizo homeland is a hemispheric cultural "space," but what does it mean to talk about the Mexican American homeland as a cultural "space"? Discussions of cultural space in literary and cultural criticism tend to foreground complex cultural and social situations connected to land and place, as Yi-Fu Tuan demonstrates in Space and Place: The Perspective of Experience.

Take the Mexican American depictions of communal order in *Shaman Winter.* This novel displays highly stylized depictions of space that are circulated publicly—for example, the documents and texts that Sonny consults in his research. These are examples of what Lefebvre calls "conceived space," models and crafted depictions of the culture—sometimes actual pictures and paintings but also diagrams, histories, illustrations, and city plans. Conceived spaces are produced by a culture's architects, urban planners, commercial illustrators, artists, and engineers. These texts are the models of how the culture or parts of the culture work and how social and cultural forces relate to each other. Such "conceptualized [or conceived] space" is the handiwork of all who deliberately construct models or facsimiles to guide the culture, whether the result is a scientific inventory, a blueprint, or an artistic rendering of a neighborhood (Lefebvre [1974] 1991, 38). Conceived spaces can also be verbal and even numerical texts that reflect the order and ordering principles that make up a community's social and cultural relations. Taken as a whole, the conceived spaces of the Mexican American community depict how potentially everything in the community relates to everything else at a particular moment.

It is this dimension of conceived space that Rafael Pérez-Torres discusses in relation to Chicano murals and posters and explores the connections they make between land and identity. He writes that "in relation to land, the thematic representation of mestizaje offers an insight into simultaneous feelings of alienation and home. Land becomes, in these visual texts, something both familiar and strange" (2006, 152). Because such conceived spaces—in this case, mural depictions of land—are shared publicly, a defining characteristic of conceived spaces, they tend to carry official status as representing the culture, or large parts of the culture, at a particular moment. People endlessly discuss blueprints, mural art, art in museums, and photographs and paintings of landscapes in professional and other kinds of publications.

Another revealing example of a conceived space would be Alma López's computer collage *La Linea.* This picture shows a rugged landscape on the border between Mexico and the United States, and on this tough terrain a young Mexican American girl walks along a wall trying to find her footing in the dangerous area between cultures. As a

Mexican American and a female living on the U.S.-Mexico border, she is reliant on her own ability to navigate the difficult terrain between cultures. López's work is addressing what it is like to navigate two worlds, especially where one culture is the "dominant space" (Lefebvre [1974] 1991, 39). Such artworks mark a moment of cultural and social understanding and are "conceived" spaces in the sense of bringing together ideas and values that map complex cultural relationships—in this case, cultural connections between Mexico and the United States.

If we look across Mexican American homes, neighborhoods, workplaces, and community centers, we see the social and idealized projections of "conceived" (public) order located within picture frames on walls and sprawled across desks as blueprints, city plans, fashion designs, floor plans, and municipal project proposals. These representations reflect images drawn from Mexican American culture as well as from the national culture. Images presented in this way act as mooring points for a community at a particular moment, and a gallery of such images and designs would reveal the style, identity, and official values of Mexican American culture in relation to the dominant culture.

There are also the private spaces of Mexican American culture that are not official representations of anything. These are the areas of "representational space," or "lived space," in Lefebvre's term, spaces that are lived in "directly . . . through [their] associated images and symbols" ([1974] 1991, 39). These lived spaces are the intimate, even hidden, spaces of Mexican American life that people inhabit and retreat to—bedrooms, living rooms, bathrooms, family rooms, lawnmower sheds, altars, utility rooms, storage cabinets, and even the highly personal spaces of drawers and closets. These spaces—even the body's hidden zones, folds, and cavities—are conventionalized and a part of culture, too, but their depictions are not circulated publicly, and their noncirculated status as private and intimate spaces defines them.

These lived-in spaces "tend towards more or less coherent systems of nonverbal symbols and signs" (Lefebvre [1974] 1991, 39). They embody "complex symbolisms, sometimes coded, sometimes not," and however personal they are, their intelligibility exists in relation to the official "conceived spaces" in the documents, paintings, murals, city plans, and so on that circulate prominently in a public display of culture. Lived spaces are often "passively experienced" and are taken for granted and even "forgotten" when not attended to (33).

In *Shaman Winter* the existence of Sonny's open channel to another time in the Spanish colonial era presents him with a conceived space that does not exist in his own day in contemporary Albuquerque. That conceived space is the Calendar of Dreams, Owl Woman's etched bowl, which tells her story and that of Andrés, Sonny, Raven, and potentially everyone else in the Americas. The Calendar of Dreams's perspective is that of the north-south orientation of the Americas (as opposed to the east-west orientation of European settlement) and includes the life of the Americas' ancient peoples and *everything* that has transpired in the New World.

The Calendar of Dreams depicts the history of indigenous people, the Spanish, and African Americans. Unlike British accounts of North America as the privileged trek of European colonists, who methodically marched westward and destroyed tribal peoples as they crossed the continent, or the Spanish story about the conquest, the ascension, and eventual fall of Spanish colonialism in the New World, the Calendar of Dreams starts with an indigenous perspective and tells about all who have come to the New World. Not an ideal view of everyone, it presents the *interested* perspective of the person who views it, the antithesis of the view from nowhere. Always tracking a specific person's journey and showing where it leads, the Calendar of Dreams's perspective is the potential of an engaged view of life in the Americas. Not in itself a repository of stories but a potential for stories to be articulated, the Calendar of Dreams is an open view of the Americas as a staging ground that has always existed as a possibility but only in this novel has become a reality.

Over the last fifty years, the broad goal of the Chicano community has been to change the lived spaces of everyday life—to make life better for Mexican Americans in their workplaces, houses, schools, and community centers. The 1960s Chicano movement tried to support those changes by advancing and promoting a revitalized conceived space, the sacred space of a once-lost homeland, Aztlán. Those attempts to model an indigenous future when people could come back to their homeland were influential and effective. We can see the success of those efforts in the changes that took place in Mexican American literature, social texts, communal reinvestment, mural art, painting, popular design, and in the images on lowrider cars, tattoos, and so forth. And like all hybrid spaces, Aztlán canceled the social prestige of a dominant legacy, in this case, the Spanish colonial legacy. Aztlán was a hybrid strategy within Mexican American culture that helped to reframe the power relationships of actual life in the Mexican American community, and to a significant degree this initiative has succeeded.

The New World as depicted in the Calendar of Dreams is another challenge and a new conceived space for the Americas in the twenty-first century. The mestizo homeland projected on a broad scale, the Calendar of Dreams is an image designed to match the expansive mestizo sense of land and place across the Americas. As the hybrid space that potentially houses mestizo stories, the Calendar of Dreams also contains Spanish and British chapters, but the New World story is no longer their exclusive possession. The Calendar of Dreams is a larger story that incorporates the history of the mestizaje along with the stories of the Spanish, the British, the Portuguese, and the French.

Since the 1960s, Mexican Americans have promoted a new understanding of land and the potential for incorporating cultural ties to land through the recognition of long-standing traditions focused on communal needs. That initiative to define a relationship to land different from that of mainstream culture has been a strategy for connecting Mexican Americans to U.S. culture and hybrid identity as they come home to the United States. Their redefining of a relationship to land has also connected them with national concerns about the loss of cultural ties and of the cultural richness that depends on an identification with land and the spirit of place. This championing of land's importance has helped to make the United States a receptive home for Mexican Americans and has energized an argument for retaining traditional ties to land that can help to create a better future for America.

Oscar Zeta Acosta's assertion of Aztlán as a Mexican American home in the United States is accurate, even though that story is complex and still evolving. This story could not be told until the modern era, when the possibilities for cultural change opened, and Mexican Americans became the people who can tell their own story. The Calendar of

Dreams, with its perspective on the Americas, is a powerful concept that provides a way to talk about the retelling of such stories. The Calendar of Dreams suggests that in the recognition of mestizo identity and in the reclamation of the mestizo homeland, Mexican Americans in the twenty-first century have discovered the stories that need retelling, stories about land, race, and mestizo peoples. Such stories tell about remaking connections to los antepasados through land and the cultural relationships to the ancestors that land makes possible.

There is a mandate in *Shaman Winter* to seize the opportunity of perspective and knowledge when it is available and to carry it forward, as don Eliseo says, to help "the human dream" to be "born again" (199b, 139). The Mexican American exploration of the relationship of land and mestizo identity, an unpacking of Acosta's statement that "Chicanos [are] from Aztlán," is another important piece in the strategy for turning the United States into a home for the Mexican American community (1973, 161). Acosta's work and Anaya's novel suggest that Mexican Americans have always been where they belong but since the 1960s have been learning to resee their connection to the land around them.

CHAPTER 4

Remapping Community

CINCO DE MAYO, LOWRIDER CAR CULTURE, AND THE DAY OF THE DEAD

The popular culture practices of Cinco de Mayo, lowrider car culture, and the Day of the Dead make available valuable perspectives on current themes, emerging trends, and preoccupations in the Mexican American community. Relatively recent innovations, Cinco de Mayo and lowrider car culture highlight social concerns and anxieties. The Day of the Dead, an established practice drawing from traditions predating the conquest, has a secure and time-honored place in many mestizo communities across the Americas. Revealing cultural evolution at the ground level of change and adaptation, these practices on occasion evolve into new forms even as we observe them. This chapter's close-up view of three practices also reveals popular culture as the potential mediator of cultural conflicts, such as when it helps to merge traditional Mexican values with contemporary U.S. social needs. Finally, Mexican American popular culture conveys the hybrid, hemispheric perspective that helps to define Mexican Americans in everything they do.

The story of making the United States into a home for the Mexican American community takes a timely and revealing turn with popular culture. Through these practices, Mexican Americans on a daily basis adjust and refocus their sense of community. This version of popular culture transcends national boundaries and enhances what Renato Rosaldo and William Flores call "cultural citizenship," mestizos stepping forward as inheritors of the region's cultural traditions (1997, 57). Those who follow popular culture know that its meanings can be fluid and can quickly change. Often cutting across social classes and communities, popular culture has the unique ability to reach heights of artistic vision but at other times may drift with the currents of fashion. As John Storey notes, at its best popular culture will be at a particular moment "clearly about 'who we think we are' and 'where we think we came from.'" At other times, it may also reveal a sense of "'where we are going.'" With patience, if we look more closely, popular culture can also show the "narrative of the self [and community in the act of] *becoming*" (2003, 909). Popular culture can provide these privileged, momentary glimpses into a community *in motion,* thus identifying the community's direction forward even before it is fully formed.

In this chapter, there will be a discussion of the historical background that launched three instances of Mexican American popular culture. Similar examples could be drawn from Mexican American art, music, film, theatre, literature, and fashion, any of which would reveal Mexican Americans processing their sense of self and community through the medium of popular culture practices. In each area, Mexican Americans would be scrutinizing their own values, negotiating with tradition, and adjusting their distinctive cultural style to fit within U.S. culture as they live their American lives.

The three popular practices discussed here will help to establish different Mexican American cultural directions—the U.S. holiday Cinco de Mayo, lowrider car culture as it exists in the U.S. Southwest, and el dia de los muertos (Day of the Dead), the Mexican national holiday for which there is a separate U.S. version. These are disparate cultural phenomena, and yet through them common aspects of the Mexican American story about creating a home will emerge. Like all experiments in popular culture, these three tend continually to reshape community. Whereas a main theme of this book's previous chapters was the reframing of ancient and traditional beliefs within contemporary culture, the examination of popular culture requires looking at microcultural adjustments, some of them changing on a daily basis, that Mexican Americans undertake to build and sustain a sense of community in their U.S. lives.

CINCO DE MAYO

The world generally regards Cinco de Mayo as a Mexican holiday that has crossed the border into the United States to be part of the culture of the Mexican American community. This holiday does help Mexican Americans to focus on certain values and celebrate others—what holidays and commemorative days generally do. With a fairly well-defined profile as the celebration of an 1862 Mexican battle against French troops, this holiday showcases U.S. social expectations as they connect with Mexican American cultural achievements.

It may be a surprise for some to learn that Cinco de Mayo is *not* a Mexican holiday, at least, not *the* Mexican holiday that people thought it was. And yet its complex history and current significance reveal some of the challenges currently facing the Mexican American community. Some take it to be Mexican Independence Day, which is on September 16. Rather, Cinco de Mayo references a legendary battle in Puebla, Mexico, on May 5, 1862. On that date, the Mexican army of about four thousand soldiers, many of them Zapotecs, defeated the French army of nearly seven thousand regulars. Invading to collect on defaulted debts, the opportunistic French were covertly seeking to install Archduke Maximilian of Austria as Mexico's ruler. The French lost this famous battle, but they came back a year later with a larger army, defeated the Mexicans, installed Maximilian as king, and kept him in power from 1864–67.

Each May 5, celebrations of this event happen all over America, and the U.S. interest in this holiday is growing. We might ask why anyone still cares about the 1862 Battle of Puebla. The explanation is that Cinco de Mayo festivities celebrating this battle proudly recognize a moment of unexpected courage and fortitude that is the essence of Cinco de Mayo. For Mexican Americans, in other words, the impact of the 1862 victory never faded, and this battle is still the stuff of legend. An outnumbered band of Mexicans defeated the well-equipped French when no one thought they could. The little guy brought down the big guy. To this day, Cinco de Mayo conveys to Mexican Americans an uplifting message about struggling against great odds and overcoming adversity in support of a just cause. This holiday asserts that "I'm still standing. Don't count me out!" That message is clear for all who participate in Cinco de Mayo. Even for non-Latinos who do not know this history, the essential message of pride and tough resistance, of being a survivor when failure looms, gets communicated.

Some will see Cinco de Mayo as a fake holiday not worth noting, a holiday that commercial interests have created strictly for profit, especially since there is no Mexican version of it. In fact, David E. Hayes-Bautista explains that Cinco de Mayo is neither a Mexican holiday transplanted to the United States and then forgotten in Mexico nor is it a holiday that U.S. companies created merely for profit. It is a *Mexican American* holiday "spontaneously created during the Civil War by ordinary Latinos living in California" (2012, 190).

Effectively a Mexican American holiday, the inaugural U.S. celebrations of Cinco de Mayo in San Francisco were intended to show "support for freedom and democracy throughout the Americas" when freedom was under attack during the U.S. Civil War. This new holiday was intended to counter war-time rhetoric generated by the north's Civil War effort. Amid all of the war-time clamor, its message was that Mexican Americans had reasons to be proud, too. From that start, the holiday evolved into its present form with an emphasis on reflecting Mexican American "experiences and perspectives," what it means to be Mexican American when times are difficult in a sometimes inhospitable environment (Hayes-Bautista 2012, 184). From its inception, Cinco de Mayo celebrated belonging to two cultures and two countries, and the long-standing practice of displaying the Mexican *and* American flags side by side during this holiday is the best indicator of what this holiday's focus has always been (191).

Many of the 50 million-plus Latinos in the United States—over 16 percent of the total population—celebrate this North American holiday each year, some because their families are Mexican American or simply because they know and like this holiday's meaning (Fry 2011, 4). Others are not knowledgeable about it but have a vague sense of honoring Latinos on their day of pride. Cities and towns all over the United States, including local civics clubs, Hispanic service organizations, and even Mexican restaurants sponsor yearly Cinco de Mayo celebrations, often drawing several thousand people at a gathering. Given that the United States adopts very few new holidays (and has comparatively few "national" celebrations), the great success of Cinco de Mayo indicates that something significant is happening with this annual event.

We might expect to see big Cinco de Mayo celebrations in Austin, San Antonio, Albuquerque, Phoenix, and San Francisco, since those are five of the ten metropolitan areas where 45 percent of U.S. Hispanics now live, areas located mostly in the West and Southwest (Motel and Patten 2012, 3). In actuality, 79 percent of Cinco de Mayo celebrations occur in California, Texas, New Mexico, Arizona, and Nevada, and this holiday is also becoming a new event in many more cities and little towns across the United States (Hayes-Bautista 2012, 5). Whether this holiday is celebrated in five of those big cities or in Oklahoma City, Milwaukee, Chicago, or New York City, its festivities include the same array of dancers in the streets, fireworks, sidewalk food venders, parades with torero children (dressed in bullfight costumes) and mariachi music. From loudspeakers at such events, there will be songs by Juanes, Selena, the Kumbia Kings, Shakira, and Flaco Jiménez. The festivities and the sea of brown, black, and white faces announce to everyone what America is becoming as a multicultural national community, and it is no wonder that these events have the feel of a Latino Fourth of July—festive, familial, and chaotic.

In line with mestizos modifying their culture to fit into their U.S. home, the pressing question concerns what this Mexican American holiday adds to that commitment. First of all, this holiday makes a strong comment on mestizo identity, as the Battle of Puebla was specifically a victory of mestizos and Zapotecs over European conquistadors. After centuries of colonialism prevailing over indigenous people, this was a fight that the Indians finally won. Mexican philosopher José Vasconcelos often asserted that the epic drama of the Americas would eventually unfold with the cultural and social rise of mestizos as a group, as I discussed in chapter 2. The victory at Puebla references this rise as the legacy of the hemisphere's past and a promise for its future.

And while the growing number of U.S. Cinco de Mayo celebrations is a Mexican American reframing of a Mexican historical event, with its optimism about the downtrodden's fortunes, this holiday is also a harbinger of U.S. cultural directions to come. Powerful social realignments in the United States are creating a "browning" of the U.S. national identity as Latinos surpass the black population as the country's largest minority community. Revealing for the future is that from 1970 to 2007 the Latino share of the young adult population (sixteen- to twenty-four-year-olds) rose from 5 percent to 18 percent—an increase of 300 percent. This trend will impact the United States and the Mexican American community far into the future (Fry 2009, 1).

With a Latino population of over 50 million people, and with experts claiming that Latinos are still being undercounted, huge changes are imminent, and such demographic shifts signal the next chapter in the U.S. story. Over 50 percent of the Latino community now owns a home in San Antonio, Riverside, Chicago, Miami, Houston, Dallas, and Phoenix (Motel and Patten 2012, 15). Hispanic median income is currently over $40,000 a year in San Francisco, Riverside, Chicago, Los Angeles, New York, San Antonio, Dallas, and Houston. Thus, the Latino community is not only gaining economic ground that will convert to economic power but is on the verge of translating economic strength into greater Latino political will (14).

Also pertinent to Cinco de Mayo is that as Latino political power increases, Latino issues and values will become even more influential in the United States. With this change will come greater awareness of the Americas as a hemisphere with its own traditions and with complex indigenous cultures that are now rising again like a modern-day Atlantis. Instead of the east-west axis of English and European colonial culture that traditionally defines the United States as a nation, Latinos—and increasingly whites—are coming to see the United States in a north-south reorientation that foregrounds Latin America, its indigenous past, and a mestizo present. This shift inevitably diminishes the focus on European culture and suggests a different model of American culture, one looking toward Latin America and not toward the cultures of the Eastern Seaboard.

From the border's other side, Mexicans also recognize that there is a formidable power sweeping across the United States, a huge "onda latina" ("Latino wave") of influence. Just a few years ago, Mexican writer and popular culture expert Carlos Monsiváis visited me at the University of Oklahoma's *World Literature Today* office, where I am the director, and spoke about the future of Latino and Chicano culture. When asked about the most powerful influence on Mexican culture, he replied wryly, "Chicanos! Everything in Mexico," he explained, "is now influenced by Chicano art and culture." He added with chagrin, "I fear that we Mexicans are becoming Chicanos, too!"

What does the invention of Cinco de Mayo as a holiday reveal about Mexican Americans? Mexican American history in the United States parallels the history of the African American civil rights movement, and when the Mexican American War ended in 1848 with the signing of the Treaty of Guadalupe Hidalgo, more than one hundred thousand Mexicans living in the Southwest were suddenly *Mexican Americans* and were stranded in a land that wanted them primarily as cheap labor or not at all. Over the next one hundred years, Mexican Americans were methodically (and illegally) stripped of land and civil rights, and through the early 1960s they were America's invisible underclass doing migrant farm labor and nonskill service jobs. Even today, after the 1960s Mexican American civil rights movement, the impact of César Chávez's United Farm Workers, and the 1970s Chicano Renaissance in culture and the arts, Mexican Americans are still struggling to escape from being the United States' perennial working poor.

But the signs of change are unmistakable. By 2007, 86 percent of Latinos aged sixteen to twenty-five were preparing for the future by being involved in a "skill-building endeavor" such as "working, going to school or serving in the military." For Hispanic males, that figure was a high 90 percent (Fry 2009, 1, 11). Latino home ownership, which peaked in 2006 at 49.8 percent of the Latino population, in 2008 fell to 48.9 percent owing to the Great Recession, but it is still an indicator of improving conditions for Latinos (Kochhar et al. 2009, 1). In 2009, only 56 percent of the U.S. population felt that their own financial circumstances might improve in the next year, but that figure for Hispanics was higher at 67 percent (Lopez et al. 2009, 1). In 2011, for the first time *ever* Hispanics were "the largest minority group at four-year colleges and universities [across the United States with] 13.1% of all 18–24-years olds enrolled at four-year colleges and universities" (Fry and Lopez 2012, 8). So while Mexican American economic life in the United States has historically been slow to improve, Mexican Americans can now look ahead with optimism to a future of political and economic empowerment.

But nationally there is also a white backlash against Mexican Americans and other Latinos living in U.S. communities in greater numbers than ever and prospering. On the intellectual far right, this backlash has brought the hard rhetoric of Samuel P. Huntington's assertions that Latinos do not want to assimilate into U.S. culture, the negative rhetoric of "self-deportation," and the commitment generally to make life as miserable as possible for the undocumented. The new barriers to voting in some states during the 2012 presidential election and Arizona's harsh treatment of the Mexican American community—for example, its ban of ethnic studies in schools and colleges—are signs of this white backlash. Donald Trump's disparaging remarks about Mexican immigrants and his acceptance of support from anti-Latino and xenophobic groups are especially worrisome indicators of this backlash. All of these changes are in response to demographic shifts that are reshaping what it means to be a U.S. citizen and what the United States will come to signify as a country.

The Cinco de Mayo phenomenon signals that what it is to be an American is getting redefined as Latinos assume a significant measure of cultural, economic, and political power. In light of such demographic and cultural shifts, the non-Latino majority of the United States may not be ready to envision or accept the political or economic rise of America's mestizos. Many in mainstream culture are concerned about massive Mexican immigration and the number of Latinos already in the United States. The 2001 U.S. Census is famous for listing all manner of Latino categories, but it finally still asked people to label themselves as "black, Caucasian or Native American." Such racial typing and the rising fear of Mexican and Muslim immigrants are trends difficult to change, but they will likely evolve further as population shifts reposition Latinos as an influential community with political power. In the meantime, there is surely still a significant potential for more backlash against Latinos that has not shown itself fully yet.

Cinco de Mayo can be a reminder for everyone that Mexican Americans and other Latinos are still striving for full participation in U.S. culture. This holiday also conveys a contemporary concern about Mexican Americans trying to position themselves in the American middle class with improving educational opportunities and fighting to stay there. To the extent that Latinos support these new, evolving initiatives, this holiday is pointing the way to America's future. That is, Cinco de Mayo—even granting the lack of clarity around its origin—is a cultural affirmation at a historical moment when some people fear the Mexican American community's growth and do not credit its rich past.

It should not be surprising that Mexican Americans identify with the outnumbered and beleaguered forces who fought the French in Puebla in 1862. Although demographic and economic signs are promising, Mexican Americans are still encountering racism and hostility. On college campuses around the United States, there are now recurrent instances of racial slurs and evidence of social discrimination against Latinos (Salinas 2015; Resmovits 2014; Duncan 2012). These problems will likely get more attention in the next few years.

But even with better cultural and economic conditions, the core unwillingness to be counted out must continue as the festive side of Cinco de Mayo grows and becomes more commercial. In U.S. Cinco de Mayo celebrations, Latinos are endeavoring to honor los antepasados and the mestizo peoples of the New World who have kept the mestizo spirit alive into the present. As Mexican Americans continue to renew this holiday and cultural institutions like it, they are working toward a better future for themselves and for the country by reinvigorating the spirit that never gives up.

Cinco de Mayo celebrations are also signaling that a rich future for Mexican Americans lies ahead as the Mexican "border" expands to include the entire country. In a poem that has been read at Cinco de Mayo celebrations many times, "I Am Joaquin," Rodolfo "Corky" Gonzales writes: "The past of blood that is mine / has labored endlessly five-hundred / years under the heel of lustful / Europeans / I am still here!" The spirit of "I am still here" will be needed in Cinco de Mayo observances for some time to come.

LOWRIDER CAR CULTURE

Lowrider car culture has appeared in the United States even more recently than Cinco de Mayo. It first surfaces as a full-fledged community after World War II. Referring to altered cars with their frames so low that they barely clear the ground, hence *low* rider, this practice is still in existence in a number of cities around the United States and abroad and includes the collecting, refurbishing, and display of cars. The practice extends across various social classes and ethnic communities but is most evident among Mexican Americans and Latinos. Providing a medium for adapting Mexican American and Latino cultural practices to be compatible with mainstream U.S. culture in regard to prosperity and social privilege, this subculture is an instance of Mexican Americans making microadjustments to their values and lives while ostensibly remodeling cars and negotiating trends in car fashion and style.

Lowrider car culture has gotten only minor attention in film and on TV, and with this lack of media exposure, this subculture is an especially valuable, uncluttered window into Mexican American popular culture. That is, since mass media have not appropriated it, this subculture is a phenomenon that is not constantly echoed back on itself through media exposure. This subculture can still provide a relatively fresh glimpse into a world that changes in response largely to its own inner dynamics and immediate community. Looking at this culture will show Mexican Americans making real-time cultural decisions as they live their hyphenated American lives.

Lowrider cars and the culture surrounding them first appear in the United States in the late 1950s as an expression of America's expanding postwar car nation. Car ownership increased rapidly after World War II partly in response to newly available bank credit, especially in the form of inexpensive used car loans (Bright 1985, 1998; Chappell 2012). And while not confined to any one region in the United States, lowrider cars first attracted attention in numbers in the southwest in Los Angeles and then in other cities, including New Mexico's Española and Albuquerque (Bright 1985, 1998; Chappell 2012; Inda 2000; Ortíz-Torres 2000; Plascencia 1983). During the postwar economic surge, there was an increase in new car sales, and this fact also made available more used car trade-ins. Pay a few hundred dollars, or perhaps a thousand, and you could own a 1960s Chevy Impala (the car that lowriders *prefer* above all others) or else a Regal, Monte Carlo, Cutlass, or Grand Am— all potential first-choice lowrider cars. With plentiful credit, a booming economy, and an abundance of used cars, the working class during this period could afford car ownership as never before.

All of these factors stimulated the rise of a new "American automobility" and an exploding "automobile nation" (Chappell 2012, 102). Any of the classic cars, but usually a General Motors car, has the potential to become a lowrider through the addition of design enhancements inside and out. A heavily customized vehicle opens the way for its owner to join a car club, and with that move the lowrider experience extends deeply into the local community (Chappell 2012, 73; Vigil 1991; Hyams 2003). In this 1970s subculture, working-class Mexican Americans could experiment in areas not heavily weighted with political involvement. They could exercise personal creativity and a sense of rebellion by focusing on cars that worked as expressions of one's cultural identity. They could remake used cars into ostentatious luxury vehicles in a way that signaled upward social movement, even when that status was not actually the case. Owners could create such cars fairly quickly and in a relatively sheltered space that accommodated personal preferences and talents.

Lowrider car culture also played a role in relation to the Chicano Renaissance of the 1970s. The 1960s Chicano movement brought new energy to the Mexican American community through public art, street protests, local and state politics, and farm-labor strikes. But after a 1970 riot in Laguna Park in Los Angeles, where several people died, much of that activity fled the streets and the public sphere. Mexican American activists and eventually much of the community became distrustful of police, the FBI, and even local government. A new time was at hand for consolidating gains from the previous decade and refraining from crossing legal and cultural thresholds that brought danger. It was no accident that the 1970s Chicano Renaissance took place largely inside of the safety of community colleges, state universities, and cultural centers. Mexican Americans never stopped advancing their own interests, but the emergence of Chicano art and culture was now happening in a protected environment that focused on the fine arts, literature, music, history, sociology, and theater.

However, not all Mexican Americans could be, or even wanted to be, a part of higher education and community centers as a way of fostering the rise of Mexican American culture. Those highly visible venues for change and cultural development excluded those with no grounding in the arts or who simply lacked the financial resources to attend college. As the protests and marches ended in the 1970s, its slogans and even the word "Chicano" gradually faded in the media. Arising amid this period of reflection and risk-averse cultural involvement, lowrider car culture provided an alternative mode for expressing Mexican American cultural pride. This subculture was a working-class, blue-collar version of the engaged Chicano life just as Chicano culture more generally was becoming largely the property of higher education, municipal programs, and the arts community.

Joining this car culture was a profound experience that went far beyond owning a car. A life style for those who heard the call to be a lowrider, the lowrider life in some barrios in Los Angeles and in small towns of northern New Mexico was an all-consuming world, where one lived Mexican American and Chicano identity through "automobility," driving and showing one's "ride slow and low." There were even social scenes in Los Angeles and elsewhere organized around famous car cruise routes, and some—like the Crenshaw district and Whittier Boulevard in Los Angeles—were legendary. By becoming a lowrider one car ride at a time, one could be a Chicano outside of the glare of politics and higher education and live that life largely on one's own terms (Chappell 2012, 102; Bright 1998).

Being a lowrider begins with the renovation of a car to give it the classic "lowrider" appearance. The car's frame needs to sit low to the ground, and this could be accomplished with the right tires but worked best through modification of the car's suspension springs or hydraulic system. A powerful hydraulic system would be needed, usually taken from a surplus airplane or a truck lift-gate, to keep the car from scraping the ground, especially to elevate the car over normal bumps but also to "bounce" the car's front end upward when the driver wanted to display or "dance" the car for an audience.

Typically, the lowrider car's exterior paint is showy with the brightest and most vibrant reds, greens, and blues, often a color blend applied in several layers of lacquer to create a unique, three-dimensional effect. Painted flames might appear around the car's grille or sides, and door handles are typically relocated in a place hidden at the door's base. Many lowrider cars even have a metal plaque mounted prominently on the car's side or toward the back to advertise the owner's name—a practice oddly suggestive of a hearse advertising a funeral home (Chappell 2012, 83–84).

But whether a lowrider car has a grille with flames, multiple layers of lacquer on its body accented with metallic flecks, dual gold-plated radio antennas, rear fender skirts, or a "continental" spare tire kit mounted on the trunk, there is one overriding goal that the car's renovation must achieve. As much as possible, a customized car should remove "all marks of the industry which produced the car" and should *re-create* everything possible from scratch to give the signature look of a luxury lowrider vehicle (Chappell 2012, 88). With new paint, upholstery, and luxury appointments, the fully transformed car should simulate "a normative bourgeois home." That is, the car should be a total environment—like a home in the sense of being a friendly, luxurious (mobile) sanctuary in a tough and sometimes unfriendly world (66).

The car's interior design should have wall-to-wall upholstery, often crushed velvet in gold or red. The car's front seats should be large and comfortable, possibly captain's chairs that swivel sideways for easy entry. In place of a glove compartment, there could be a wet bar with ice on demand. Some lowrider cars even have fountains with circulating water installed in the back seat (Chappell 2012, 78). To have the best interior, the cab must be free of unadorned surfaces so that every part of the car's interior is modified with new upholstery, lights, and food or drink dispensers. The primary goal is to create an environment completely dedicated to luxury and (most importantly) the appearance of luxury.

The lowrider car's interior and exterior must work together to signal a common theme or style. Perhaps there will be a few words inscribed beneath a layer of lacquer on the trunk or on the hood, or there could be a dazzling portrait of Jesus Christ or the Virgin of Guadalupe. There could even be a painting of the owner's hometown, and if there is a written text on the car's body, it might convey the owner's adopted life motto about destiny or good fortune or being a vato loco. But whatever the details, the car's total effect should arise from the close coordination of these exterior and interior enhancements (Chappell 2012; Bright 1998; Plascencia 1983).

The successful interior design should convey "lowrider baroque aesthetics" (Chappell 2012, 78). That is, the "baroque" car effect will be the accumulation, or stacking, of after-market design elements such as specialty carpeting, luxury paneling on the car doors, neon lights inside and outside of the car, wet bars, and so on. The aim of these "stacked" adornments is for the car to be as unconnected as possible to practical use and to be defined exclusively in elite, luxury terms, as if luxury existed in a world separate from practical transportation. A lowrider car will usually not be gas efficient or economical to maintain, the point being to show off one's ability to display something dazzling and grand.

Finally, having such a car advances the proposition that the owner has a special claim on success, perhaps is lucky, or is a formidable person. The car is about making this statement on the owner's behalf—like an applause track—so that whether one is driving or standing before the car in a driveway for a photograph, the car's appearance communicates volumes about the car owner's personal stature.

The lowrider social scene, whether set in Los Angeles or Española, New Mexico, is often associated in the popular imagination with gangs and crime, a misleading association originating in films and TV shows. Lowrider car specialist Brenda Bright notes that lowrider cars and their culture rarely arise from gang environments and most often are the products of a hometown community and family combining resources to support the renovation of a car (Bright 1998, 594). Buying expensive cars and transforming them into elite luxury vehicles require resources beyond a working person's means, and uncles, cousins, nieces, and neighbors must donate or barter their labor, car parts, and accessories to underwrite such a project, hence anchoring the car owner ever more closely to family and friends for financial support (596).

The successful, customized car will embody a fundamental paradox. Lowrider car culture and its claim on a luxurious life simulate the lifestyle of the privileged, even while the car itself becomes a focus for the owner's own working-class family and community. A lowrider car often has few features that define actual luxury cars—advanced safety features, efficient engines, and sophisticated technology in support of the car's operation. And the luxury atmosphere associated with the car does not extend beyond the small world of car display. Owning such a car nonetheless must signify local prominence, being famous all over town, since owning a lowrider car is about spectacle and making a good impression. The lowrider car does provide "a space for subjects to exercise agency in configuring the ties between private and public spheres" (Chappell 2012, 68). The car owner, in other words, has a certain power over the building and showing of the car, but this prerogative is akin to an overly expensive single trip to Disney World, Las Vegas, or a single night in a five-star hotel. Owning a lowrider car signals the *desire* for worldly achievement and stature, but these high aspirations will recede to the background faced with the reality of how a lowrider car is produced and the unique role that it plays for its owner.

In anthropologist Ben Chappell's work on lowrider cars (the first book-length study of this subculture), Chappell describes many of these complex and conflicting values. He details an insider's view of the lowrider car world, which tells about a community deeply committed to car renovation, public display of cars, and personal pride, ranging from how a community initially rallies to support a car owner through how a car club operates and interacts with other clubs. At one point, Chappell returns to interview his original informants and discovers that the Custom Kings (a pseudonym for the club he worked with) has disbanded, the members going their separate ways. Some went on to other clubs. Some went solo and began displaying their cars without club support. Others sold their cars to pay bills. Even the Custom Kings's cruising route, Riverside Drive, closed permanently to lowriders, and most of its businesses banned them (2012, 206).

What terrible crisis happened that could destroy the Custom Kings? Maybe a devastating event befell the old neighborhood, an industrial accident, or a death. Perhaps there was a violent crime on Riverside Drive or a misunderstanding between lowrider clubs and the police. These questions hang over the Custom Kings's story, and no single answer ever emerges. There is never an event to explain why the club disbanded or why its members went their separate ways, or why the lowrider world, or at least this version of it, collapsed so quickly.

We can fill in that a thousand small weaknesses destroyed the club. The price of gas at the pumps went up steeply, and there was also some difficulty, it turns out, in lowrider families trying to make financial ends meet with raising children, the cost of college tuition, divorces, caring for elderly parents, family doctor bills, and the ongoing cost of maintaining the cars. Life and the details of supporting a family got in the way of maintaining a luxury car. The difficulty of surviving in the lowrider world—staying on good terms with the community and police, bills, children, grandparents, and continually reinvigorating the life of their club—destroyed the Custom Kings more than any single event could. Over time, their community and all that they had patiently nurtured weakened and was destroyed, suggesting that their enterprise could not change quickly enough and was perhaps too fragile in its inner makeup to survive.

The Custom Kings's story conveys that there is an admirable boldness in living the lowrider life. A lowrider has a vision, is creative, and must always be resourceful. But lowrider fate also demonstrates that, in this instance anyway, their communal ties and marginal finances always teeter on the brink of disaster and, finally, inevitably, brought them down. The Custom Kings were able to lift themselves to heights of acclaim with dazzling car design achievements with prize-winning cars, but then they fell hard when they could not sustain that life amid the ordinary demands of family and community life.

THE DAY OF THE DEAD

The Day of the Dead as an instance of popular culture is a world away from lowrider culture in regard to having extensive historical roots. This holiday, the last example in this discussion of Mexican American popular culture, is rooted in Mexican culture and ancient Aztec tradition. Every culture in the world has some version of a yearly observance honoring the dead, often in summer or fall in connection with seasonal planting. In Mexico, the Day of the Dead is celebrated on November 1 and 2 and is a hybrid ritual of traditional Aztec and Catholic practices. These observances over two days, honoring deceased family members and friends, include the preparation of special foods, most notably pan de muerte and white sugar candies and sculpted sugar toys. It is common all over the Americas to create altars dedicated to the dead's memory, visit grave sites in cemeteries, and pray for the deceased. Many consider the Mexican Day of the Dead, a national event observed across Mexico, to be the premier version of this practice, and most see this holiday as a time to be mindful of one's own mortality and everyone's impending death.

The history of this practice dates to a time before European contact in the Americas. Early sixteenth-century Aztec culture before the Spanish conquest had rituals for commemorating death and dying, including an entire month (August) of observance on the Aztec Calendar. For the Aztecs, the concept of death was intimately tied to life through the model provided by fertility figures such as Coatlicue, the goddess with two snakes' heads—one for life and one for death. The Aztec god Mictlantecuhtli oversaw dying and ruled over the land of the dead, but it is Coatlicue who conveys the elaborate sense that life and death are united through a cycle of change that can never be broken. Her province as the goddess of life *and* death and even her physical features (with two snake heads) convey the intimate relationship of life and death in Aztec and many Mesoamerican cultures.

The interest in honoring death, which extends across the Western hemisphere, is common to most cultures in the Americas with the idea that at least once a year the dead may journey back to the living for a brief stay to commune with family and friends. Much like the Aztecs, "the Maya, Olmecs, Mixtecs, Zapotecs, Aymara, Quechua, and other agricultural-based aboriginal peoples of the Americas," as Regina Marchi notes, believe that "maintaining harmony between the world of the living and the dead" is the highest priority (2013, 276).

As currently practiced in Mexico, these rituals are celebrated on the same days as Catholic All Saints Day and All Souls Day and involve "decorated breads, paper cutouts, and plastic toys" and "sculpted sugar candies in the form of skulls, skeletons, and caskets." Versions of these same artifacts have been used to celebrate Day of the Dead for hundreds of years, and anthropologist Stanley Brandes notes that these artifacts tend to convey, whether in ancient Mesoamerica or deployed today, the story of an "irreverent, macabre confrontation with mortality" and the constant reminder that life, frequently short and unpredictable, especially in Mexico, can end in death at any moment (1997, 270).

The observances over two days, whether in Mexico or in the United States, have a domestic and a public side. In people's homes today, families display marigolds so that its scent will guide the dead back to their relatives. Families construct home altars to display images of the dead, their personal effects, and religious icons and prepare the dead person's favorite foods. Children play with sugar toys shaped like skulls, skeletons, and caskets while the family remembers and prays for departed relatives and friends. As all of this is happening, families reflect on the dead's accomplishments and attractive personal qualities while alive.

In the current Mexican version of this holiday, people also go to cemeteries, clean relatives' grave sites, and eat meals there. In some large Mexican cities, people display life-sized escenas, tableau scenes placed in parks and other public venues. These scenes feature mannequins styled as skeletons (muertos) performing the mundane tasks of daily life. The muertos appear to be frozen in mid act as they go about serving tea, attending sermons, dancing, or working in a carpenter's shop. The escena figures are happily pursuing their daily lives while remaining oblivious to the fact that they are dead. The studied nonchalance of the muertos foregrounds the paradox that the living, who look upon these escenas, may also fail to identify their own journey toward death and may not see that they, too, edge ever closer to dying and could succumb at any moment just as have the muertos before them.

In the United States, the traditional tendency to avoid the specter or any serious recognition of death or else filter death through polite euphemism would not have interested the Aztecs in any fashion. Maintaining an intimate, harmonious, and intentional relationship with death was this Aztec holiday's primary goal, and Aztec practices moved people deliberately to have that awareness of death (Mitford 1963).

The most impactful of the three examples of popular culture presented here, Day of the Dead is an especially reliable guide to the changing directions of Mexican American culture as it adjusts and makes accommodations to life in the United States. Mexican Americans have in several ways reconfigured this holiday to be workable on U.S. soil.

They have created their own version of it with significant differences and use the U.S. variants to close gaps between Mexican and American attitudes about death and differing approaches to commemorative rituals for honoring the dead. For the Mexican American community, the Day of the Dead becomes a medium for adjusting important cultural assumptions about religious and nonreligious understandings of death in ways that work in their American lives.

And while Day of the Dead in the United States has grown in popularity enormously since the early 1970s and is now widely celebrated, it is still in many ways an unlikely choice for a celebration. In the U.S. version, photographs of deceased relatives and friends are on display on home altars, much as is done in Mexico, and oftentimes artifacts are accompanied by frightening images of death and miniature candy coffins and skeletons. American houses are decorated with deathly imagery and religious icons, and people buy Day of the Dead cookies and sugar treats for their children. This death imagery in many ways, in other words, re-creates Halloween, and in some cities in Mexico and the U.S. children even mark Day of the Dead by visiting neighbors to trick-or-treat and ask for calaveritos, small sugar skulls and candies. And since this holiday starts just as Halloween ends on October 31, the Day of the Dead overlaps with Halloween, suggesting that the two holidays are serving the same need. Yet the fact remains that the U. S. version of this holiday is becoming more popular each year, especially with young people (Griffin 1995; Marchi 2009, 2013).

The explanation for this U.S. holiday's popularity lies in the cultural discourse that Day of the Dead creates between U.S. and Mexican culture. The U.S. version of this holiday was inaugurated on November 1, 1972, the year that also marks the start of the Chicano Renaissance. On that day, Self Help Graphics and Art (a community center) in Los Angeles sponsored the first U.S. Day of the Dead street procession with dancing, muertos on floats, and gothic styles of decoration. This U.S. version from that start had less of a religious orientation than there would be in Mexico and was more like a raucous New Orleans Mardi Gras celebration (Marchi 2013, 281–82).

On that same date in San Francisco, La Galería de la Raza (another community center) celebrated Day of the Dead with a similar procession and inaugurated public instruction for creating personal altars and escenas. The celebration and the free instruction were an immediate success, and in both cities people danced, sang, and celebrated in a uniquely Mexican American, festive style of revelry. To this day, the annual Day of the Dead festivities at La Galería de la Raza in San Francisco attract twenty thousand people and are the largest of the observances for this holiday (Marchi 2013, 281–82).

The importation of this holiday to the United States has changed it from the Mexican version in at least two ways. There is the U.S. tendency to downplay the religious content when building altars or organizing processions. Altars still display religious icons but are also playful with pictures of celebrities, folk heroes, and colorful reminders of popular culture. In a somewhat secularized version of the Day of the Dead, at least by Mexican standards, this holiday does overlap with Halloween. With this shift also comes a change of venue for this holiday. "In the U.S.," as Marchi notes, "art galleries, schools, community centers and other public secular spaces replaced churches, cemeteries and private homes as sites of Day of the Dead rituals" (2013, 283). This move to go into public venues instead of churches broadened the holiday's appeal and allowed for a different kind of involvement with a mix of Latino and non-Latino and Catholic and non-Catholic participants. Going into public spaces also made the holiday more of a broad "commemoration of the collective 'ancestors' of all U.S. Latinos," regardless of their nationality (2013, 283).

The second change involves injecting political commentary into Day of the Dead celebrations to advance social activism. While the Mexican practice is narrowly local with strong religious themes and some sexual and gender satire (outlandish cross-dressing, etc.), the U.S. Day of the Dead practice highlights social issues such as immigration, especially regarding deaths at border crossings, the plight of AIDS patients, and the violation of Mexican American civil rights. The U.S. version promotes public discourse on current social issues and has been a valuable tool in building community. Mexican Americans did not want, as Marchi notes, "merely to reproduce the rituals of Mexico in California" and in other American cities, so "Chicano artists reconfigured the celebration to make it *relevant* to their lives and experiences"

(2013, 283; italics added). All of these changes substantially retrofit this holiday to engage U.S. social issues and to be directly pertinent to Mexican American lives.

These general dilutions of the Mexican style of this holiday have not worked for everyone. A number of commentators have worried that "Day of the Dead [in the United States is] progressively losing its authentic and autocthonous character" (Brandes 1997, 275). Believing the substance of this holiday to be "at risk," they have protested the loss of an "original" significance and the dilution of authentic Mexican practices. One must judge such a complaint, of course, against the fact that the *entirety* of Mexican American culture, almost always in actual practice, is a series of appropriations and "betrayals" of the existing Mexican practices (Brandes 1997, 275). Therefore, it is not surprising that Mexican Americans shoulder the responsibility of making the Day of the Dead relevant and pertinent to their U.S. lives.

The contrast between practices in Mexico and the United States point toward different conceptions of death. In Mexico, many children die as infants or at very young ages, and so death is a daily fact of life and has been so for hundreds of years. The Mexican practice tends to face death with little buffering and encourages living with the reality of death and dying. There is no choice but to face the fact of death as directly as possible. Mainstream Americans, as Jessica Mitford documents (1963), tend to avoid or disguise death's blunt reality. A Puritanical culture little interested, at least officially, in candid spectacles concerning death, the body, and sexuality, the United States is also a wealthy and privileged culture that focuses on youth and material abundance. The United States has largely chosen, as many have observed, to confront death (or at least cope with it) in small doses when it is convenient to do so.

There are religious elements in the U.S. version of this holiday, to be sure, but the U.S. importing of political and cultural issues shows the Mexican American reliance on creating hybrid cultural mixes to reconcile cultural differences between the United States and Mexico. The U.S. version of the holiday honors death but does not invest in the Mexican well-articulated relationship of life and death and foregrounds, instead, uniquely Mexican American political issues and social

concerns. This style of honoring and yet modifying traditional practices in hybrid forms evident here is a signature of Mexican American
culture.

This overview of Day of the Dead practices today also shows something that a casual observer might initially miss—the abundant presence of sugar in Day of the Dead practices in both countries, a revealing
clue about Mexican history "hidden" in plain sight. The ubiquitous
appearance of sugar in Day of the Dead practices is difficult to miss
entirely and appears to be adding interest in the holiday for children
to keep them involved even when the solemnities of this holiday can
be excessive for young people. During this holiday in both countries,
white, granulated sugar is everywhere. It is molded into crosses. It is
sculpted to become festive Day of the Dead skulls and skeletons. It is
formed into small boxes to look like miniature coffins. There are even
intricate motion toys with moving sugar coffin lids and sugar arms and
legs on skeletons.

In Mexico and some parts of the United States, parents and teachers
instruct children to write their names on the foreheads of sugar skulls
(calaveras) and then display them on an altar. Prior to the Day of the
Dead, one can move through any Mexican or Mexican American market place or grocery store and find long rows of sugar "skulls, animals,
cadavers, [and] caskets," especially skulls (Brandes 1997, 287). The phenomenon of connecting huge amounts of sugar to this holiday, pairing
sugar and death, appears at once innocent but also conspicuous.

What connects sugar and death? Why should they be paired? The
answer lies in the ancient history of the Americas. The original tie of
sugar to death dates to the sixteenth-century and the Spanish colonial
era, a time when sugar was an important commodity crop for the
Spanish. The Spanish produced and processed sugar for the New Spain
market and sold it in large amounts. Mexico played a prominent role
and eventually exceeded all countries in the region in sugar production
and consumption (Brandes 1997, 287).

Massive sugar production also happened in Peru, Brazil, and
the Caribbean—precisely the areas singled earlier (in chapter 2) for
their commentary on mestizaje. Sugar was formidable in the lives
of indigenous people, and whereas its wholesale adoption as a food

commodity in the daily diet did not reach working-class Europeans until the mid-nineteenth century, indigenous peoples in the Americas in the late sixteenth century had already incorporated sugar into their diets and spent much time producing it (Brandes 1997, 287).

The sixteenth-century Spanish succeeded with this labor-intensive crop difficult to bring to market only because they enslaved massive numbers of indigenous people to do the back-breaking work. The Spanish worked its slaves to death, and many succumbed to diseases and abusive treatment by the Spanish. Overwork, infectious diseases, poor living conditions, and frequent mistreatment killed native peoples during the conquest at dizzying, legendary rates (Brandes 1997, 287).

In their 1970s groundbreaking work, Sherbourne Cook and Woodrow Borah show that indigenous populations in New Spain declined in staggering numbers in the century after the conquest. From 1519 to 1620, the indigenous community in New Spain declined from 25.2 million people at first contact to a shocking low in the seventeenth century of about 730,000. While there were numerous causes, mainly connected with mistreatment, abuse, and disease, the Aztecs themselves connected the many deaths with sugar production. Over the course of the sixteenth and early seventeenth centuries, they ramped up their version of Day of the Dean to highlight the presence of sugar. They made and displayed sugar figurines, much like the ones made now, to acknowledge the huge presence of sugar and death in their lives (Cook and Borah 1979, 1, 100).

In the Caribbean, a site of intense sugar production, the situation was even more shocking. In that region, indigenous people were sugar plantation workers, and the Spanish drove them with endless work and brought about the "virtual obliteration of the [whole] indigenous population" (Brandes 1997, 289). Thus destroying a whole community, the Spanish eventually had no one who could work the sugar fields and had to replenish the islands with new workers. They imported African slaves and created yet another population of colonized and oppressed people. That importation of Africans led to the burgeoning mestizo and interracial communities that the casta system in the eighteen century was designed to control, as I discussed in chapter 1 (Brandes 1997, 289).

In light of this history of indigenous peoples and Africans in the Americas, there is an explanation for sugar's prominence in colonial New Spain and in modern Day of the Dead festivities. In contemporary practices in Mexico, the United States, and elsewhere, the connection between sugar, colonialism, and death gives testimony to the massive imprint of the Spanish colonial period on the Americas. In the extensive use of sugar to make skulls, skeletons, caskets, and assorted Day of the Dead toys, there is historical trace evidence of a connection between death and sugar "hidden" in plain sight that dates to the sixteenth and seventeenth centuries. Sugar figurines from the Spanish colonial period, if they could speak, would tell a complex and dark story about sugar, overwork, disease, and the overwhelming commonality of death in the Americas after the conquest. Native peoples made sugar figurines to commemorate death during the Spanish colonial period, and one can only imagine that such figures must have appeared as terrible momento mori to sixteenth- and seventeenth-century indigenous people who were themselves working in sugar production and faced abuse and death every day.

Another irony about the Mexican Day of the Dead and the historical forces that drive it is that in modern times, beginning in the late nineteenth century in Mexico, artist José Guadalupe Posada originated the whimsical approach of cartoon-style skulls and skeletons that is common in Day of the Dead illustrations. This popular stylization sidesteps the grizzly aspects of death and dying and circulates the iconic imagery of Catrina, the socialite muerto, and other playful, cartoon versions of graveyards and imminent death.

Posada's drawings, with cartoon skeletons performing the mundane tasks of socializing and working, have the special appeal of looking spry and alive even as they represent death. Most of his images are conveyed in sugar figurines, as well, and it is common in Mexico and the United States to find wood, plastic, and sculpted sugar versions of them for sale year round. Posada's light and popular style has even become the signature look of Day of the Dead festivities almost everywhere. These images and also the plentiful presence of sugar during this holiday are powerful, if disguised, messages from the past that seem to play as trifling allures for children. Nonetheless, the underlying historical reality of these figures and the historical connection of sugar and death are powerful traces in present culture of the Spanish colonial past.

In most published descriptions of the Day of the Dead or accounts of Spanish colonial history, there is little or no mention of the death of millions of indigenous people in sixteenth- and seventeenth-century New Spain. On occasion, Cook and Borah's figures have been revisited, and sometimes they have been challenged, but they have never been substantially dismissed or revised. Also, in most published writing about this period, the dark side of New Spain's colonial past is often under-played or omitted altogether. Stanley Brandes, Keith A. Sandiford, Pal Ahluwalia, Sherbourne Cook, and Woodrow Borah, among a few other Latin American scholars have advanced this material with unflinching candor and have refused to ignore or dismiss this part of the Spanish colonial heritage. These scholars have steadfastly foregrounded sugar's actual significance in the Americas for greater recognition and under-standing of the plight of mestizos in the Spanish colonial period (Cook and Borah 1979; Brandes 1997; Ahluwalia 1999; Sandiford 2010).

In the twenty-first century, a variety of indigenous peoples across the Americas still honor the dead with similar if not the same rituals intended to establish a balanced view of life and death (Marchi 2013, 276). In public displays, this holiday's followers generally take their cue from Posada and adopt a light and celebratory attitude toward the Day of the Dead, an attitude that parallels the more serious contemplation of the dead during these celebrations. Also, many commentators who discuss the Day of the Dead elect to focus on preconquest practices as a way of side-stepping discussions of the indigenous holocaust that happened in sixteenth- and seventeenth-century New Spain. This high-lighting of the precursors of Day of the Dead festivities in the time before colonization detours around a difficult and painful history con-cerning many millions of native peoples—deaths on the order of five times the number of people who died in the World War II holocaust.

These three popular culture practices, all cultural events still current and evolving, provide a ground-level view of three different directions in contemporary Mexican American popular culture. These practices demonstrate that Mexican Americans are trying to bridge the gap between cultures and stay focused on social and cultural success in their American lives, as is most immediately clear in Cinco de Mayo practices. They are also aware of their continuing social status in American culture as the working poor, as can be seen in the world of lowrider car culture. Even if Mexican Americans and others do not know all of the details and the relevant history behind these practices, lowriders know that their own legacy in the Americas has not always been fully in view for all to see. The Day of the Dead practices give the example of sugar as historical trace evidence pointing in the direction of a still largely hidden, dark history in the Americas. Mexican Americans are using these practices to express uncomfortable truths as vehicles for adapting to U.S. life on a daily basis, dealing constantly with the important cultural issues evident in each area.

Cinco de Mayo asserts a Mexican American tenacity, hope for a better day, and pride in the hybrid mix of Mexican and American identity that this holiday foregrounds. For many Mexican Americans and Latinos, this important cultural practice resonates each year with new urgency and as a cautionary tale about never becoming complacent or ceasing to struggle. Conveying a message about the fight against adversity, and with no Mexican counterpart, Cinco de Mayo speaks in a clear and nuanced voice on behalf of the aspirations of the Mexican American community.

Lowrider car culture is a Mexican American innovation in celebration of working-class life and the American potential for innovation and invention. It celebrates Mexican American identity and being a Chicano, and it references Mexican American culture's remarkable energy and inventiveness. It also documents real-time struggles for survival among the working poor and records moments of heroism that are being played out every day by millions of Mexican Americans.

The Day of the Dead references a broad array of Mexican American religious art, the history of this hemisphere, and folk and social traditions. Those traditions begin in Mexico and cross the border with the Mexican American community's determination to make changes needed to live in the United States. Borrowing from Mexico and later reframing for U.S. consumption, the Day of the Dead engages with Mexican American history and tradition and continues to evolve in unpredictable ways as an important cultural innovation.

In 1972, when the artists and celebrants in San Francisco and Los Angeles inaugurated the first U.S. Day of the Dead festivities, they drew on deep Mexican cultural and religious history. Like other Mexican artistic and social traditions brought to the United States (murals, the practice of curanderismo, religious imagery such as the Virgen de Guadalupe, Doña Sebastiana, and the corrido song tradition), this holiday needed to be reinvented to be relevant to Mexican American cultural needs and aspirations (Marchi 2013, 279). The Day of the Dead's continuing success shows that its practices consist of cultural issues and transformations in which authenticity is being reconfigured in strategic ways to serve the Mexican American community in the present.

The strength of these practices is that they are sensitive to social needs and change and constantly connect Mexican and American cultural values and articulate a Mexican American voice, one that reconfigures religious and cultural practices in ever new forms. The enthusiastic involvement of Latinos who are not Mexican American in Cinco de Mayo, lowrider car culture, and Day of the Dead festivities and also the recognition of these practices across the Americas point to their success in successfully bridging traditions across the hemisphere.

The cultural and political themes that Mexican Americans regularly bring to these practices underline their commitment to cultural involvement and social engagement—in a word, the desire to be Mexican American *and* American and move toward solutions to cultural and social dilemmas in the United States. The Day of the Dead's first celebrants in Los Angeles and San Francisco were especially focused and wise in making these old/new practices connect deeply with the Mexican past as well as current U.S. issues and concerns. It is no surprise that this holiday's cultural grounding has given it continual momentum and endurance as a dynamic and positive force in the Mexican American community.

These three examples of popular culture show the Mexican American community at different moments and in different environments at home where they are. John Storey has written that cultural meaning "is always the site and the result of struggle," and with these popular culture practices the Mexican American community is locating points of social and cultural struggle and is finding its way "home" as it redefines terms for living in the United States (Storey 2003, 53). Mexican American popular culture, responding almost by the moment to rapid cultural and social changes, has the flexibility to push the Mexican past further away or bring it closer and then reverse that process as needed, as the Mexican American community uses popular culture to find its way home.

Through these popular culture practices, Mexican Americans are actively adjusting their culture and developing it in their relationship with U.S. mainstream society. These practices show that as Mexican Americans recognize and meet the cultural challenges that connect with who they are and what they (we) need to accomplish as a community, they generally succeed. When they veer from that agenda or fail to reinforce their deepest commitments, they weaken and falter. These practices from popular culture show how Mexican Americans are shaping their community in the United States and also enhancing their sense of cultural citizenship.

If popular culture can reveal current directions regarding "'who we think we are' and 'where we think we came from,'" it is asking not about settled cultural truths but about Mexican American cultural and social paths into the future. Mexican Americans need to know "'where we are going'" and understand themselves in the "[the act of] *becoming*" precisely so that they can make effective cultural investments and find the way "home" with confidence (Storey 2003, 909). Those who are living the reality of Cinco de Mayo, lowrider car culture, and the Day of the Dead are adjusting the microsteps of social change to refind and strengthen the Mexican American community's direction forward. Demonstrating that the relationship of historical legacies and present needs can be redirected in productive ways, popular culture practices show Mexican Americans assuming that responsibility and advancing their community a few steps at a time to continually move closer to home.

CHAPTER 5

Recovering the Body
LITERATURE, PAINTING, AND SCULPTURE

How we view and define the human body and its status in society are some of the most overlooked and yet important concerns of contemporary culture. Different perspectives on the body bring with them different relations and responsibilities in regard to one's own identity and that of other people and society. Mexican American writers, artists, and cultural critics have been pioneers not only in focusing on issues connected with the body but on the contrast between Mesoamerican and European models for understanding its significance in the Americas. The literary and artistic works that they have produced explore what it means to have a white or a brown body and the consequences of having a body invisible to the community at large. Critiquing Western conceptions of the body and traditional racial distinctions expressed as "natural" dimensions of the body, Mexican American writers and artists are signaling a further erosion of the cultural and theoretical foundations for traditional definitions of race.

There is a revealing moment in the Mexican American response to having a *brown body* in a white culture in Oscar Zeta Acosta's *The Autobiography of a Brown Buffalo*, one of the most well-known of Mexican American texts. Early in this novel, standing before a mirror in his bedroom, eyeing his "brown buffalo" body, Acosta notes his own "peasant hands," huge "brown belly," and an "enormous chest of two large hunks of brown tit" (1972, 11). The passage closely resembles Richard Rodriguez's *Hunger of Memory*, in which Rodriguez writes that as a child "with disgust I would come face to face with myself in mirrors." He explains that "I grew divorced from my body." "I was too ashamed of my body," he writes. "I wanted to forget that I had a body because I had a *brown* body" (1982, 125; italics added). Finally, in *How to Be a Chicana Role Model*, Michele Serros, while brushing her teeth before a mirror each morning, narrates that as a teenager she would "squeeze [her] nose" to make it look thinner and less indigenous. "I've been doing this since the seventh grade," she reports. After comparing her nose past and present, she volunteers that "my nose has actually become smaller . . . less *Indian*" (2000, 13–14; italics added).

Guiding readers to a focus on the body and related social issues on behalf of mestizo culture, Acosta, Rodriguez, and Serros foreground their own responses to being brown and separate from mainstream U.S. culture. The "peasant hands" that Acosta notes even give a passing nod to social class and life on the economy's periphery with little access to social and economic resources. Perplexed and obsessed about their brown bodies, and in conflict over identities that render them socially "invisible," they invite readers into the five-hundred-year-old labyrinth of the body—enslaved, free, brown, white, off-white, visible, and invisible—as it is known in the Americas.

Mexican American writers and artists from this period foreground the fact of the human body and the social issues that it raises. An often overlooked, or at least undiscussed, concern of Western culture, for reasons that I will address, the body preoccupies Chicano Renaissance writers and artists like few other topics. Both familiar and alienating, one's home and yet foreign, comforting, uncanny, and strange, a reference to the hemisphere's past and yet anchored in the present, brown bodies in these works are raising questions about tradition and change in the Americas. For historical and cultural reasons going to the heart of what *Mestizos Come Home!* is about, the mestizo, brown body raises profound questions about racial identity and social justice in the United States and across the Americas.

Chicano culture's fascination with the human body during the years 1960–90 (and in some cases beyond) shows the body to be a starting point for discussing concerns with race, communal health, personal well-being, and social justice. Writers and artists foreground the body as an especially revealing dimension of culture from the Spanish colonial period through the present. To appreciate and decipher this major focus on the body, we need to understand what these writers and artists were responding to. Is there a uniquely mestizo perspective on the body that differs markedly from Western ideas and views about what the body is? Mesoamerican and Western philosophers say there are significant differences that identify versions of the body as belonging to one culture or another. They shed light on different approaches to the human body, but the best evidence for modern conceptions of the body will come from Mexican American literature and art, from works that focus on the body as belonging simultaneously to the modern world and to a contemporary postcolonial legacy. In a word, we can inquire into what these writers and artists have done to show that mestizo bodies differ from traditional Western notions about the body, are living in a new day, and matter.

In this chapter, such large-scale inquiries about the body and life and culture in the Americas will suggest perspectives for understanding the mestizo body as a dynamic cultural icon and present telling evidence for understanding the culture of the Americas. We will see that this inquiry is part of an often unrecognized project in the Americas to reclaim the body in a social, economic, psychological, and real-life sense. The Mexican American interest in the body is intended to bring forward what is happening to actual marginalized and abused people in their community when nothing else gets through to mainstream culture. Writers and artists found a way, in other words, to cut through social misdirection, obfuscation, and the often hidden realities of social injustice. Their insight was that reclaiming the body in a simple and direct way can, with great power, reveal issues immediate for those who are forgotten, socially marginalized, and withering as a community. Their further insight was that issues connected with race were making brown bodies invisible and obscuring what was happening to an unhealthy, forgotten, and abused community. The Chicano initiative to pose these wide-ranging questions by displaying the body in poor health and in pain and to persist in getting answers to those questions provides Mexican Americans with yet another route to finding their way home in a culture that has often ignored them.

WHY MEXICAN AMERICAN WRITERS AND ARTISTS FOCUS INTENTLY ON THE HUMAN BODY

In the United States in the 1950s, prior to the Chicano Renaissance, there was ample reason to be concerned about Mexican American bodies and lives. With a post–World War II boom in Western economies during the years 1949–70, it was a time of sharply rising incomes and even a welcome decline in economic disparities between social classes (Iceland 2003, 499). The average U.S. family income during this period rose 66 percent, but Mexican American families earned only 62 percent of the U.S. median income (499–500). With great prosperity developing for almost everyone else, Mexican American unemployment rates were still twice the national average. With one-third of the Mexican American community working in agriculture and four-fifths in semi-skilled and unskilled jobs, types of employment with perennially low wages, one half of all Mexican American families lived in poverty on less than three thousand dollars a year (Mintz 2016, 2).

Such bleak economic conditions during a time of general prosperity signaled that Mexican Americans were stranded with distinct vulner-abilities on the economic periphery. Tomás Rivera's novel from this period, . . . y no se lo tragó la tierra / . . . And the Earth Did Not Devour Him, a novel with documentary aims, sought to dramatize in moments of journalistic clarity these economic realities, played out as poor community health, limited health-care services, high rates of illiteracy, little attendance in primary schools, no participation in higher education, and an absence of support from social services. Like Acosta, Rodriguez, and Serros, Rivera directs readers to the body as an accurate barom-eter of what was actually happening in the Mexican American com-munity when nothing else could emit the same clear signal. Detailing the human toll of abject poverty for the most vulnerable—the young, the elderly, those in bad health, the overworked, and so on—Rivera foregrounded the *body* in distress as possibly the only reliable way to break through white culture's lack of attention to communicate that his community was in deep trouble.

Rivera was responding to the fact that mainstream America was ignoring the tragedy of Mexican American abject poverty and debased lives. While their plight was not a secret, it got little attention from mainstream culture; his response was to show what was happening in the most elemental way to actual human bodies. Willing to display the worst in the most direct terms, he foregrounds a child accidently shot in the head, who "didn't even jump like a deer does" but fell "like a dirty rag" into a water tank (Rivera 1992b, 86–87). He shows a "wetback" murdered and placed in a child's bed so that the child discovers the body "like a snake [when] in reality [it was] the wetback's arm," and he is terrified (100). Rivera reveals a Latino Gallery of Horrors with tubercular, coughing bodies. There are young and old bodies of migrant farm workers collapsing from sun stroke. There are children whose bodies are burned to a crisp while their mothers work long shifts, and many other young and old bodies stumbling and falling as they succumb to deplorable conditions.

Highlighting broken, maimed, and discarded people, Rivera wagers that the specter of the body's destruction will speak loudly about a community's fate when nothing else will. He saw that while those in power may always claim to be champions of equal liberty for all, the fact of actual bodies living the reality of extreme poverty tells a completely different story. Rivera saw a bigger picture of hidden and invisible Americans and was bold enough to ask why brown bodies are consistently the working poor, remain on the social margins, and do not matter to mainstream culture. Conveying what Latinos knew well but which non-Latinos and literary critics of this period often misread and took as literary "gothic effects" in his work, Rivera was giving candid testimony about a community on destruction's edge, a tragedy that no one else in mainstream culture seemed to notice. Believing that no bodies were disposable, he found a literary strategy for promoting change. His wager was that tragedy and grotesquerie would communicate the need to save a community from destruction when nothing else could.

At the same time, the focus on the human body began to show Rivera and others that larger issues were at stake, suggesting that critiquing the body's predicament and the way that bodies are viewed could be an important first step toward understanding the past and race as they were impacting the postcolonial present in the United States. The body was beginning to matter in unpredictable ways. In time, he saw that his focus on bodies in pain could open doors on profound social and cultural issues in the Americas. He was depicting damaged bodies to probe Mexican American and U.S. cultural values during the Chicano Renaissance, values connected with community that allowed some bodies to prosper while others were neglected and discarded, the effects of which would persist far beyond his work or this period. But he also began to see the body not only as a standard of judgment about current social conditions related to health but as a metaphor for areas of inquiry connected with economic and social life, what it means to be human, more broadly in the Americas.

In other words, this is not only Rivera's story. Since the 1960s, Mexican Americans have been involved in the massive project of redis-covering what the focus on the body has to reveal about life and culture in the hemisphere, an undertaking that is challenging to all societies, but especially those structured around racial values and strict social hierarchies. Working through literature, painting, sculpture, and social thought, in the Chicano Renaissance Mexican American writers and artists began exploring artistic and imaginative ways to understand and reclaim bodies from their marginalized, debased, and "lost" state. They were testing assumptions about what it means to save their community and about societal values in response to Mesoamerican and Western perspectives on culture and the body. Their work contributed to this hemisphere's real project of "recovering" the body after its loss to the Spanish casta system five hundred years ago. They were becoming aware not only of what was happening to actual bodies but of the issues raised by those discoveries for life in the Americas.

Literary and visual art in this period shows Mexican Americans trying to configure different versions of the body to fit into Mexican American and mainstream culture. They asked what the body is, how bodies are situated in community, and how bodies—usually thought to be fixed, physical objects—can be a hybrid mixture of cultures, prac-tices, and traditions referencing vastly different values and worldviews. How could the body mean one thing to one culture, and something else to a different culture? At times, this focus on bodies was an inquiry about who was hungry and homeless, and it shed light on mestizo families and communities in crisis. At other moments, it was a broad set of questions about what it means to be brown in a white culture, how to reclaim the mestizo body for modern culture, and how iconic bodily images relate to the Americas as a cultural and social realm.

Their special focus on the brown body was intended to reveal cultural relations between Mexican American and mainstream culture as well as form a reliable index of communal health and sustainability. Living the reality of inadequate housing, poorly paid service and manual-labor jobs, limited access to public education for children, no real opportunity to attend colleges and universities, and meager participation with mainstream culture, Mexican Americans in the 1960s were building communities but receiving no credit for their contributions to the national economy and culture. With no large-scale social initiatives on the horizon to remedy their concerns, writers, artists, and cultural critics initiated the Chicano Renaissance in part to shield and protect brown bodies from disaster, to make life better, a move that entailed rebuilding lives and advancing the community's interests during a time of cultural and social crisis.

Their efforts resulted in a heightened profile for the body in literature and art, which, as Rivera's work shows with great clarity, amounted to sounding an alarm about vulnerable people and families at risk. In economic good times, social institutions work to protect fragile bodies from physical assault, disease, starvation, inadequate housing, inclement weather, and toxic environments. Those institutions provide a shield for the unprotected during a crisis by coordinating governmental and volunteer services. In the Mexican American community during the 1950s, families and poor people had no such social buffer and felt the full brunt of personal violence, assaults on health, and social and cultural isolation, much as they do in poor communities today. As Rivera's fiction demonstrates with distinct candor, social institutions (churches, public health services, public schools, the Red Cross, and the business community) in this period failed the community, and, without a safety net in place, Mexican American bodies were falling directly into harm's way on a daily basis (Ortiz and Telles 2012, 44). Writers and artists signaled this crisis as directly as they could by foregrounding the body as a living index, one that never lies, of communal health and sustainability.

In response to this crisis, writers and artists, including Helena María Viramontes, Rodolfo Gonzales, Lorna Dee Cervantes, Estela Portillo Trambley, Rivera, Anaya, and others called for the restoration of social institutions, improved health care, enhanced job opportunities, better relations with U.S. mainstream culture, and renewed cultural and economic prospects for the future—all of which came under the Chicano Renaissance umbrella. These crises from the 1950s to the 1990s further prompted writers and artists to decide whether to embrace the version of the body that they knew from their own cultural traditions (the Mesoamerican body) or claim the "white" body marketed to them in the form familiar to Anglo-Protestant culture. Mexican Americans in every walk of life were facing the choice of *how* to assimilate at the next step of cultural engagement, and their decision would be made according to which version of the body likely had a better future—a question still in play today.

Experimenting in literature and art by combining different versions of the body based on cultural models in the Americas, Mexican Americans were exploring questions long forgotten about the conquest, history, race, and privilege and were often arriving at a familiar conclusion. Making important discoveries and rebuilding their own cultural infrastructure, they were noting the United States' failure to signal at any level that mestizo bodies mattered. They asked how white bodies in the Americas had come to prosper and to be treated with respect, while brown bodies were dismissed and had become culturally invisible to all but themselves.

Asking how their community fit into the U.S. mainstream, they saw the care and protection given to white bodies and the "life of the mind," the world of culture and privilege, far removed from the realities and needs of the marginalized. The general promotion of the mind over the body was not a new development in the mid-twentieth-century United States but one rooted in Western values and philosophical thought. Some also saw that the elevation of *mind* over *body* also suggested a collective blindness toward bodily needs and the social realities of the working poor, those who performed basic, "menial" (but indispensable) jobs and who lived in toxic environments that, in time, also became an assault on poor and vulnerable bodies. The valuing of the "life of the mind" as a perspective was a general dismissal of poor people and the body's significance in societal health evident in substandard health care and education for Mexican Americans, the underserved children of the poor, and those associated with manual labor. The "life of the mind" could be translated as the invisibility of poor bodies and communities that served the privileged classes, poor communities with degraded neighborhood environments, inadequate housing, and substandard health conditions.

Mexican Americans chose to focus on the body, in other words, when no one else was paying any attention to their plight. Their decision to "recover" the body as an issue was at first part of that emergency strategy for their plight to be recognized. Subsequent, more encompassing cultural questions followed, broad issues that came with the recovery of the body and that tapped into questions about history, life, and community in the Americas. These larger cultural questions quickly matched in importance the economic concerns of the post–World War II years.

HOW CHICANO WRITERS AND ARTISTS UNDERSTAND AND DEFINE THE HUMAN BODY

When Chicano writers and artists of this period depict the body in daily life, they are looking for clues about cultural values and expressions of belief. Like the casta assignments of racial identity discussed in chapter 1, they were seeing that depictions of the body are neither "natural" nor God given. As Vasconcelos, Quijano, Grosfoguel, Anzaldúa, and other racial theorists show, depictions of the body are never just one thing or naturally "given," and are always evolving. Any depiction of the body, as Richard Sennett notes, leads people to "repress mutual, sensate awareness, especially among those whose bodies differ." He is saying that bodies are presented in meaningful and culturally encoded ways to reflect their culture's values, and powerful classes inevitably tend to "deny the needs of bodies which do not fit the master plan," generally the poor and those who work with their bodies (1994, 23).[1] Ideas about what the body is and how it functions will always express official beliefs and social and cultural commitments and help to disseminate those values as broadly as possible. We know this, in part, because ideas about the body change from one culture to another and differ markedly far more than people normally need to acknowledge or have occasion to admit. People come to see as fact the racial and bodily distinctions that their culture constructs for them as natural. The way that we understand the body, in short, is always culture specific, revealing the beliefs and values of the culture that produced that particular version of the body.

From this perspective, depictions of the body speak for the culture and express its values as reigning ideologies, highlighting a certain body size, stature, skin tone, overall appearance, or connection (or lack of connection) to social groups and hierarchies. Drawing on the details of race, class, and gender to depict bodies in ways that promote, or sometimes question, a culture's values, depictions of the body convey narratives about the values of the cultures that produced them, narratives that tend to reenforce common beliefs and the community's rationale for assenting to those beliefs initially. A body's "story" in any one instance tells about the current status of a community's well-being and health. Credible and successful depictions of the body—presented as "real" and accurate—reflect official and often state-sponsored values in the culture. On occasion, we may think and act as though there is a single and "natural" depiction of the body, but we will always be able to work backward from such depictions to discover a culture's specific ideological commitments and values.

Hence for Mexican American writers, artists, and others knowledgeable about Western culture in the Chicano Renaissance, there was little surprise in identifying mainstream culture's dismissal of the body and health issues in poor communities. Western culture has famously judged the body, *any* body, unfavorably, a tradition that was again playing out in U.S. social and cultural life. This point has been well documented concerning longstanding traditions in Western culture that are decidedly *anti-body*, play down the body's importance, and frequently rally against the body and bodily concerns in any form as disruptors of culture. One can trace this tradition to Plato, who notoriously viewed the fact of the body as an affront to the noble human spirit, which he viewed as always arising from an elevation of human nature as a mind—as if the mind, existing separately from the body, could live separately. He saw the body, plagued by disease and destined for decay and death, as the weak, even disastrous, side of being human and the Achilles' heel of being alive.

In the United States, we can see early moments of rebellion against this dismissive attitude toward the body as it is referenced in the work of Chicana poets in the early Chicano Renaissance. As a group, they were trying to reclaim the body's presence and its relevance in the Americas. With a common focus on female figures famous for the abuse of their bodies, the La Malinche and La Llorona themes, these poets dealt with the "bodily," material implications of what it means to be a mestiza in a white culture. They gave fresh treatment to themes that developed from two overlapping cultural traditions casting women as destructive figures who nevertheless mark the border zone where bodily needs, gender, "nature," culture, and social status combine to strand brown bodies on the cultural margins.

In the early Chicano Renaissance, many poems from these writers deal with the female body in the Americas and tell how a single woman, La Malinche, suggestive of the Biblical Eve, was the immediate cause of Mesoamerica's fall to European domination. La Malinche is a figure arising from an interpretation of events surrounding the conquest of Mexico from 1519–21. This Aztec young woman, whose real name was Malintzín Tenepal and whom the Spanish called "Doña Marina," became Hernán Cortés's interpreter when he brought his army of supposedly friendly visitors to the Aztec empire. She became Cortés's lover and had a child with him. As Tey Diana Rebolledo comments, "when Cortés was ordered to bring his Spanish wife to the New World, Malinche [the name she has been given in the folkloric, condemning version of this story] was married off to one of his soldiers, Don Juan de Jaramillo. Cortés' child with Malinche [went] to Spain to be educated, and Malinche died young, in relative obscurity" (Rebolledo 1995, 62).

Around these basic historical facts have grown traditions about La Malinche lacking recourse for her mistreatment, panicking over losing her child, and killing it. The embellishments of this story, in association with the eventual, brutish Spanish conquest of Mexico, became part of a tradition of seeing Doña Marina as "La Malinche," the "traitor and whore," whose betrayal of her culture through bodily indiscretions was responsible for losing Mesoamerica to the Spanish (Rebolledo 1995, 96).

This story about La Malinche is thought to be the origin of several narrative details in the La Llorona legend. La Llorona (literally, the crying woman) comes from a tradition in Mexico and the U.S. Southwest of stories for children about a woman who appears in the night to steal and drown children in a nearby river or lake. Named for crying over the loss of her own children, she appears to revisit her grief each night as she replaces her dead children with living new ones. Details vary, but this story consistently focuses on the predicament of having lost her children for reasons relating to a previous "adultery, infanticide, or child neglect, and sometimes homicidal revenge, excessive hedonism, and self-indulgence as well" (Candelaria 1997, 93). La Llorona was too trusting of a deceiving man and violated social decorum connected with sex and marriage. She pays for her indiscretions forever—hence La Llorona as a cautionary tale for young women not to stray with their bodies outside of traditional courtship and marriage. There is an inevitable "phallic propaganda" in this tale's attempt to color La Llorona, and by extension all women, as usually reckless with their bodies, antifamily, and even anticommunity (94).

Mexican American women writers have faced a double bind when dealing with such Western-inspired, misogynistic material about the female body. They reject turning away from traditional culture and abandoning it en masse, since doing so means losing contact with their own past and cultural traditions. The problem is that it is culturally devastating for any Mexican American with strong ties to tradition to deny huge chunks of the cultural past, even when parts of that tradition are harmful. It is also difficult to extract damaging parts of a tradition from its greater context, so Mexican American women have needed a strategy for dealing with misogynistic traditions that cast a shadow over their lives.[2]

A number of contemporary poems from this period deal with La Malinche and La Llorona in a way that reframes this material to minimize the misogyny and point to the body as a primary reference for understanding culture in the Americas. The principle that each poet follows is a rearrangement of poetic material and *not* its removal. Works by Lucha Corpi, Carmen Tafolla, Angela de Hoyos, Margarita Cota-Cárdenas, Erlinda Gonzales-Berry, Alicia Gaspar de Alba, and Sandra Cisneros, among others, reinterpret the La Malinche–La Llorona tradition and reject as empty the idea that a young woman acting as a translator for Cortés had any impact whatsoever on the conquest and fall of Mexico and Mesoamerica. To blame La Malinche for the history of the conquest is a false, proxy argument for condemning women's impact on all of culture.

These texts argue that Doña Marina deserves awe and respect—as Lucha Corpi shows in the poem "Marina"—as Marina Mother, the Marina Virgin. In this historical reframing, Doña Marina is the mother of the first mestizo child and, by extension, the mother of *all mestizos* in the Americas, not someone to be cursed but a figure to be exalted as the Mesoamerican mother of all. Carmen Tafolla highlights this view of Doña Marina—Malintzín Tenepal in Nahuatl, the language of the Aztecs—in her poem "La Malinche." The legendary mother of a people and of a rich cultural tradition, Tafolla's Malintzín Tenepal should not be denigrated as a "Chingada" ("screwed") loose woman but as the great mother of the Americas (1993, 199).[3]

Sandra Cisneros goes even further to put the body back on the stage of the Americas by identifying in intimate, bodily terms with the Virgin of Guadalupe, the female body associated most directly with the hemisphere's culture. In the bold manner that Cisneros is known for, she compares her own genitalia and breasts to those of the Virgin of Guadalupe—in effect, describing two brown women with identical bodily features. In "Guadalupe the Sex Goddess," Cisneros talks of wanting to lift the dress of the Virgin and discover if she has "chones" ("underpants")." Does her "panocha" ("vulva") look like Cisneros's, and are her nipples dark, too? (1996, 51). Attempting to reclaim the female body *as* brown and Mesoamerican, Cisneros resets bodily reference points in relation to this sacred figure and concludes with a sense of her own reframed and revalued Mesoamerican body. In her view, the body is back.

Gloria Anzaldúa—mestiza, lesbian, and feminist—goes one step further to rebel against mainstream culture in the Americas and its dismissal and retrieval of the body for mestizo culture. She identifies her Mesoamerican body as having the potential to be malleable and respond directly to the world around it, a non-Western sense of the body in dialogue with the environment, a body that is *"un ama-samiento . . . an act of kneading, of uniting and joining,"* a changeable and fluctuating body, a constantly forming body that is "every woman's sister or potential lover" (Anzaldúa 1987, 78–79). Her point is that the Mesoamerican body, in contrast to the Western sense of the body as a free-standing *object,* is multivalent and not fixed in its orientation as an object must be. Anzaldúa's power as a writer comes from her own *un*willingness to abide by fixed bodily markers associated with Western gender categories and to focus instead on having a mestiza (multivalent) body that is in constant, direct dialogue with its environment and other people (4). She creates the striking image of the body as a dynamic field in which issues of identity and community continually change, evolve, and reshape themselves in a reflection of the environment's and other people's dynamic nature.

Anzaldúa references the Mesoamerican view of the body with an overlay of Western culture and society concerning social life and gender. With an insightful sense of how Mesoamerican and Western models of the body may compete within a single person, she here references her own life to dramatize her social isolation from mainstream culture and how the Mexican American community's economic stagnation undercut cultural and civic life to leave vulnerable bodies, in this case her own, in ever greater danger. As we saw in Rivera's work, this is the harm done to the body that happens when public health care and other social institutions are absent or fail, in Anzaldúa's case leading to her premature death in 2004 due to type 1 diabetes.[4]

All of these Mexican American and Chicana writers are contributing in their own ways to a conversation about Mesoamerican conceptions of the body, attempting to recover the body in the Americas. They are drawing from sources passed down through ancient traditions in the Americas and still in evidence in contemporary mestizo perspectives, a tradition of viewing the body as a continuum of mind-body experience and interactions with the environment. In this Mesoamerican tradition, the body—*not* the mind—is of the utmost importance in explaining human behavior, preferences, and values. The Mesoamerican way of looking at the body frames it as *central* to everything that is human, both personal and cultural. The body in this view, a world unto itself, is *never* something that can be marginalized, thrown away, or neglected like so much refuse.

The Western view of the body is virtually the opposite of what these writers show about the Mesoamerican perspective. The Western view leads back to the ancient Greeks and the idea of a strict mind-body separation. Plato saw the body as an object, the part of humanity lacking in vitality, a permanently unresponsive appendage attached to the mind— the dead weight that the mind must inhabit and drag around (Bordo 2003, 1). Western philosophers have traditionally framed the idea of the mind-body split in their own understanding of the human body, religious faith, personal relations, and the unveiling of truth. Almost always marking the body as the weak or inferior partner in that split, the clear downside of being human, they have consistently elevated the mind while condemning the body's intractable and perishable nature. All of these beliefs and distinctions contribute to the Western rationale for seeing the body as an untrustworthy necessity, a necessary evil— the unavoidable bad news about being human and being alive.

This comparison of Mesoamerican and Western views of the body— as a vital center versus a near lifeless, heavy burden—reveals areas of disagreement that are related to the marginalized status of the body in the Chicano Renaissance, all suggesting what the body is, what it can achieve, and why it matters or does not matter. The Mesoamerican body, for example, is a sphere of energies and relationships, a living energy field with a movement that "fuses and expels, absorbs and discards, and through this motion is in permanent contact with all elements in the universe" (Marcos 2009, 43). The Western body, by contrast, is a finite and lumbering "heavy bear" (barely alive) that houses the mind but exists as a physical limitation that blocks at every turn the mind's surging nature and great potential for vitality (Bordo 2003, 1).

The Mesoamerican view posits the body as intimately enmeshed in a complex social network with other people and always in touch with the social and physical worlds—always in dialogue and responsible for its actions.[5] The Western body, by contrast, stands alone, only loosely associated with other bodies through kinship, race, social class, and the world of work (Bordo 2003, 1). Whether the body in the West is rendered as invisible or in some sense unresponsive accomplishes the same goal of drastically devaluing what the body is in order to elevate the mind and people associated with the mind. At the extremes of the Western body's dismissal, those with lower social status are "invisible" to those in power, exactly the situation of Mexican Americans and others doing manual labor jobs in the Americas in service to the master plan and privileged social classes that employ them (23).

In the Mesoamerican view, the body is a hub of living social and environmental connections, a realm of possibility and unpredictable. In the Western view, the brown body, or any body, is a kind of raw material, not fully or adequately human, that exists to be shaped, categorized, and assigned an allotted place in a strict social hierarchy, as it was in New Spain's casta system and in the postcolonial exploitative work force. Currently, much as it was in Spanish colonial times, those who are affluent have bodies that resemble those in power at the higher levels, the white bodies of the elite. Those in the lower social classes, the brown bodies, are rendered invisible as they perform service roles for the privileged.

Philosopher Susan Bordo notes that in the West "the scheme" for understanding the body "is [also] frequently gendered, with women cast in the role of the body" and men as mind (2013, 5). This "cultural associating of mind with masculinity and body with femininity," as Judith Butler also notes, is a long-standing assumption in Western philosophy (1990, 17). The body's feminine (corrupt) identity and lower social station historically have worked like a dark foreshadowing of what lurks as ephemeral, unreliable, risky, and frightening about the body and its needs (Bordo 2013, 5). For their part, projected as "mind," men are able to escape to be free of the body's imperfections associated with being a woman, blood, decay, and mortality.

Brown bodies in the Americas in the present, not fitting the master plan in what is still a distant reflection of the casta system, are socially marginalized, treated as invisible, and covered over like bodies hidden after a crime. Body "loss," in other words, is a reality in the contemporary United States, where brown bodies are the personification of manual labor, performing a disproportionate number of unskilled and service jobs for affluent social classes. Too often "hidden" from those who benefit from their labor, brown bodies are alienated further by being disproportionately imprisoned and themselves are the frequent victims of violent crime. Hidden from view, but in plain sight as service providers and manual laborers, brown bodies often participate only marginally in mainstream culture and have controlled access to the corridors of power.

Mexican American writers and artists have focused on these distinctions and what it means to be a brown body living on the social margins as female, as male, as incarcerated, as a brown body invisible to the dominant culture, a person experiencing the white world through brown skin. Brown bodies have been "lost" in the Americas in that they are not valued, and we can now add that Acosta, Rodriguez, and Serros were viewing their bodies with both longing and loathing precisely because their bodies are disconnected from anything significant in American public life. Hence in the language of "recovering the body" in this chapter's title, "recovering" means refinding suppressed bodily knowledge that undoes invisibility through a rebuilding of mestizo community and a reconstructing of the history of mestizo bodies in the Americas through, among other channels, literature, art, culture, and community participation.

What is the mestizo body in the Americas? As Mexican and Chicano writers and artists depict it, the Mesoamerican body—in this case *not* the "brown body" of the Spanish casta system but the one defined by

Mesoamerican culture—is the representation of a vital potential in experience. It is not an *object* to be scrutinized, as is the body in the West, but a *site* of activity that includes an overlapping sense of one's physical being, other people, and interaction with the environment. It is for this reason that curanderismo, indigenous healing in the Americas, focuses in its treatments on the body's interactions with the environment as the basis for healing, seeking to adjust, in other words, the body-environment relationship. The Mesoamerican body is a hybrid version of a body that is part self, environment, and other people in a dynamic sphere of possibility and change. Western artists, poets, and philosophers (especially phenomenologists) have often conceived of such approaches for talking about the body, but their speculations are outliers and not the dominant tradition in the West, where the body is dead.

In Mexican American culture, the Mesoamerican body will inevitably be associated with cultural and political subversion. Since the Spanish created their version of the brown body as part of el sistema de las castas, mestizos have struggled to maintain their own vitality to counter Western culture's overbearing influences. The intention of mestizos to act in ways that keep their culture and themselves alive, maintaining a vital connection to their worldview and origins, has continued in the culture of the Chicano Renaissance. That legacy through the present is expressed through vital conceptions of the body and the healing practices of curanderismo.

HOW CHICANO WRITERS AND ARTISTS DEPICT AND INTERPRET THE MESTIZO BODY

Many Mexican American women writers have made the project of recovering the body over recovery of the homeland the driving force of their work. In line with this choice is the work of Sandra Cisneros, Demetria Martínez, and Denise Chávez, writers who focus on the dimensions of women's culture, both through and beyond La Malinche and La Llorona in relation to the body. They focus on experience not commonly explored or emphasized in modern fiction by men, such as

the entailments of having a woman's body, both its strengths and diffi-
culties, and the specific cultural and social context of being a woman.
They explore a woman's perspective as determined by the material,
governing facts of physicality, bodily needs, and a woman's particular
relationship with other women and men. Doing all of this from within a
culture that promotes the male perspective as a normative view, a male
"gaze," they have found ways to recover the personal, bodily experience
of being a woman through having a Mesoamerican, vital body that
matters.

The attempt to recover the body in social relationship with others,
with the potential to reshape every dimension of social life, is perhaps
the most radical of undertakings. With their recovery of the body in
a social context, these writers and artists are attempting to reframe
being a mestiza by deliberately violating social decorum and cultural
norms, essentially taking the lead in their own lives and refusing to
live in men's shadows. Chicana writers take up the role of "bad girls,"
"Mujeres andariegas, mujeres callejeras" ("women who wander and
roam") to refind the significance of their own bodies and a new sense of
direction in their lives (Rebolledo 1995, 183).

These writers find ways to explore the "female space of the body" in
relation to women's culture and lives, the calculation being that gaining
knowledge of such "spaces"—bodily spaces of interaction, penetration,
intimacy, and social discourse—will enfranchise and reorient women
in culture with a Mesoamerican orientation to the body's importance
and interdependency with others (Rebolledo 1995, 197). That recovery of bodily knowledge could give women a different relationship to
the material conditions of their private, social, and political lives, thus
positioning them to act on their own behalf in new ways to revitalize
women's culture.

Sandra Cisneros's *My Wicked Wicked Ways* and *Loose Woman*
dramatize her recovery of the contemporary body as modeled on the
Mesoamerican body and a new set of Chicana attitudes and strategies.
The Chicana persona that arises from her work is bold, savvy, and
irreverent—an exuberant and nonapologetic transgressor of rules that
keep women from leading fuller lives. The photograph of Cisneros

on the back cover of the *Loose Woman* paperback edition conveys the playfulness that animates her work. Dressed in a black evening dress with a plunging back and an evening jacket slung lightly over one shoulder, she invites the viewer to engage on equal terms and says in her direct stare that we should not assume anything about her intentions. We are viewing a "loose woman," as the book's title announces, but we need to let her tell us what "loose" means. The photo of Cisneros on the cover of *My Wicked Wicked Ways* is an even more explicit provocation in which Cisneros, in a skimpy black top, cowboy boots, almost-empty wine glass at her side, and an alluring smile looks toward the viewer as if beckoning toward some imminent but unstated involvement.

In poems such as "You Bring Out the Mexican in Me," "Down There," "Las Girlfriends," and "Loose Woman," Cisneros is playful and "loose" in the manipulation of stereotypes. Instead of arguing against the racist idea of a Mexican woman as a fiery, primitive sexual body, a "hot" Latina, she dons that persona in "You Bring Out the Mexican in Me" and succeeds in revealing it as an artificial mask, deftly and with subtlety. A colorful sexual being in many of the book's poems, often describing romantic encounters and relationships gone bad but never herself as a victim, she is a woman actively working to maintain a sense of the human body and a full range of responses. She is loose in the sense of remaining open to experience, of being relaxed in her various roles, and of not closing emotional channels prematurely. "Loose" as a description also works in that Cisneros must violate long-standing patriarchal norms of female modesty as a style in order to open herself to new possibilities as a woman.

Her most vivid impression comes in the total, nuanced view of women's bodies and lives. Creating an intimate space for women's inter-actions and experience that will be immediate and powerful *to them,* she confirms that their bodies are alive and respond to pleasure, to their own bodily sensations, to menstruation, to each other, and to men. Cisneros explores regions of a woman's experience often juxtaposed to social concerns as sites for encountering herself in relation to the world, thus publicly discovering and declaiming her bodily space.

It should come as no surprise that her perspective has little to do with a man's view of women but with the spaces of women's bodies as women know and inhabit them. This perspective is most evident when Cisneros foregrounds the details of having a woman's body that men do not wish to know at all. The calculated effect of Cisneros's attempt to develop a woman's perspective is particularly clear in a passage from "Down There" that presents the reality of menstrual blood as central to a woman's manner of relating to the world, the image of blood and the association of a vagina as an inkwell calculated to be unassimilable in a male's idealized view of women. The poem says that a woman must shape her experience in relation to the material facts that she knows, her life and her cultural identification with her body.

The fact that the terms of this female space, much of it bodily space, may seem unusual is part of Cisneros's strategy to counter the view of women often filtered through patriarchal norms. By directly referencing and revealing the bodily lives of women, Cisneros critiques traditional values and perspectives while suggesting a new Mesoamerican frame, in which bodies *matter*, to guide women. She foregrounds crises of self-esteem, energetic lovemaking, the Virgin de Guadalupe with exposed chones, and orgasms to create an appropriate bodily space for women and an implicit but bold challenge to male (and Western) idealizations of women's bodies as fixed, dead objects.

In Denise Chávez's (1948–) Texas and New Mexico fiction, the focus on women's bodies also depicts women as powerful agents with great personal and cultural vitality, women as largely uncharted expanses of beauty, energy, and strength. All of her works can be seen in this vein as a celebration of women's bodies and women's culture. In Chávez's hands, there is a surprising avoidance of traditional notions of women as standards of beauty and maternal nurture. She celebrates *every* aspect of being a woman, *every* woman's body unconnected with male approval, as if to say, "nothing that is woman is alien to me."

There is a powerful glimpse of Chávez's striking evocation of Mesoamerican bodily energy in her first novel, *The Last of the Menu Girls* (1991), a book detailing the experiences of Rocío Esquibel as a "menu girl" who works in food service at Alta Vista Hospital and then later as a teacher in the public schools. Rocío wants to know about female beauty and emotions and cannot immediately answer in what ways women are beautiful, especially "their flesh and souls aligned in mystery" (1991, 63). Her most intense focus on women's bodies happens when she dances for her dying great-aunt Eutilia. Rocío is blunt in describing Eutilia's dying body and her own response when she writes, "Great Aunt Eutilia smelled like the mercilessly sick. At first, a vague, softened aroma of tiredness and spilled food. And later, the full-blown emptyings of the dying: gas, putrefaction and fetid lucidity" (14).

Trying to cure the cancer in her aunt's body, Rocío "danced around her bed in my dreams, naked, smiling, jubilant. It was an exultant adolescent dance for my dying aunt. It was necessary, compulsive. It was a primitive dance, a full moon offering that led me slithering into her room with breasts naked and oily at thirteen" (14). In this passage remarkable for its lyricism, Rocío narrates that "I leaped into Eutilia's faded and foggy consciousness where I whirled and danced and sang: I am your flesh and my mother's flesh and you are . . . are. . . . Eutilia stared at me. I turned away" (14–15). She adds that "in the darkness Eutilia moaned, my body wet, her body dry. Steamy we were, and full of prayers" (15).

This performance resists easy, complete paraphrase, and yet she clearly conveys a deep acknowledgment of the female body, its vitality, sensuality, and imaginative power. Stripped of all concerns about looking pretty for men and bowing to social decorum narrowly conceived, Rocío reaches into a well of compassion and empathy and shares the commonality of having a woman's body with the aunt who, in her dying and decaying state, has little else. The fact that Rocío chooses to speak to her dying aunt, or rather to her dying aunt's body, through the medium of her young, vibrant body in an ecstatic dance, her breasts pressed hard against a screen door, is a telling gesture of the body's importance. In this contest concerning which model of the body will dominate, the brown or the white, the vital, Mesoamerican body dances for Eutilia and wins.

Demetria Martínez (1960–), a New Mexican writer, highlights the female body in personal experience, spirituality, and politics—three areas that define her writing. She challenges long-standing notions

1.1 Anonymous eighteenth-century painting of the casta racial identities at the Museo Nacional del Virreinato, Tepotzotlán, Mexico. The format of presentation, four rows of four, progressing from least mixed to most mixed racial categories, is traditional for displaying casta paintings.

1.2 *De español y negra: nace mulata* (From a Spanish man and an African woman is born a mulata), 1774, by Andrés de Islas. Courtesy El Museo de América, Madrid.

1.3 *De Mestizo y de India, Coyote* (From a mestizo man and an indigenous woman, a Coyote), 1763, by Miguel Cabrera.

Courtesy Elizabeth Waldo-Dentzel Collection.

5.1 *Robert and Liz*, 1984, by John Valadez. Pastel on paper, 60 in. × 42 in.
Courtesy John Valadez.

5.2 *Our Lady*, 1999, by Alma López.

173

5.3 *I Lied*, 1996, by Alex Donis. Silk-screen on litho poster, 30 in. × 21 in. Collection of Philip and Anne Colburn. Courtesy of the artist.

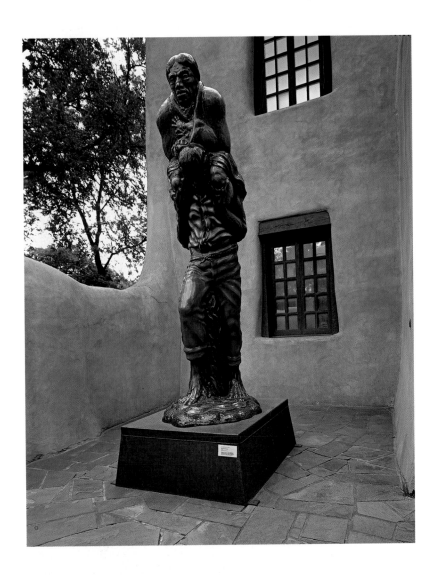

5.4 *Border Crossing*, 1989, by Luis A. Jiménez Jr. Polychrome fiberglass, 128 in. × 40 in. × 55 in.

Collection of the New Mexico Museum of Art. Purchased with funds from the Los Trigos Fund, Herzstein Family Acquisition Endowment Fund, Friends of Contemporary Art, Margot and Robert Linton and Rosina Yue Smith, 1994 (1994.73.1). Photo by Blair Clark.

5.5 *Fiesta Jarabe*, 1991, by Luis A. Jiménez Jr.
Courtesy Jessica Villarreal and Brian Boeckman, University of Houston.

regarding women, non-Western peoples, and the colonized. While many Chicana and Latina writers focus on the issue of Chicano and Latino empowerment, few writers in any tradition insist on seeing the implications of power in the spheres of personal experience and the body, religious belief, and international politics. Martinez's commitment to connecting religion, politics, and power through the body is the basis for the far-reaching scope of her work.

In her visionary novel *Mother Tongue,* the narrator lives her young adult years ignoring her body and taking care of someone else. She is Mary when she first meets José Luis and María when experience changes her. The devoted American host and mentor of José Luis Alegría, a Salvadoran political refugee, she orchestrates their love affair as a way of hiding from herself. She writes, "I handed my body over to José Luis like a torch to help him out of his dark places." She concludes that at nineteen years old "to love a man more than one's self was a socially acceptable way for a woman to be insane" (1994, 27).

Martínez's understanding of the body comes in focus when José Luis Alegría, delirious with posttraumatic stress disorder, attacks María. Her discovery from this experience is that she was harboring a repressed memory of being sexually abused, an event that happened when a seven-year-old María was left alone with a neighbor, a man with a "minus sign" smile. As abuse memories tumble back, there is "something about hands crawling up my thighs, thumbs under panties" (1994, 165) so that "the place of pleasure becomes the place of fear" (166). She reflects that the "world" was flat to this man who could coldly harm anyone. Such a person was "dead in the eyes" and capable of canceling "whole populations," hence the "minus sign" smile (167).

The memory's immediate effect is for Mary to recover her vital, Mesoamerican body. Once the painful memory returns, "the ghost of the man with the minus sign smile fled," and Mary opens her body to pain and truth. Her comment is that the "demon" created in her body by the repressed experience fled because "he could not bear the sound of my true name" (168). Over the next several years, the *new* María learns the speech of her "mother tongue," speech emanating from body and feelings.

The larger insight from *Mother Tongue* is that engagement and commitment happen when a person's emotions and beliefs are aligned with the body, with who she is, and with what she believes. When María is the young "Mary" and lives a counterfeit life through José Luis, she is a walking ghost of herself in a Western setting. Mary is held hostage and cannot break free until the wall erected against fear falls. María is then free to engage, to love, and to commit to the larger world of change and possibilities for social justice. Mary's body is a Western body with its life in the mind but dead below the neck. When she frees herself of hidden traumas, she reunites her Mesoamerican bodily vitality with who she is and becomes María.

Cisneros, Chávez, and Martínez form an essential trio for understanding the Chicana recovery of the body in that they accomplish three distinct tasks. Cisneros moves boundaries to bring the body into play so that Chicanas can address the taboo areas and the issues of power that previously have gone unaddressed. Chávez discovers the beauty and power of the Mesoamerican female body that had disappeared before the Chicana recovery of it. Martínez then inventories and maps the issues at stake in the suppression of the body and the connection between the personal, spiritual, and political realms. Without taking possession of one's own body, without being willing to understand what the body has to convey, very little is possible, which is the message of three Chicana writers who are committed to truths known through the Mesoamerican body.

Three Mexican American artists also bring forward brown bodies and foreground the Mesoamerican vitality of each. The first is John Valadez, a Mexican American painter born in 1951 and based in east Los Angeles. With a large corpus of work as a muralist, painter, and photographer, he is associated with 1970s photo-realism, paintings that present Mexican Americans and Latinos, urban settings, and landscapes with photographic accuracy and a documentary aim. Focusing on the barrio of east Los Angeles, he does not so much document as probe and test the social practices, ethical norms, and values of the Mexican American community, resurrecting the brown body as a revealing center of vitality.

In *Robert and Liz* (1984, see figure 5.1), a portrait done in pastels, Valadez creates a masterpiece in which bodies speak subtly and powerfully about why they matter. In this work, Robert and Liz stand for what appears to be a casual camera snapshot. In this awkward pose, they play out the drama of a vital Mesoamerican body responding to a "dead" body. Robert stands to Liz's right, his shoulders squared to us, looking at the viewer. To his left, leaning in an off-balance, contraposto stance, Liz embraces Robert with her upper body only, her posture suggesting that she was pulled off balance. Their different stances create a tension, suggesting that the couple may be at odds with each other.

Their clothing tells more. Robert has two stains on the front of his t-shirt, and his hands and tattooed forearms are spotted with grease. His discolored t-shirt and jeans are work clothes that he felt no need to change. Liz's sweatshirt and jeans appear new, the clean clothes of someone staying at home or promptly changing after work. In these details are two different stories. Liz's arms are brown, but her face is lighter while Robert's face, arms, and hands are brown, suggesting indigenous ancestry and possibly working outdoors. With a dramatic contrast in their faces, Robert has a conventional male mask, a recurrent stoic expression that holds others at bay and keeps him emotionally distant from everyone. He will present the same face with the same expression to the world no matter what he does or where he goes. With life only in his eyes, his facial expression and his body will not change regardless of what emotion he feels because his body and face are disconnected and unresponsive to each other.

By contrast, with no set look to her face, no recurrent mask, Liz reveals what she is feeling as she feels it. She appears worried as she looks down and past Robert. We do not know what troubles her, or whether the problem is Robert or something that she must tell him, but if her mood changes, her facial expression and her body posture will change, too. Without a fixed mask to hold back the world, she appears vital and open, perhaps painfully so, to the same degree that Robert is masked, closed, and well defended.[6]

Robert and Liz appear to be on two sides of a divide. With his male mask and rigid body, he is stoic and guarded. With her expressive, open face and agile posture, Liz communicates accessibility and Mesoamerican bodily vitality. In the past, they have had success as a couple or they would not be together now. And whatever is troubling Liz could be a personal dilemma that she will share with Robert or it could be the recognition of an impasse that will end their relationship. In either case, this work focuses on the details of Robert's and Liz's brown bodies according to several broad patterns. The drawing's detail and presentation reveal Robert and Liz as people with complicated and intricate lives who deserve the attention that we bring to their bodies as evidence of who they are.

The drawing's details suggest that these people matter. Their brown bodies matter. The drawing's overall message is that Robert's and Liz's lives count because they are people with interior lives and plans for the future, and they are worth examining closely and taking seriously. Their working-class bodies may be invisible to others, and Robert's body may be deadened by Western culture and the routine of his life as a male, but in the time of this work their bodies, requiring close scrutiny and care to decipher, tell us that the details of their lives are worth interpreting. Robert and Liz together advance an argument for recognizing a complex, deeply felt human experience. Expressing their aspirations and discoverable interior worlds, this "snapshot" portrait shows that these brown bodies need to be taken seriously.

The same logic of refinding Mesoamerican vitality is at work in one of the most controversial depictions of the body in Mexican American art of the late 1990s. Born in Mexico and raised in Los Angeles, Alma López is a celebrated cyber and video artist, a printmaker, and a photographer. Already well-known in Southern California through the late 1990s, she came to national attention in 2001 when her work *Our Lady* (1999, see figure 5.2) was included in an exhibit in the Museum of International Folk Art in Santa Fe, New Mexico. A computer montage that samples traditional images of the Virgin de Guadalupe, *Our Lady* presents two women with photo-shopped Aztec emblems arranged around the first, in the guise of the Virgin de Guadalupe, and a large Viceroy butterfly behind the other bare-breasted figure with a nipple ring.

At the center of *Our Lady* stands performance artist Raquel Salinas. She has long hair, a defiant facial expression, and traditional Aztec images and roses on her cloak. She is clad in a bikini made of roses—the flowers traditionally associated with the Virgin de Guadalupe—and under her feet is another young artist, Raquel Gutiérrez, who appears where the traditional image of a cherub usually stands. Behind Gutiérrez, positioned like angel wings, is the giant wing spread of a Viceroy butterfly. The Viceroy is a butterfly that mimics a Monarch butterfly for protection and has become an image and a scenario appropriated by the transgender community as an allegory for sexual reorientation (Latorre 2008, 133). This work's overriding effect, and a matter of serious concern to many Hispanic and Catholic viewers in New Mexico, is the creation of a scandalous version of "the Virgin of Guadalupe in a bikini" (Calvo 2004, 202).

Upon being installed in Santa Fe in 2001, this work "sparked heated objections from a mob of protesters." Mexican Americans in northern New Mexico were up in arms and rejected seeing naked female bodies in place of the Virgin de Guadalupe's traditional image. With protests "led by community activist José Villegas and New Mexican Archbishop Michael J. Sheehan," there was a robust debate in the community and in the national press about depicting sacred figures in art. Alma López became a cause célèbre, with calls to close the exhibit, remove her work, fire the museum staff, and even kill the artist (Latorre 2008, 133).

The loud and violent protest against *Our Lady* was surprising. Displaying a brown female body and sexualizing the Virgin de Guadalupe had already happened years before in Sandra Cisneros's commentary (1997) and in the work of Chicana artist Yolanda López who, in *Portrait of the Artist as the Virgin of Guadalupe* (1978), had shown the Virgin in running shoes below a contemporary cotton dress. In 2001, it was not immediately clear why the communal uproar occurred in response to *Our Lady*.

López's innovative work in foregrounding a contemporary mestizo body along with the Virgin's Mesoamerican body may have been too successful in another way. On the one hand, López's bold display of the female body closely links it to a famous religious icon connected to both the Mesoamerican and Catholic worlds. The vitality and "attitude" of Raquel Salinas (the figure in the center) suggests a close comparison of a Mesoamerican sacred body and contemporary young women with alternative sexual orientations. In other words, López reframes a religious icon in a contemporary setting with computer-generated graphics to highlight the Virgin's "feminist and queer potential," as the presentation of the two women in the work expresses (Calvo 2004, 204). It is one thing to modernize the look and relevance of a religious icon and to attribute to her the energy of the Mesoamerican body, but the protesters in Santa Fe objected that López was resetting the Virgin's appeal and the Mesoamerican body as having immediate relevance to the LGBTQ community, an association that drew criticism.

López had correctly seen the power of the iconic mestizo body in Mexican American culture to challenge social institutions such as the church and also conventional gender expectations. There is no icon more meaningful in Mexican American culture than the mestizo body, especially that of the Virgin de Guadalupe. But López and the museum curators failed to gauge the strong response that followed when López redirects the Virgin's appeal to a LGBTQ demographic. The shock of her work in 2001 showed that Hispanic lesbian women were attempting to make changes and creating a home for themselves in the United States, and they correctly saw the mestiza, brown body as a powerful medium for articulating the rationale for such change.

Adorning Raquel Salinas with icons from the Mesoamerican cultural past, López wanted to recover mestizo, Mesoamerican bodies in this work by letting them speak about same-sex relationships. The public reaction to this work was based on the association of the Virgin of Guadalupe, female sexuality, and the suggestion of a lesbian brown body with the Mesoamerican body's vitality. The Mesoamerican body in this work has been recovered to speak directly about its own gender interests. López's work demonstrates that the scope for understanding the Mesoamerican body parallels larger issues concerning how the body is regarded in the West, and the relegation of the body, as Susan Bordo documents, to women and the traditional association of women with a "negativity," an association that López disputes (2003, 5).

The Mexican American painter Alex Donis, born in Chicago in 1964, is a Los Angeles–based visual artist whose work is also part of an initiative to create a welcome environment in the United States for the Hispanic LGBTQ community. He addresses the issue of the body in the broadest possible terms. Like López, he manipulates a traditional Catholic icon in a powerful cultural setting. At first glance, his silkscreen on offset poster called *I Lied* (1996, see figure 5.3) is a highly conventional presentation of the Virgin Mary in the Catholic sacred art tradition. The exquisite face of a young woman is framed with white and blue robes, and she gestures with her hand in the traditional manner to indicate her "burning" (passionate) heart. This is the traditional invitation for the Virgin Mary's followers to petition Jesus through her powerful intercession and her flaming heart.

The flaming, passionate heart is an image usually associated with Jesus, while the "immaculate heart" represents Mary's nature as someone free of sin and is more commonly associated with her. Jesus's passionate heart is the Catholic icon representing God's love for humanity. In this case, her gesture is a reminder that her body in Catholic terms is the sacred vessel that brings redemption and salvation into the world. She is looking toward the viewer with a steady, soft gaze, and in the background behind her is a large break in an otherwise heavy cloud cover. In Catholic iconography, the cloud's opening informs viewers that through her intercession there is a path for believers to be in harmony with the Father.

Everything that can be gleaned from this silkscreen image in the first few seconds of viewing is then radically called into question in toto as the viewer notices two pale words under Mary's chin—"I lied." These words are intended to be shocking, since they appear to thwart traditional associations with the Virgin's body—purity, paradise, the tradition of connecting her with the hortus conclusus, the Medieval "enclosed garden," God's miraculous intervention when Mary conceived the Christ child, steadfastness, chastity, the possibility of grace and harmony with the Father, and so on.

We also see that the color scheme in the work creates a second motif connecting the white letters of "I lied," her white robe, and the white clouds behind her. This "white" pattern connects all three images and suggests a conceptual equivalence among them, a significant theme that the work's composition emphasizes. While *I Lied* is saying that all traditional associations to the Virgin Mary's body are misleading and false, the white color scheme appears to map a different set of connections—clouds, robes, and words—that suggests an alternative revelation of truth separate from the painting's rebellious message.

This second message can be put in dialogue with Mexican American cultural works and art that deal with the body, the significance of her words concerning her body's vaunted purity. The viewer can recall Bordo's comment that the Western body is often taken to be "feminine" and that women in the West have been closely associated with bodily life and its frailties. In this work, Mary is saying that as the "virgin" she cannot continue to assert that she rises above the great taint of having a body and also live in a world where women are associated with decay, aging, and death. The Blessed Mother, who, like men, is traditionally thought to transcend the body, is the sacred vessel, but her words decry and directly reject that misrepresentation. The blunt assertion of "I lied" argues that the conflation of women and the body must be recognized as a cultural lie and an act of violence historically done to women. At this late stage of Western culture and the modern world, women cannot continue to be the body's exclusive caretakers and also be the ones always condemned owing to their negative association with the body.

I Lied says that women are neither reducible to their bodies nor content with having to avoid bodily life to be free of the "feminine" bodily taint. *I Lied* says also that men should not be licensed to deem women inferior based upon a false and self-serving Western patriarchal authority associating women with the body and nature-Earth and men with mind and God. A powerful, sweeping gesture, *I Lied* says many things, and it principally tells viewers that change is at hand and mainstream culture cannot continue to cover over and degrade the body as a supposedly feminine and disposable dimension of experience.

Mary's gesture toward herself has the significance of a recovery of her own body *as a body* with an existence and significance outside of the Western exploitation of women as responsible for sin and the fact of having an "imperfect" (not male) body. In this powerful work, Mary is asking the viewer to recover and reinterpret the female body, *her body*, much as Mexican American writers and artists such as Cisneros, Chávez, Martínez, Valadez, and López are demanding this rethinking in regard to the brown body, the plea in each case being to recover the human form's vitality.[7]

WHAT WE LEARN FROM THE HUMAN BODY IN THE BROAD CONTEXT OF THE AMERICAS

Themes connected with the body and its status in the West get dramatically reframed in the work of Mexican American artist Luis A. Jiménez Jr. (1940–2006)—a sculptor and painter who, until his death, was based in Hondo, New Mexico. The many indigenous details and icons that Jiménez scatters around his works ask to be interpreted and understood as referencing the culture and history of the Americas. One of his goals is to expose depictions of the brown body as a damaging legacy dating from the Spanish colonial period. His critique of the traditional social construction of the brown body is intended to lift that burden from mestizo bodies and free them from the colonial condemnation under which they have suffered for almost five hundred years.

Jiménez's work "embodies what Chicano scholars have identified as a Chicano sensibility and aesthetic" (Brenson 1997, 11), a description that references the combination of a representational and romantic style but also Jiménez's working-class figures who are mostly Mexican American. Jiménez created masterful depictions of the brown body as it has been constructed, reimagined, and manipulated in Western culture. Fully aware that the Spanish invented the idea of racial identity according to phenotype (bodily details), and that they also created the idea of the brown body as a possession to be managed and controlled, Jiménez attempts to unveil the postcolonial significance of the brown body as a historical correction to that tradition. Developing sculptural figures that critique racial traditions and their constructions of identity in the Americas, he also signals the *end* of race as an institution and a practice.

His exaggerated brown bodies help us to see race's failure in the modern era to explain human nature and social relations. In light of what modern culture has learned about the political dimensions of race as a concept and the lack of any genetic or natural foundation for that concept, he sees the concept of race as coming apart, dying, and almost at an end.

His argument is that the marginalized brown body in the Americas functions like a blank screen on which affluent classes have projected their fears—the classic ones dating from Plato's time concerning aging, decay, and death. Connecting through his work with other writers, artists, and public intellectuals who focus on race and the brown body in the Americas, Jiménez foregrounds his version of the body as a colonial construction with a starkness and sophistication that have been, on many occasions, shocking to viewers. Through his work, viewers are alerted to deeper cultural shifts regarding race and the recovery of the body in the late twentieth century.

Exemplary of the style and subject matter of Jiménez's work is *Border Crossing* (1989, see figure 5.4), a large public-art work showing a man standing eight-feet tall and dressed in jeans and a sleeveless shirt. On his shoulders sits his hunched-over wife holding their child, and together they are forging the Río Grande River, possibly to find work in the United States. The second exemplary work is *Fiesta Jarabe (Fiesta Dancers)* (1996, see figure 5.5), another public-art work, in which two people stand ten-feet tall with colorful and impossibly shiny clothes, the skin on their faces so dark that one can barely discern their features. The woman has hands too large for her body, and both dancers have unusually thick shoulders and strong torsos. These and other bodies in Jiménez's work dominate his sculpture and painting, the body presenting an opportunity for him to display and critique race *and*, through the plastic, shiny medium that he works with, the commercial excesses of contemporary culture.

Jiménez has commented that *Border Crossing* and *Fiesta Jarabe* were the only two pieces that he ever worked on together,[8] both works presenting a couple with unusually powerful bodies. In *Border Crossing*, bodies, with the woman on her husband's shoulders, define the piece. In *Fiesta Jarabe*, male and female dancers are colored in earth tones, and the skin and clothes of each figure are shiny with an ultra–high gloss urethane coating that is the industrial finish common to his work. *Border Crossing* may well be a "signature work" for Jiménez, as some critics have said, but the same must be said of *Fiesta Jarabe,* a brilliant work of the same period, style, and color range (Brenson 1997, 19).

One strong appeal of Jiménez's work is not merely the overview of Mexican American culture and themes, but the attention he gives to *the body,* the inherent superiority of sculpture to display the human body, and his invitation to examine the nuanced presentation of brown bodies. *Fiesta Jarabe* is especially distinctive as a work outside of Western canons of beauty and appeal. The tall, female dancer has well-defined, large shoulders and oversized hands resting on her hips. The sharply angled features of her face, especially her jaw and protruding brow, are severe, and her heavily muscled arms are bent, as are her legs, in the posture of physical readiness, thus defying conventional Western expectations of feminine modesty. There are also no smooth, flowing curves anywhere on her body, nothing to suggest that she is weaker than her male partner. Jiménez draws special attention to her body by stripping away *all* Western aesthetic conventions for depicting body symmetry, balanced proportion, and normative standards of feminine beauty.

Both figures have dark skin, especially the male dancer.[9] In defiance of much popular art, where there is often a homogenized, normalized view of ethnicity, Jiménez makes dark skin an important reference for the dancers.[10] The dancers' skin, especially the man's, and the atypical presentation of the woman's body draw attention to these figures' bodily stature and demeanor. These are bodies not conventionally decorative or "beautiful," suggesting that Jiménez is intending to break through Western aesthetic traditions of rendering the brown body as an exotic, attractive other.

We see this point most clearly in relation to Jiménez's earlier maquette, the small model for *Fiesta Jarabe* made for this project's development in 1985. This model shows a traditionally conceived female dancer with slender arms, small waist and hands, light skin, and gradual, smooth curves defining shoulders and torso (Brenson 1997, 15). The earlier image is dead in appearing utterly conventional, while the finished product is alive in its grotesquerie. The maquette shows what *Fiesta Jarabe* would have been if it were executed in line with European aesthetic conventions. These two versions of *Fiesta Jarabe* present an instance of the Mesoamerican body competing with the Western body, and the Mesoamerican body in the final work wins.

The evidence in *Fiesta Jarabe* shows that Jiménez moves methodically in stages *away* from the conventions of European beauty and the Western body as depicted in the maquette. With unusual bodies defying easy categorization, the final version shows Jiménez rejecting traditional Western aesthetics. A viewer unfamiliar with his art could see the final work as grotesque and misshapen. It is, and he apparently wants to avoid making non-Western people in his work look like Westerners who accidently have dark skin. Jiménez forces viewers to see bodies that convey complex messages about social exclusion and cultural marginalization, counters to Western visual depictions of indigenous people—the maquette's version of beauty or a sleeping Mexican with a sombrero covering his face. Just as the bodies in New Spain's casta paintings were "lost" and had no names (literally, one of the casta categories translates as "I cannot understand you") because their Spanish, "white" blood had been corrupted with indigenous and African influences, the bodies in Jiménez's work are mestizos, too, that otherwise, without his exaggeration of their features, would be framed with Spanish and European culture and would quickly vanish as anonymous and "invisible."

At the same time, *Fiesta Jarabe*'s figures are not mestizos showing brown bodies as they "really are" but monstrous, grotesque, nonwhite bodies that exist outside of Western norms. The result is a view of bodies with unexpected features that have broken free of Western *and* Mesoamerican cultural aesthetics and that are displayed as nonassimilable examples of being nonwhite, bodies that by design neither fit the "master plan" of looking Western nor are presented as conventionally brown and invisible. With these unusual figures, Jiménez exposes traditional practices of dismissing brown bodies in the Americas as not fully human, references to bodies that the affluent classes can register as not like themselves—the invisible bodies that mow American lawns, work in meat processing plants, clean homes and hotel rooms, and take care of white children. Drawing attention to oppression by rendering bodies with exaggerated features makes these bodies visible again.

We are reminded that the Spanish elite during the colonial period did everything possible to guard against letting such "monstrous" bodies as these exist outside of a controlled social hierarchy and racial context. The Spanish in the colonial period tried to categorize and control the recognition of mestizo bodies, just as eighteenth-century race theorists did in Europe, as we saw in chapter 1, to control the recognition of dark skin and the *Homo monstrous* people who were mixed racially or had other "abnormalities." Jiménez is calculating that at this point in the Chicano Renaissance by constructing figures that are close to cartoons in their presentation he can show those depictions to be harmful and irrelevant and break free of Western and Mesoamerican norms of aesthetic beauty. He violates almost everything that eighteenth-century traditions, or modern traditions, have done to shape and control racial categories and, in the process, brings those traditions to a close.

We can see Jiménez's aim more clearly by connecting these two sculptural works with the eighteenth-century casta system. Always highlighting sixteen racial identities (the ones most often cited, as there were many others), that system commonly had a first row of four paintings that identified Spaniards as the embodiment of being white, the originating reference that makes the casta system work. A second row of four paintings typically references the almost white mestizo racial identities that come from the union of a Spaniard and indigenous person. A third row shows the not white category of four paintings produced by mixing several ethnic identities to create racial identities far removed from being Spanish. The fourth row of paintings shows races that the Spanish described as "polluted," the category that includes Africans, the identity for which there is no restart, no blood mending—no possible return to being white through a succession of marriages to Spaniards. This is the row of paintings that the Spanish gave no proper names and instead used terms such as "I can't understand you" to designate them as permanent outcasts and outsiders (Katzew 2004, 36).

Jiménez's work parodies racial identities drawn from the casta system's fourth row. By referencing figures in *Fiesta Jarabe* outside of Western aesthetics and racial hierarchies, he creates an exaggerated version of all bodies that are invisible to mainstream culture and the privileged classes. When we see the figures of *Fiesta Jarabe* with the urethane shiny surface over clothes and skin, their impossibly large physical dimensions, and their non-Western aesthetic features, we see a vivid display and exposure of the *artificiality* of all Western racial identities—cultural constructions political in their origin that do not correspond to any human reality. In this way strategically exaggerating bodily features, Jiménez parodies and destroys the racial logic of the casta system by creating grotesque figures who do not fit *any* standard categories of racial identity. In so doing, he references the work of eighteenth-century race theorists and scientists who created terms to describe those whose abnormalities and dark skin excluded them from belonging to normal, "scientific" racial schemes.

Creating a parody of the people who do not fit anywhere, with their impossible physical dimensions and their shiny plastic skin, a constant reminder of the constructed nature of racial categories, Jiménez critiques the specter of traditional brown bodies in the Americas and exposes their dehumanizing effect. His goal is to reveal the appearance of racial categories as artificial and irrelevant and forever undercut the legitimacy of the Spanish colonial version of the brown body, in this way exaggerating racial effects beyond the possibility of any recovery.

His success with such parody is well-known. In 1999, I witnessed the lead-up to a major exhibit of Jiménez's work in Norman, Oklahoma. Jiménez's many sculptures were installed around the University of Oklahoma campus. His work was everywhere. Once those works were in place, there was a widespread, negative reaction from the community when *Fiesta Jarabe, Border Crossing,* and many other Jiménez works were available for public scrutiny. Angry and resentful, the community saw themselves as besieged as so many "grotesque" bodies invaded their town, campus, and lives.

But then something unexpected happened. Within weeks after opening *Working Class Heroes,* and after an artist's gallery talk and many opportunities to meet the artist, view, discuss, and process his work and its implications, people changed their minds. People began to see his work as raising issues about race and the *representation* of race in the Americas. The climate of opinion about his work gradually shifted, and people came to value it for the critique of racial categories that it presented. The community initially felt threatened by his unconventional figures, but viewer by viewer, visitor by visitor, family by family, they came to value what his work sought to accomplish by exposing the reality of white fears projected onto brown bodies.

The wide swing in the community's response suggested that a fundamental change in perspective, unusual for a whole community, took place. Within three months, the vast majority of the community acknowledged that *Working Class Heroes* was one of the most powerful and successful art exhibits to come into their community—ever. At similar moments in other communities, Jiménez's work has succeeded in exposing harmful cultural assumptions to enable the recovery of bodies from the brown body abyss. Jiménez wanted viewers to see that these impossible bodies were undercutting and exposing the artificiality of race as a category. His aim was to lift the burden of *brown* from actual people so that bodies that were hidden and effectively "missing" from the Americas and the culture's social consciousness could return—in effect, showing that mestizos do not have *brown* bodies in the traditional sense, only bodies.[11] Jiménez was wagering—truly a *wager* and not a certainty—that the extremes of parody in his work could destroy the legitimacy of traditionally conceived brown bodies as a racial category.

The evidence is that Jiménez's work succeeds, as his large and appreciative following still shows, because through parody it opens the way for viewers to disengage from the specters of race still doing damage after so many years. The Spanish created the brown body to control a variety of mixed-race people and establish their social and cultural authority in a colonial environment. When the postcolonial version of the brown body finally gets destroyed, as is now happening, viewers can explore mestizo cultures no longer blocked in their vision by these colonial categories and legacies. The casta racial tradition that began in the eighteenth century ends, at least symbolically, with Jiménez in that his work reveals not only the potential but the reality of brown bodies no longer functioning as markers for a person's worth and social prestige. Jiménez identifies the specter of the brown body as racial artifice, a screen on which people have projected their fears of disease, decay, and death—what brown bodies have represented for the Spanish and white people in the Americas for almost five hundred years.

WHAT CHICANO WRITERS AND ARTISTS HAVE DONE TO RECOVER THE BODY

This discussion began with Oscar Zeta Acosta, Richard Rodriguez, and Michele Serros viewing in voyeuristic fashion their own brown bodies. Why did their bodies appear grotesque to *them?* Why had they become voyeurs of *their own* brown bodies? What underlying revelation did their bodies hold for *them?* The writers and artists in this tradition of commentary as I have traced it give an important answer to these questions. They reveal mainstream culture's projection of fears and misplaced associations of death and destruction onto the empty screen of the brown body. As the descendants of colonized people, Acosta, Rodriguez, and Serros were repulsed by seeing the colonial reconstruction of their bodies reflected back to them. In effect, they became voyeurs by viewing themselves through the dominant culture's eyes. They did not see their own bodies but white culture's fantasy projections of brown bodies, bodies that are associated with the "feminized," decaying body of the West that Susan Bordo critiques. At such moments, Mexican American writers and artists lift away the cover of Western aesthetics and dark fantasy projections to exorcise what Spanish colonial culture created and left behind for others to sort out so many years later. The goal of Mexican American writers and artists who critique the brown body, as Jiménez's work exemplifies, is to expose the lack of any foundation for such dark racial fantasies and, undercutting their legitimacy, put those racial fantasies to rest once and for all.

These writers and artists did their work during a period in late twentieth-century U.S. culture when the scrutiny of race as a category was an active endeavor. Like others in that period, they saw that the time had come for a profound rethinking of race, especially since genetic research, with little fanfare, had steadily been dismantling the "natural" or genetic basis for all racial categories as expressions of a natural order for judging people's worth. Genetic scientists have shown the presence of diverse genetic markers in the most remote communities, demonstrating a complex, genetic cross-indexing around the globe. Their results consistently reveal a diversity of markers *within* communities and among peoples who are presumed to have developed in relatively "pure" lines of genetic descent and influence. Geneticist Howard M. Cann notes that "human genome diversity studies have clearly shown that the large part of genetic variability is due to differences *among* individuals within populations rather than to differences *between* populations." This view of genetic diversity, locating the presence of most genetic difference inside of communities rather than separating them, destroys the genetic basis for racial categories and unique social identities based on race. Genetic science completely removes the rationale for elevating some social classes and races above the supposedly mixed lineages and heritages of subordinate classes (Cann 1998, 443). This work reveals that human diversity, not genetic "purity," is humanity's actual condition the world over and is the new normal.

Alma López, Yolanda López, John Valadez, Alex Donis, Luis Jiménez, and many other Mexican American artists identify race as a political tool. Owing to alterations in class and social dynamics, a new global awareness created through digital media and technology, as well as the work of race theorists such as Omi and Winant, bell hooks, Aníbal Quijano, and Cornell West, Mexican American artists are reframing *race* as a social construction and revealing it for what it is on several levels. Also entering this conversation is the work of Latino Critical Race theorists such as Tara J. Yosso, Dolores Delgado Bernal, Veronica N. Vélez, Angela P. Harris, and others, whose work overlaps with this book in numerous ways. These writers have done important work to focus on the social construction of race as a category and the cultural and social barriers blocking social justice for Latinos, especially highlighting the need to validate the evidence of personal experience (Solorzano and Yosso 2001; Delgado Bernal 2002; Yosso 2006; Vélez et al. 2008; Delgado and Stefancic 2011).

All of these writers and artists have glimpsed the powerful potential for a cultural reframing of the perception and enactment of race as a social construction. Their challenging work draws on a "modern" understanding of brown bodies originally created when the Spanish decided to distinguish among enslaved communities with color codes such as brown, red, or black.

Losing the power to dictate social hierarchies and shape lives, race is no longer "natural" or commanding in its reach. Artistic and cultural visions during this period prompt an awareness on several fronts to show how the brown body as a social and cultural construction has persisted into the present but now has been exposed as a sham, a politically motivated strategy for social control. Mexican American writers and artists remind us that when the Spanish created the *brown body* they were not creating actual bodies but roles that have persisted for too long. Spanish brown bodies were markers of an historic impasse, having to do with the impact of the conquest, and in this chapter I have shown that the time has come to recognize that this impasse has been lifted and race is no longer a viable social category.

In crucial ways, the reign of race is over, and Mexican Americans are now bringing closure to this chapter of the Americas' history. It is now our lot to help culture and society to reequilibrate around new postcolonial references and identities—hence the strategic importance of Chicano literature and culture as part of the response to racism in the twenty-first century. Racism as a practice still lives, but images such as Valadez's typical brown bodies, López's erotic Mesoamerican women, and Jiménez's radical parody of brown bodies all challenge the racial underpinning of Western aesthetics and signal the future, imminent closing of a remarkable but also hugely destructive era in the history of the Americas.

The mestizo body's fortunes in Mexican American culture and in the Americas are among the most important issues for all to interpret and understand. The mandate to recover the body in Mexican American culture may seem a world away from the discussions of mestizo identity, land, popular culture, voice, and Mexican American literature in the Chicano Renaissance. But the issue of the brown body and the prospects for understanding it connect to all of these areas. The Chicano movement broadened its perspective from the immediate concerns of migrant farm labor, social marginalization, lack of participation in local and national government, health crises, and poor educational opportunities and outcomes to go to the furthest reaches of life in the Americas and the reconceptualization of society and culture. The historical progression of these changes from the early 1960s to the present shows a fast-action film focusing on labor strife, social mobilization, emergent labor unions, guerrilla theater on flatbed trucks and dirt stages, the poetic reclaiming of Aztec culture and the concept of land, the rise of Chicano literature, and the recovery of the mestizo body.

Such developments derive from a gradual realization, a true insight, in the Mexican American community that too much has been lost and too many people have suffered for this community to fail to come home to the United States when it can. By mid-twentieth century, it was clearly time to reclaim Mexican American identity, social life, and a new direction for the future. The indigenous relationship to land, the Aztlán homeland claim, the recognition of mestizo identity, and the mestizo body's reclamation have moved steadily away from an exclusive focus on Mexican American life conceived in the narrowest of terms. Needed was a critique of broader issues in contemporary society, concerning the direction of mestizo culture in the Americas. The perspective that emerged, as the discussions in this chapter show, has the potential to challenge received notions and conventional and entrenched understandings about race and community in the Western hemisphere.

The success and impact of the writers and artists who are recovering the body in Mexican American culture are foreshadowed in the cultural remappings of Mexican American writers from the 1960s through the 1990s. In documents such as *El Plan Espiritual de Aztlán*, Anaya's "Aztlán: A Homeland without Boundaries," Anzaldúa's *Borderlands/ La Frontera: The New Mestiza*, and Cisneros's *Loose Woman*, among others, it becomes clear that a renewal of Mexican American culture required a rethinking of every aspect of communal and social life, including the fate of the body and body consciousness.

Without these alterations and challenges to mainstream American culture, Mexican American social documents and literary texts would be of passing and possibly no significance. The dramatic alterations of private life and Mexican American culture as reflected in literary texts and art mark a transformation occurring in the Mexican American community. This is a transformation drawing upon powerful forces in the community to critique the residue of colonial influences to empower Mexican Americans to reinvigorate their community and create a new life in the United States.

Mexican American writers and artists attempt to rethink the context of community, life, and home in relation to the body. This body focus, touching on a great variety of bodies writing books and creating art, laboring, dancing, running, crossing borders, sexually vital, family engendering, undernourished, and eventually dying conveys a vision of what was hidden before when Mexican Americans and other mestizos in the culture were living their lives in the shadows, invisible to the culture at large. With a new focus on the body, no longer the *brown* body, there is now a welcome sense of knowledge that has finally been revealed. The new focus on bodies has shown that the recovery of the body is a major avenue of mestizos trying to come home. We started this discussion by attempting to listen to what the bodies of Acosta, Rodriguez, Serros, and Rivera had to say about themselves and their life in the Americas. We end this discussion by still listening to bodies, and we need to be committed to keep listening to what they have to say.

* III *
THE LITERARY RESPONSE

CHAPTER 6

Tomás Rivera and the Chicano Voice

Tomás Rivera is one of the writers and educators most responsible for the cultural and social directions taken by the Chicano Renaissance in the 1970s. As a novelist, educator, administrator in higher education, and public intellectual, he provided leadership when it was needed most for his community. His frank assessment of his community's way forward in U.S. culture, as we saw in chapter 5, helped to create important directions for effective change and development. Along with Rudolfo Anaya, he helped to establish the "voice" of Chicano culture, setting a constructive tone and designating a set of values and perspectives—a lasting contribution still in evidence today. His work, vision, and example can continue to be a source of inspiration for Mexican Americans and all who want to understand this community's unique contributions and character. By recovering a sense of his life and work, we deepen our understanding of Mexican American and Chicano cultural values and goals needed for the future.

***

When Tomás Rivera came onto the Mexican American cultural scene in the early 1970s, he signaled—along with Rudolfo Anaya, Rodolfo Gonzales, Estela Trambley, and a few others—the start of the Chicano Renaissance. This was a period of promising new beginnings, and Rivera's novel . . . *y no se lo tragó la tierra* / . . . *And the Earth Did Not Devour Him* (hereafter *Tierra*) expressed a powerful vision for how the Mexican American community could reinvigorate itself. Through his writing and work in education, and with his unusual dedication and energy, Rivera seemed to embody that vision in himself. A great writer and always a champion of education for Mexican American

199

young people, Rivera became in 1979 the chancellor of the University of California at Riverside and was his day's most prominent Hispanic educator.

THE EMERGENCE OF A LITERARY
AND CULTURAL VOICE

Rivera's major contribution to the 1970s Chicano Renaissance came with his judgment that fiction must "talk" as it had not done before "about a Chicano as a complete figure," a complex, multidimensional human being (Bruce-Novoa 1980, 150–51). He saw not only that Mexican Americans were marginalized in public life, but in fiction and in culture they were often stereotypes with little sense conveyed of who they were, what motivated them, and what they aspired to. Fiction could begin to show this "complete figure" only when it was written by Chicanos themselves, and he continually supported the work of other writers. His consistent advocacy on this fundamental issue gave him a voice not just as a single writer but as someone speaking on behalf of the Mexican American community. The "talk" that Rivera referenced needed to be a "voice" that spoke for the community about its values and conveyed a full picture, strengths and weaknesses, of being Mexican American. His enduring cultural significance comes in part from the function that he fulfilled in being one of the people, a key figure, creating that voice. His contribution to this discussion shed a new light on the Mexican American community at a critical moment in its history and culture.

As part of the Chicano Renaissance in the 1970s, he also wanted to reframe Mexican Americans in relation to mainstream culture and show how they fit "into the spectrum of the Americas" (Bruce-Novoa 1980, 150–51). He argued that recognizing his community's humanity was a gesture in harmony with the New World legacy of valuing social justice and freedom from oppression. Could Mexican Americans join that initiative in the Americas? He believed that they could. Optimistic about the hemisphere's potential for social justice, he also saw the need to change the perception of Mexican Americans, a need that still exists. Believing that Mexican Americans could shape the U.S. future owing to the role that they played in the Americas in the past and present, he developed a profound optimism, unique to his own vision and perspective, based in what he took to be "the spiritual strength [of Mexican Americans]." He believed in their potential to bring meaningful social change to the United States (Bruce-Novoa 1980, 150–51).

Rivera could see that Mexican Americans during his time were already stepping forward to explore their culture and who they were, and he intended to create a "voice" to capture that cultural energy and make known their attitudes, values, and identity. He was adopting a voice in the sophisticated sense, as M. H. Abrams notes, that is the "equivalent in imaginative literature" of "Aristotle's 'ethos,'"—the expression of values and beliefs that coalesce as a cultural perspective and in various ways can then be "heard" (2009, 228). The emergence of such a voice often signals that a community has reached a threshold, in this case, Rivera's estimation that the Americas' past combined with his community's current aspirations were creating a new sense of possibility for Mexicans Americans in the 1970s and beyond.

This voice functioned like other voices in American literature in representing cultural values at a particular historical moment. New cultural voices emerge at moments when past conflicts and cultural impasses are being reconciled and it becomes possible to express what they can convey. Rivera's *Tierra* brought forward such a voice as had *Huckleberry Finn* (which defined a new sense of race and morality for its day), *A Narrative of the Life of Frederick Douglass* (which celebrated an African American moral liberation from white America), and *The Awakening* (which critiqued the circumstances of women's lives in the late nineteenth century). Like these signal texts and the Chicano classics "I Am Joaquin" and *Bless Me, Ultima*, Rivera's *Tierra* was announcing that aspects of Mexican American culture were ready to be projected to a larger audience. What was possible and potential in Mexican American culture before this voice existed was afterward poised to become a cultural reality. Implicit in his decision was the prediction that important Mexican American achievements would be forthcoming in literature, art, and social thought.

Focusing on "the concept of justice so important for the American continent," he wanted Mexican Americans to reengage the U.S.

mainstream in new ways (Bruce-Novoa 1980, 150–51). He understood that Mexican Americans needed a strong sense of their own community but also a sustainable, nonexploitative relationship with U.S. culture. He referenced the potential for mestizos to find social justice in the hemisphere and wanted to contribute to cultural initiatives that could support such goals in the United States, a potential that played out as the Chicano Renaissance starting in 1971. Owing in part to his work and that of his friend Rudolfo Anaya, others followed and began writing literary works with complex Mexican American characters, involved interior lives, and a self-conscious awareness of themselves and their cultural inheritance.

To further support goals that would strengthen his community, Rivera became a public intellectual, a scholar, a teacher, and an administrator. In these complex roles, he encouraged his community toward greater self-reliance, the active advancement of its cultural interests, and reconceiving their relationship with the national culture. He wanted to bring Mexican Americans "home" in the sense of sinking roots where they were—in many cases, on land that used to be Mexico—and finding greater civic involvement locally and nationally to revitalize their community. He wanted them to find a more nearly balanced relationship in their lives and in their relations with the country at large. Rivera and Anaya urged independence for Mexican Americans to live and thrive. The 1970s Chicano Renaissance thereafter developed as an arts culture and social movement supporting this new awareness of being Mexican American beyond anything that Rivera might have imagined. By the 1980s, Chicanos were finding a different relationship to mainstream culture through literature, art, and community building much as Rivera and Anaya had asked for.

Rivera died in 1984, when much of what he planned was under way, and now years later there is the danger of a generation of younger writers forgetting the extent and clarity of his vision and what he made possible and is still making possible for all of us. *Tierra*, his short fiction, his essays, and his poetry invited Mexican Americans to celebrate community but also to accelerate the process of U.S. acculturation in some specific ways, mainly urging self-determination in culture, community, and the economy. Rivera raised a flag of hope on behalf of his community's future, and that vision is still pertinent and much needed today. Actively engaging the literary scene during the 1970s, Rivera toured the Southwest with Rolando Hinojosa and Rudolfo Anaya as each read from his work in venues such as book stores and coffee houses. All three had a deep understanding of the historical importance of this undertaking and their community's need for them to succeed in producing a voice for the Mexican American community.

In the early 1970s, the new Chicano literature advanced through the work of a few writers, but by decade's end it became a robust wave of creativity and fresh cultural directions on many fronts. It is true that Rivera's own lifetime publishing remained modest in volume owing to his commitments in higher education and his premature death in 1984. But after so many years, *Tierra* and much of his other work still have a powerful vision to share for claiming cultural citizenship in the United States and the Americas.

Rivera and Anaya challenged everyone in the Americas to be more inclusive in conceiving of citizenship and to a broader view of American culture and society. They wanted Mexican American writers to operate on the largest hemispheric stage possible, a vision inspiring to many writers from this period, but now there is a need to encourage younger writers to understand Rivera's achievements and benefit from his vision. Anaya is still a highly prolific and influential writer, and Rodolfo Gonzales (who wrote "I Am Joaquin") made his mark by writing a single, influential poem. By looking carefully at three writers, we are focusing on sites where the Chicano Renaissance first surfaced and was becoming evident to everyone. If we add the Denver Youth Conference that I discussed in this book's introduction, we have four cultural moments where we can say that something important was beginning to take shape and attract attention. With insights still to share about cultural new beginnings in Mexican American culture, *Tierra* needs to be recovered and brought back to our awareness as an important resource for the Mexican American community. We still need what it has to show us.

Central to *Tierra*'s success as a novel was that it examined adverse living and working conditions that prevailed in the Mexican American community over several decades, from around 1940 to approximately

1960, with a power and directness that no other works had shown. *Tierra* was sounding an alarm about the dire circumstances of an impoverished and neglected community. Revealing adverse working conditions, substandard public education, degraded housing, and nonexistent health care, Rivera shows that most U.S. social institutions in this period before the Chicano movement were disastrously failing Mexican Americans. His novel's markers for communal vitality—community health standards, access to basic education, routes for accessing higher education, rising income level, and ability to maintain and nurture cultural traditions—were indicating that a complete disaster had befallen the Mexican American community from 1940 to 1960. It was faltering by every reasonable standard of health and communal sustainability, and this failure still remained largely invisible and of little concern to the national community. Focusing on the need to reset social goals and aspirations, *Tierra* was nearly alone in documenting the loss of social cohesion and communal health. He was reporting on deplorable living and working conditions in the Mexican American community and was pointing a new direction forward.

During the 1960s, Mexican Americans were protesting both the Vietnam War and unfair farm labor practices in California. And despite a generally favorable economy through the 1960s, unemployment among unskilled workers (including Mexican Americans) ran between 5 to 7 percent, with especially limited job opportunities for the young (Acuña 2000, 330). Mexican Americans had little participation or representation in local and federal government, and under economic pressure to assimilate into the American melting pot, they were slipping ever further into being the permanent working poor. Mexican Americans needed new ways to approach their situation as a community, and Rivera felt that he could help to define that need. His most immediate goal was simply to tell the truth about what was happening to his community, a truth that no one else in mainstream America seemed interested in hearing about. Analyzing impoverished lives and foregrounding the need for large-scale change, he fulfilled the task of reporting on his community and also bringing to it a new self-awareness, one that foregrounded communal strengths and failures and helped to identify new cultural and social goals.

Tierra was prominent, in other words, along with "I Am Joaquin" and *Bless Me, Ultima* as a work inaugurating a new period of cultural and social goal setting. Whereas before this period "Chicano" for some meant anything written by Mexican Americans—such as Leonor Villegas de Magnón's *The Rebel*, Daniel Venegas's *The Adventures of Don Chipote; or, When Parrots Breast Feed*, or José Antonio Villarreal's *Pocho*—in the 1970s, under *Tierra*'s influence, "Chicano" came to mean something more specific. After Rivera and Anaya, "Chicano" meant the commitment to community development as a goal more important than mere assimilation into U.S. culture. As a prototypical Chicano text, *Tierra* set this goal and that of strengthening community, and in doing this it created expectations for what other "Chicano" works should address, what they would look like, and what they should accomplish.

HOW TO *REREAD* TOMÁS RIVERA'S WORK

There is a need to *reread* Rivera's work not only because his memory is fading for younger readers but because his work has invaluable perspectives to share—ones that we cannot do without. Like *Bless Me, Ultima*, Ana Castillo's *The Mixquiahuala Letters*, and Helena Viramonte's *Under the Feet of Jesus*, *Tierra* has a sophisticated and in some ways still difficult narrative structure—in this case, with short chapters arranged in a nonlinear order. For most readers, this presentational format is at first difficult to read. Reading *Tierra* is a little like deciphering a play script in which crucial information is missing that will be added later in actual performance. Even by today's standards, *Tierra* is an avant-garde experimental text that pushes the boundaries of narrative experimentation, what readers can readily understand. *Tierra* is a challenge to traditional storytelling with unattributed dialogue and stream-of-consciousness techniques that are still difficult to interpret.

At the same time, this novel was similar to other Chicano novels of its day in being strongly autobiographical. Early Chicano writers often led colorful and frequently difficult lives with childhood poverty, the struggle for education in white schools, and maneuvering to enter the publishing world when the big publishing houses did not understand or value new and challenging works. In Rivera's case, the premise of his fiction was simple. He focused on a Mexican American migrant-farm family and a boy's recounting of a year in his life, a time in which this child, like Rivera, worked in the migrant fields from Texas through Oklahoma, Kansas, Nebraska, and beyond. In telling such a story, Rivera wrote a kind of "portrait of the artist" confession of a life to dramatize the discovery of a vision of community amid the most adverse of circumstances in shanty towns and in agricultural fields soaked in pesticides and toxins. By novel's end, Rivera guides his young narrator toward a vision of social change, a vision that will help to create a sense of possibility and a constructive tone for this period.

Tierra is the interesting case of a major text that can be puzzling to readers even after over forty years since its publication. Owing to its elliptical narrative and cryptic, unglossed references, *Tierra* frames its content minimally and creates barriers for critics wanting merely to paraphrase it. When the book first appeared, most critics tacitly admitted to having little sense of how to analyze it.[1] With fourteen micro "chapters," some of them less than a page in length, and thirteen vignette sections, some with only a few sentences, and with a fragmented, highly experimental style of referencing characters and events throughout, this novel was a classic "problem novel" like William Faulkner's *The Sound and the Fury* and Virginia Woolf's *The Waves*—books that, in effect, had to create their own audiences. With such experimental irregularities of novel form, even its status as a *novel* was not assured. By all accounts a great twentieth-century literary masterpiece, "a landmark of Chicano creative expression" (Olivares 1985, 66), this novel still needs to reveal its inner workings. Everyone agrees that it generates an interesting and revealing cultural voice, but how it does that has remained unclear and a mystery.

In an overview of the book, we can say that this novel focuses on a migrant family's relentless travels as it constantly leaves to reach the next migrant farm job. The novel is structured around brief chapters and episodic scenes creating rapid stops and starts, possibly suggesting a view of the world through a moving truck window—flashes of landscape blurring through the glass in a succession of fragments. His narrative suggests the staccato rhythm, delays, and speed of stopping and starting during a work day.

Another clue to this novel's operation is Tómas Rivera's hovering presence in this novel as the *author*, the degree to which Rivera's own story overlaps with that of *Tierra*'s unnamed narrator. Rivera projects himself into this work by giving glimpses into his own childhood as a migrant farm worker, including his education, his literary preferences, and even Chicano literature's cultural and historical influences. All of these references, some of them in the novel and some from his essays and an interview, work to frame *Tierra* as a complex autobiographical *and* historical work emerging from a moment of transition in migrant farm culture in the 1940s and 1950s—a historical moment prior to the Chicano movement's attempts to rectify the injustices of Rivera's world.

Providing many close parallels to *Tierra,* especially with the unnamed narrator's epiphanies and personal crises, Rivera recounts his own high school awakening to the beauties of English and American literature, especially Walt Whitman's religious visions. In a famous interview with the Chicano critic Juan Bruce-Novoa, he recalls Whitman's vow to "sing the body electric," that is, to live in the moment and revel in personal challenges even amid communal and personal adversity. During that time, Rivera "dropped out of the Catholic Church," explaining that "really, I just didn't want to have anything to do with religion." By "high school graduation[,] I was reading about religion and I became pretty cynical." "Walt Whitman," he adds, "[became] my replacement" for religion (Bruce-Novoa 1980, 144). Likewise, Rivera narrates the fictional boy's rejection of Catholicism as a disappointing institution that did not fulfill its promises to poor people and, leading him to be suspicious of dogma in every form, prompted him to replace religion with a spiritual presence (a vision borrowed from Walt Whitman) in the natural world around him.

The connection among these issues was resistance to "any kind of dogmas," any conclusions and beliefs forced on the Mexican American community especially from white culture and privileged social classes (Bruce-Novoa 1980, 147). With such attitudes, Rivera intended to reject *every* institution that failed the Mexican American community, especially while proffering platitudes promising the opposite, and turned away from cultural idealism in almost every form. He rejected any path that encouraged the community to ignore social and economic exploitation and look past the need for social change. In fiction and interviews, he counseled investigating the underlying causes for the hard conditions of migrant farm life—the grinding poverty and the absence of economic opportunities, the lack of community self-determination, and alienation from mainstream culture. Even "a slave is an investment," he commented, but "a migrant worker? You [as a farm owner] owe him nothing. If he came to you, you gave him work and then just told [him] to leave. No investment" (151). Rivera portrays this first awakening in his own story, much as he did for the boy in *Tierra*, as a refocusing on the material conditions of Mexican American economic and social life and foregoing any attachment to empty ideals.

Another important "awakening" occurs with Rivera's discovery of the famous Chicano scholar Américo Paredes. Before writing *Tierra*, Rivera browsed library shelves (possibly at the University of Oklahoma, where I teach and Rivera was a student) and found Paredes's book on Texas folklore, *"With His Pistol in His Hand."* The name "Paredes" startled him, he notes, as "I was hungry to find something by a Chicano or Mexican American." This book "proved [that] it was possible for a Chicano to publish" and also "that it was possible to talk about a Chicano as a complete figure," a human figure, and not just a minor or background character in a world dominated by whites (Bruce-Novoa 1980, 150). Rivera's primary commitment was to find a way to talk about Mexican American culture to people in the mainstream and bolster a sense of its common humanity.

Encouraged by Paredes, Rivera vowed "to document the [experience of the] migrant worker para siempre . . . so that [his and her] very strong spirit of endurance will go on under the worst of conditions [and] should not be forgotten." To accomplish this, he committed to being a writer who advocates for his community. A vivid example of doing that came in his "documenting" the lives of migrant farm workers who were in the broadest sense the "undocumented." This literary "documenting" of the "undocumented," with all of the legal overtones and ironic resonance to our situation today, was Rivera's powerful way of acknowledging the daily drama, heroics, and suffering of those who were invisible to the rest of the culture (Bruce-Novoa 1980, 151).[2]

Rivera especially indicted institutions that were failing to support the Mexican American community—organized religion, education, social services, and public health. Critiquing such institutions, because doing so means rending the social fabric as most people in mainstream culture know it, may necessarily look monstrous and "grotesque" before it succeeds. He knew that he risked looking like an insurgent writer and recalls the Mexican writer José Revueltas's description of Chicano writers as a "grotesque people," primarily in regard to their willingness to innovate and make changes. Revueltas cites "grotesquerie" because "you [Chicano writers] take every risk [to critique the world around you] without fear of being humiliated" (Bruce-Novoa 1980, 159). At first startled, Rivera eventually agrees that "it's true. I go to teatro [theatre] presentations y hay cosas alli bien grotescas [and there are really grotesque things], and yet they're so damn human. They have substance. That's one of the qualities [of Chicano culture] I find" (160).

The "grotesque" dimension of Rivera's own journey means the pursuit of social truths and realities that mainstream culture resists acknowledging, making the Mexican American unknown appear grotesque to others. In *Tierra*, for example, the unnamed boy chooses to confront the "devil" at midnight at a "crossroads" in a desperate act of rebellion, a childish strike against the social status quo when no other ready targets for rebellion are at hand. The unnamed boy decides to commune with the devil if doing so will make a difference in his community's life. Both this crisis at a "crossroads" and Rivera's personal story posit "grotesque," unselfish encounters to find a new direction forward.

When José David Saldívar remarks that "Rivera's concept of identity in *Tierra* . . . is essentially an existential concept" involving the "process of becoming" (1991, 169), he could be referencing Rivera's own story as well as his character's fight to keep his spirit alive. The boy's story in *Tierra* begins when he hides under a neighbor's house and spends the day recollecting events in the migrant farm community over the last year. In this way isolating himself to discover how he fits into his world, he envisions leaving his home in Texas and then journeying full circle back there—his personal journey only ending when he can emerge from under the house with a new understanding of how his world comes together and what action on behalf of his community he could take.

Like a Greek chorus reflecting the community's judgment, this novel's voice narrates these scenes and events, expressing the community's viewpoint, regrets, and approval, as the narrative shifts abruptly from isolated scenes to snippets of action and dialogue and back again. In the film version of this novel, the director Severo Pérez seeks to capitalize on this theatrical but fragmented presentation when he transforms *Tierra's* extremes of disjointedness in the screenplay for his 1995 film. Attempting to make the narrative accessible for a film audience, Pérez strays from the novel's fragmented style, naming the narrator Marcos and designating him as a reassuring guide through various events throughout the film. Pérez also rearranges and deletes scenes that did not fit the linear style of cinematic realism that he needed to transform this experimental novel into a film.

THE RISE OF RIVERA'S VOICE

Imposing this well-made structure on this experimental novel produced a successful film but did not reflect the novel's narrative. More promising for an understanding of this novel is to focus on the creation of its "voice" by examining its chapters and vignettes in their original arrangement. This approach will make the assumption that this novel successfully creates a voice with a social and cultural role to play for its community, as readers have attested. Readers and writers in the 1970s responded to that voice, and, in effect, we can work backwards to see how that cultural voice was created. With this approach, we will be trying to determine how this novel creates a communal voice that helps to inaugurate the Chicano Renaissance in literature and culture.

Tierra's voice is a composite of beliefs and values that characterize Mexican American culture. Its chapters and vignettes can be separated into groups referencing certain of the beliefs and values that make up that voice. For example, there are several early chapters that establish the boy's identity as a mestizo and position him as an outsider in the mainstream white world that he tries to interact with. His identity is established in "El año perdido," the first chapter, as a Mexican American child working with his family in the migrant stream that runs from his home in Crystal City, Texas, and through many midwestern states. He is a child isolated from other students in the schools he attends, a "Mex." He is denied a haircut in a "white" barber shop. He is forgotten by a white priest who had offered moral support but then never remembers to be present for this child.

The first and last chapters of *Tierra*—"El año perdido" ("The Lost Year") and "Debajo de la casa" ("Below the House")—create the frame of a boy hiding under a neighbor's house for a day to process events of the last year and possibly overcome his personal disorientation. Searching for a new cultural direction and a way forward for himself, his family, and community, the boy is caught in paralyzing circumstances. These chapters reveal that he is personally "lost," his whole community is adrift, and both need a new cultural and social orientation to survive.

"El ano perdido" also shows the boy's discovery that for him words, thoughts, and events have ceased to cohere, straining his sense of reality and his sanity. He does not know when his lost year of disorientation began. Did he dream or actually experience being confused and disoriented? He doubts whatever answer he might find to such questions (Rivera 1992b, 83). The spatial, temporal, and psychological disorientation apparent in "El año perdido" is part of the boy's "existential dilemma," as Saldívar mentions, in that it isolates him from mainstream culture and raises questions about his future. These questions come up in the next four chapters (2–5) depicting a series of events pointing toward his social exclusion from mainstream society and his community's dire economic situation with no hope in sight.

In *Tierra*, there are also chapters and vignettes that show the boy's Mexican American hybrid culture. His community is a mixture of cultures, as is evident in the novel's overlaying of Chicano Spanish (inflected with English grammar and vocabulary) and the social prestige associated by some characters in knowing English to connect with mainstream culture. The boy's family seeks out both curanderas (natural healers, in this case, a spiritualista, a spiritual guide) and Western doctors for health care, choices showing the family's mixed-culture perspective.

There are also chapters and vignettes in *Tierra* pointing toward recognition of the broad, cultural stage of the Americas as the context for everything happening in this novel. In the Bruce-Novoa interview and in Rivera's poem "The Searchers," Rivera proposes a perspective that incorporates his community into the scheme of the Americas. He sees the Americas as characterized by people continually in motion in search of "truth" in their lives. Native peoples, the Spanish during the colonial period, and Mexican American migrant workers are all such "searchers" who traverse the region to find their own version of truth. The boy's community is always in motion, which situates this novel's action as well on the same broad, hemispheric stage of those who "search" in the Americas. Always in motion, migrant farm workers are searchers, too, and they are a continuation of this historic cultural pattern. The connection between the venue of the novel's action and the Americas' broad stage is also made through the community's mestizo identity and hybrid culture.

The boy's personal and educational development through experience points toward the necessity in his world of being an active agent for social change, for taking responsibility for his community. The contrast here is between the boy's success in shaping events around him and the community's tendency toward passive responses to education and the prospect of altering their fortunes when they are overly reliant on the baseless pipedreams of "when we arrive" in the book's last chapter. While the boy becomes "lost" and disoriented in the book's introduction, by the book's conclusion he has become potentially a person ready to be responsible for his community and to take steps to improve it.

Social activism and education are two of the book's major themes. The boy begins with pain and calamity in his world but then ends with a critique of that world as needing broad social reform and a new cultural vision. The novel through chapter 5, the whole first part of the book, depicts a world where economic hardship and inadvertent, even accidental, tragedy happens almost daily, such "accidental" harm being this world's norm. The chapter entitled "Los niños no se aguantaron" ("The Children Could Not Wait") tells the tragic story of a young migrant farm worker shot by a white field foreman. The boy was drinking water during the hottest part of the day, and the foreman fired his rifle to nudge the boy back to work, but the shot accidently kills the boy. The event's starkness is conveyed in Rivera's description of how the boy "didn't even jump like a deer does. He just stayed in the water like a dirty rag[,] and the water began to turn bloody" (86–87).

Rivera references social activism in the next chapter, "Un rezo" ("A Prayer"), where the narrator's mother prays for her oldest son's return from Korea. The fact that the son is actually dead haunts this chapter, as does the irony of a Mexican American son serving in Korea when there is great social injustice for Mexican Americans at home. In the fourth chapter, "Es que duele" ("It's That It Hurts"), the young narrator tells his parents about being expelled from school after white boys provoke him into a fight. These are instances of social exclusion masquerading as mere accidents of fortune.

These stories gel in their significance with the addition of the gothic tale "La mano en la bolsa" ("Hand in His Pocket"), the story of Don Laíto and Doña Bone, two sociopathic predators in his community. The young narrator boards with this childless couple for three weeks to stay in school while his parents travel to other jobs. The food that the old couple feeds him appears "green and it smelled really bad when she was cooking it" (98). The couple demands that he steal for them. And while the community considers the couple "good" people, buena gente, the boy knows that they are in reality thieves and killers. This story ends when the couple murders a "wetback" who pays Doña Bone for sex. The couple forces the young narrator to dig the man's grave, and they trick him into discovering in his bed "what felt like a snake but was in reality the [dead] wetback's arm." The boy then flees the bed as "the old couple burst into [sadistic] laughter" (100).

Amid this dark sequence of events, the chapter is introducing the idea of a pattern of social causation for personal mishaps. Don Laíto and Doña Bone exploit the community for narrow personal gain, and this fact foregrounds what the boy has been contemplating—that personal misfortune may have unseen social causes that this couple represents. The next step in his practical education is to connect unfortunate social and economic circumstances as possibly *causing* individual acts of misery and suffering in his community. The couple inflicts on others an intensified, nightmare version of the injustice inflicted on all Mexican Americans in their working and private lives, and the unnamed boy "awakens" morally with a new sense of ethical violation in the world's events. Once he can make that connection, seeing that "mishaps" in the book can merge into a larger pattern of social injustice and destructiveness, no longer mere innocent and unconnected events, he is taking the first steps in being able to critique his community's dire circumstances and plan for change.

This same point is made regarding the violence of social degradation in "Los niños no se aguantaron" ("The Children Could Not Wait"), where violence against Mexican Americans is shown to be a social reality and part of the lived horror of the boy's unjust social world. Addressing the idea that bad intentions may exist behind episodes of misfortune, such stories move the boy toward a larger vision of social injustice that could reveal the actual cost and social impact of a failing community.

In the pivotal chapters "La noche estaba plateada" ("The Silvery Night") and " . . . y no se lo tragó la tierra" (" . . . and the Earth Did Not Devour Him"), the boy at last is able to summon his courage, a big step, to critique the profoundly unjust reality of the social order around him. In one of the book's culminating scenes, the boy, like an Old Testament prophet, challenges traditional notions of God's divine plan and demands answers to why people in his community suffer and have little hope for the future. There is a psychological breakthrough in these chapters as the boy reacts to tragedies depicted in the book as revealing social injustice. With this new awareness, the boy begins to question all ethical foundations, including God's existence and divine retribution for sin. His reasoning is that with all of the destruction and "evil" in the world, and with no one held responsible for it, there is no social justice, no world order, and possibly no God.

The asking of such questions in these chapters is a stunning reversal for the boy—a turning point in the novel's development of the boy's social vision. The fact of rampant social injustice in the community suggests to the boy that adversity exists as a broad pattern and that it can be focused upon and understood. So at midnight, he goes to a grassy knoll at a crossroads to find the devil to ask about the world's social injustice. He waits, but no devil shows up, and he then reasons that "if there's no devil maybe there's no punishment." His ultimate worry is that if the devil does not exist, "maybe there also isn't [a God]" (105). In the following passage, he faces that second frightening conclusion: *There is no devil, there is nothing.* The only thing that had been present in the woods was his own voice." He responds with momentary despair but then also with a stronger feeling of being "extremely content about something" when he himself begins to take ownership of the fortunes of the community around him. Realizing that evil does *not* govern the world, he comes to see that people create much of its evil, and this thought is new and liberating to him (106).

His discovery's full force comes in the title chapter, " . . . y no se lo tragó la tierra" (" . . . and the Earth Did Not Devour Him"). After the boy called for the devil and found nothing, the next day his father suffers a sun stroke. The boy laments that "God could care less about the poor" (109). He has the same response again when his brother "began vomiting" from sun poisoning, and the narrator moves ever closer to a social critique of a situation that requires new understanding and an active response (111).

This book's central drama occurs next when, at wit's end over these catastrophes, the boy stands alone in a farm field, summoning his courage and utters the dreaded words that "cursed God." He then teeters precariously between different worlds of belief. Rivera writes that "for a second he saw the earth opening up to devour him," reflecting the religious tradition that says that the Earth swallows whosoever curses God. But then he "felt his [own] footsteps against the earth, compact, more solid than ever" (111). He finally tells himself "that the earth did not devour anyone, nor did the sun." People, not demons and spirits, are responsible for human lives. Surprisingly, "he [now even] felt capable of" accomplishing great things, of "doing and undoing anything that he pleased." He "looked down at the earth and kicked it hard and said[,] 'not yet, you can't swallow me up yet. Someday yes. But I'll never know it" (112).

The full scope of his discovery is not so much theological, a challenge to spiritual beliefs and God in any direct way, as his critique of the material and social conditions of Mexican American life. Cursing "God" is only the boy's way of indicting the unfair social order around him. He yearns to improve that life, exactly as the Chicano movement will do in the period after this story's setting. This young boy now focuses on the big picture of social conditions and contemplates the possibility of effective social change. The next five chapters (9–12) reinforce the boy's discovery that he *can* critique social conditions on behalf of his family and his community.

In "Cuando lleguemos" ("When We Arrive"), the second to the last chapter, an omniscient narrator reports the hopes and fears of migrant workers returning home from work in the migrant stream. "When we get there, . . . I'll turn back." "When we get there I'm gonna see about getting a good bed for my vieja," and so on. The chapter's refrain, "when we arrive . . . ," "when we arrive . . . ," encapsulates the community's hope for the future even when there is no rational basis for such hope. The narrator critiques the palliative effect of such empty aspirations. He judges these attitudes to be the same complacency that has kept his community from working toward needed change. "I'm tired of *arriving*" (italics added), he complains. The "real truth" is that, under present circumstances, with no participation in the culture and little developed skill or training for cultural engagement, "we [in the Mexican American community will] never arrive" (145).

The final chapter, "Debajo de la casa" ("Below the House"), focuses the boy's thoughts about social injustice and closes the book's frame as the boy hides beneath a house while contemplating the social patterns in his life. Once lost, the boy now locates himself in the present moment, at a particular historical time, under a particular house, with a specific Mexican American family moving around above him. While nothing outward in his life has changed, the boy now sees everything differently and has learned "to discover and rediscover and piece things together. This to this, that to that, all with all" (152). He locates himself in a meaningful social and historical reality perhaps for the first time. Previously a person marooned in a dysfunctional community, and living amid great adversity, and fighting distractions all around him, he begins to see the life of family and community and what it could mean to nurture and support those lives. Having "made a discovery" by critiquing his community's social values, he views himself now as someone capable of making great changes, someone who can make a difference in his world.

The transformation in the boy's outlook advances an argument for change in the community based on an understanding of the community's needs. The frame story and the novel's first and last chapters present the personal cost to the narrator of living in a world without social justice and without hope based on a practical vision. The boy's evolving perspective in the middle chapters shows the impact of the community's social stagnation. Finally, the book closes with the critique of the mentality of living in a stagnant community and points toward renewal through the possibility of investing in a vision of the future and new social initiatives.

Whereas "La mano en la bolsa" reveals the brutality of social injustice for Mexican Americans when the unnamed boy stays with the sociopathic couple, piercing the rationalizations for social inequity, "Cuando lleguemos" reveals the baseless, empty myths that the Mexican American community at present relies upon to survive. The chapters in between develop several themes about the degradation and violence that plague Mexican Americans in their lives on the fringes of the American economy. In these chapters, moments of inadvertent violence and cruelty are reframed as patterns of social injustice and the violence done to good people. These are stages in the boy's maturing vision but also in his community's coming of age. This book finally argues for the necessity of choosing between (1) the stymied and deadly social world of the present and (2) the possibility of rebellion initially identified with the devil and the boy's challenge to the social status quo, the vision that will be the actual signature of the Chicano movement and the Chicano Renaissance.

The boy's recognition of social injustice in chapter 7 and the discovery that there is no devil leave him with no rational choice except active engagement with the world to improve it. This evolving response to the prospect of change redirects his perspective toward the cause of his community's degraded lives. Whereas the book's first chapter represents the unnamed boy's personal problems, the chapters after that gradually advance a critique of the community's social and economic situation. The book's final chapter focuses on the boy's changed outlook as a basis for future social action to alter the community's fortunes.

In this book's last chapter, the boy has altered nothing in the world around him (he is only a child), no social change or community rebuilding, and yet his attitude about the possibility and need for social action has been transformed. Prior to chapters 6 and 7, the boy had a mentality and an ethos reflecting the Mexican American community before the Chicano movement. From chapter 6 to chapter 7 and beyond, the boy becomes, in effect, a "Chicano" in terms of communal activism and budding political awareness—his sense of the urgent need to act on his community's behalf.

By telling his own story to overlap with his novel, Rivera aligns his biography, the region's history (a region with people in motion), his novel, and "The Searchers" to create a voice that arises from the pages of these several texts. *Tierra* narrates a story about the Mexican American community's need to champion its own cause as a community, but it is his composite, larger narrative of several texts that creates the distinctive "voice" that is a real achievement. This voice emerges to speak in this novel about Mexican Americans and the nature of social change and the urgency to cultivate and bring forward the focused social awareness that will become the Chicano movement.

Rivera examines the transformation of personal and communal values in the historical period from 1940 to 1960, the period when his own family worked in the migrant stream across the Midwest. His family and community, removed and alienated from mainstream culture, lived in poverty and poor health and struggled against social disintegration. His nameless narrator also records the impact of these economic and social forces shaping his community during this historical era. The story culminates with the discovery of a voice through which to combine the divergent parts of the community's complicated life, what the unnamed boy also seeks personally from his time spent in the crawlspace beneath a house. When that voice speaks, it signals that the boy has become aware of his own alienated perspective and is beginning to see the potential for change. He moves into a Chicano, politicized perspective toward the possibility of community improvement, thus creating the potential for a better life for Mexican Americans. Critiquing the material conditions of social life as they shape community is an important function of voice in this novel, and that voice's persistence is a powerful signature of Rivera's work. The focused intensity of the boy's perception and the distinct images that convey his world combine in Rivera's work to critique social conditions and to initiate the journey toward social justice.

Social critique is imbued in Rivera's secular vision with "the passion of prophecy," a secular view that nonetheless has the power of a spiritual vision (1992a, 291). He speaks in the Bruce-Novoa interview about the "transplanted cultures from Europe, and the fact of the indigenous cultures still being here." In writing *Tierra*, he claims, "I wanted to throw light on the spiritual strength, on the concept of justice so important for the American continents" (Bruce-Novoa 1980, 151). Positing an identity and a sense of self that is characteristic of the Americas as a cultural sphere, he foresees "the capacity and possibility of a much stronger and complete intellectual emancipation" in the Americas than was possible in Europe (151).

Such strength to change comes from the commitment to a cultural and social "sense of movement" and the great importance of being a "searcher" in the Americas for social justice. The unnamed narrator and the other families in *Tierra* resist cultural disintegration by searching for truth as migrant farm workers. "They [migrant farm workers] always kept searching; that's why they were 'migrant' workers," Rivera explains (152). With religious and mythic overtones, he concludes that such searching is "an important metaphor in the Americas," and "to me [migrant workers] were people who searched" for truth (152). The boy narrator wants to see his community build on the truth that they enact in their searching and actually move forward to revitalize their community. In the narrator's words at *Tierra's* end, his goal is "to discover and rediscover and piece things together. This to this, that to that, all with all" (152).

Rivera's voice in this work captures the personal intensity of a young boy in crisis alongside the cultural expansiveness of the hemisphere as a staging for the Americas' cultures. Rivera contrasts the reality and particularity of what happens in the Americas to cultural abstractions and generalities that are European imports. Here Rivera returns to his distaste for imposed dogma, whether it comes from religion, from the public schools, or from European culture. He believed that the truth of the Chicano voice and his own truth as a Mexican American must come from lives actually *lived* in the Americas. He believed that the Mexican American community, in a way that encompasses psychological, political, and spiritual life, had suffered under the imposition of European cultural dogma instead of living with its own knowledge of social conditions and the hemisphere's unique history. "Truth" for Rivera must come from the Mexican American community's experience and social situation and from its economic repositioning in the present. He held to this vision of truth based on the particularity and uniqueness of experience *within* the Americas as a distinctive cultural staging.

THE EMERGENCE OF THE CHICANO VOICE

Projecting a hemispheric cultural identity and a perspective on the Mexican American experience is not unique to Rivera but is defining for the Mexican American and Latino worldview—in part, because of Rivera's influence. That worldview foregrounds the unique history of the Americas, critiques the role that race has played as an organizing force across the Americas, and explores the relationship to land and the importance of the homeland concept. Rivera also has a strong mestizo sense of the materiality of the human body in the Americas, the defining importance of understanding the legacy of los antepasados (the ancestors), and the need to actively advance the cause of mestizo community. Rivera's "voice" attempts to capture these "truths," and the rise of a Chicano voice in his work comes from this focus on these commitments regarding what it means to live in the New World.

It is also clear why this novel is difficult to analyze and interpret. To read this book effectively and to see how its narrative functions require a focus on the novel's relationship to Rivera's own biography, especially his migrant work experience, the involved labyrinth of *Tierra's* experimental, microchapters, the history of the Americas, "The Searchers," and the approach that reveals the narrative's generation of a voice—all opening the way to further social interpretation of this complex work. A narrow focus on the formalistic, restrictive notion of this novel's form—what is on the page in terms of images, motifs, themes, and so on—will fail without the broader view that includes Rivera's biography, his migrant-labor background, and the backdrop of the Americas as dimensions of voice.

The ways that *Tierra* speaks from the Mexican American community's perspective signals an emerging Chicano awareness. The fact that

Rivera's community heard that voice is one indication that his work on behalf of Mexican Americans succeeded. His voice created a mandate for the Chicano Renaissance to build on strength by moving forward in literature, the arts, and social thought. In the present, his voice has not always reached the broad audience of those who came after him, and the discussion in this chapter is intended to open the way to a new understanding of his work.

It is now possible to identify four tenets that, arising from Rivera's work, create a direction forward for the Chicano Renaissance, reference points that this arts and social movement actually followed to orient itself. These tenets combine to produce this novel's voice. But in that this novel helped to create a direction for the Chicano Renaissance, its voice and the cultural values and beliefs that make it up can also be advanced as tenets guiding the cultural, artistic, and social developments of the Mexican American community in the 1970s and beyond.

These cultural tenets can be stated as follows:

1. Validate the hybrid nature of mestizo identity and of being a Mexican American. This tenet comes as knowledge about the boy's exclusion from the white community. Everyone in the narrator's community is a mixed-race person living on the periphery of mainstream, white culture. The narrator is isolated from other children in his school, and the fact that he cannot get a haircut in a white barber shop is an invitation to reapproach and understand mestizo identity in a cultural and historical context appropriate to the Americas. The boy will eventually rebel against such discrimination and begin to focus his identity differently.

One of Rivera's primary messages is to recognize being a Mexican American as a hybrid identity and that this identity has its own context of significance. A mestizo may be invisible to mainstream America, which imposed a strict line of division between being Mexican and American, and he knew that being a Mexican American created a peripheral identity in the United States, one that needed to be framed in a liberating way within the larger staging of the Americas.

Rivera was attempting to refocus the meaning of having a mestizo identity. It is a fundamental contribution of his vision that he presented being a mestizo as a subject and an identity critical to understanding life in the Americas. He wanted mestizos to see that they had a meaningful and revealing history and that they could shape their world's future. Recognizing mixed-race people as the norm in the Americas of the modern era, Rivera wanted to be part of advancing that recognition in the New World.

2. Commit to exploring Mexican American culture as a variety of mestizo, hybrid culture. The hybrid nature of Mexican American culture is everywhere present in the values and practices depicted in this novel. The family consults doctors *and* curanderas, specifically a spiritualista, and this novel focuses on the materiality of the body with an indigenous emphasis on the importance of what happens to brown bodies. Rivera was also sensitive to the fact that Chicano culture was an emerging phenomenon in the Americas coming into being during his life time. He was aware, sometimes painfully so, that as a pioneer he was writing about a "grotesque" hybrid culture that mainstream American culture little recognized and at critical junctures even ignored and rejected. Rivera, Rudolfo Anaya, Rodolfo Gonzales, and other early Chicano authors faced the great difficulty of getting published and of being recognized for their unprecedented achievements, and this experience, sometimes awkward and sometimes painful, left a deep impression on Rivera and the writers of his generation.

He also understood that Chicano culture, as an emergent culture, would move through different cycles of development and, at times, would continue to appear "grotesque" as it experimented with different initiatives and ways of presenting itself. He wanted to acknowledge mestizo culture in the Americas and allow for new ways to present and understand Mexican Americans in the present. *Tierra* itself is the best example of an unorthodox, "grotesque" product at a certain phase of an emerging culture in that it was a dramatic break from the Anglo-American novel tradition and a challenging text to decipher and appreciate. Like all important, large-scale departures from literary history, this mestizo, mixed-culture novel has gradually created its own readership.

3. Acknowledge the broad historical and cultural setting for under-standing the Chicano community in the hemispheric view of the Americas. The theme of people in motion searching for a "truth" in their lives runs throughout this novel, and Rivera also makes that pattern explicit in the Bruce-Novoa interview. The theme of "searching" on the stage of the Americas establishes that this novel belongs in that cultural setting. This tenet involves a dramatic change of perspective. The coordinates for Rivera's work are not those of traditional American literature with its New England fascination but the north-south coordinates that come with seeing the Americas as the context for this hemisphere's life and culture. This perspective includes the traditional contributions of European cultures, but Rivera's is a broad view that also focuses on the New World's mestizo peoples up through the current period.

This perspective is resetting the cultural compass to orient toward the whole of the Americas as the proper reference for cultural and demographic developments, a stage grander than any single chapter in that larger, hemispheric story. Rivera's work makes the connection between his own life as a migrant farm worker and the traditional legacy of people "searching" for "truth" all through the Americas. Continual searching is not a failure of community but a cultural signature that defines the Americas as a cultural and social sphere where its citizens seek the "truths" that are theirs to search for and claim.

4. Commit to an activist approach to building community. *Tierra* moves toward a culminating transformation in the title chapter where the boy narrator finds the courage to act forthrightly based on his own beliefs and concerns. He becomes a person who will change his own life and invest in his community to help it grow and evolve. The boy, who is not afraid to curse God when he feels abandoned and betrayed, will also be the man courageous enough to engage with the Chicano movement to make his community better, a transformation that will make him a community builder.

A central theme in *Tierra* is the need for the community to act on its own behalf, and a "Chicano" dimension of Rivera's voice is its commitment to advance the Mexican American community in economic, political, and cultural terms. The major development for *Tierra's* unnamed boy is to conclude that the inertia he sees around him leads nowhere. While we do not watch the narrator mature and take respon- sibility to rebuild his community, the novel's critique of social passivity (always returning to the dream of "when we arrive") directs him to be socially proactive and engaged, as the Chicano movement itself will do in rebuilding its community for a better future. The unnamed boy's transformation at novel's end says that he is prepared to move beyond the empty platitudes about a better day. His new charge, growing out of his discoveries in the crawlspace under a house, is to embrace the chal- lenge to make a difference for his community by taking responsibility for himself and the world around him.

These four tenets coalesce to form a cultural voice and signify a community's growth, the commitment to strengthen community and extend its cultural and social impact. The voice that this novel helps to create focuses on the day-to-day life of being a Mexican American migrant farm worker, and that focus is one of this novel's strengths. The background texts for *Tierra,* especially Bruce-Novoa's Rivera interview, "The Searchers," and Rivera's knowledge of the Americas also help to situate *Tierra* in relation to core tenets that create a new voice for the Mexican American community. These tenets, different parts of a single voice, show that the Chicano community, more than an ethnic label, is a perspective, an attitude, a way of living in the world, and a particular awareness of the Americas' past. The Chicano "voice" gen- erated through these tenets speaks about the ancient peoples of the New World as los antepasados, the Americas as the mestizo homeland, and the mestizo as the Americas' citizen. Rivera's voice also resembles the many voices of the present Chicano and Latino world that he influ- enced. These voices are calling the Mexican American community to come home, as *Mestizos Come Home!* shows and as Rivera intended, and they are gradually speaking about the future of the United States as the home that he envisioned so long ago.

CHAPTER 7

Write Home!

CHICANO LITERATURE, CHICANO STUDIES, AND RESOLANA

Gaining recognition in the early 1970s, Chicano literature and Chicano studies distinguished themselves with important achievements in literature and social thought. Finding early success with a talented first wave of writers, Chicano literature gave Mexican Americans a forum for exploring their own culture and a direct line of communication to the nation. Chicano studies instituted courses and programs in higher education to recognize the Mexican American community and assist young people to prepare for a better future. Chicano literature and Chicano studies together chronicled Mexican American life, helped the community to clarify its goals, and sought to establish new economic and social ties with the U.S. mainstream. These initiatives of the 1970s continue as successful ways of understanding culture and community. In the early twenty-first century, the promotion of resolana (a traditional town hall approach to governance and generating new knowledge) creates especially helpful perspectives to enhance those initiatives.

In the early 1970s, Mexican Americans took a major step toward being at home in U.S. culture when they launched Chicano literature, the sixth area of Mexican American cultural innovation treated in this book. Like the generation of a Chicano "voice," Chicano literature was not a reframing of culture already in place, as was the case with mestizo identity, land, the body, and popular culture. It created something new, with Chicano studies following in tandem. Chicano literature and Chicano studies—most helpfully discussed together, as I will make clear—touch on every aspect of community in complex ways. These were cultural achievements larger than anything that Mexican

Americans had attempted. . . . *y no se lo tragó la tierra* and *Bless Me, Ultima,* early milestones of the new literature, were breakthrough novels foreshadowing this literature's rapid development. These works caught the attention of the literary world and galvanized other cultural and social projects in the Mexican American community. At decade's end, this sophisticated, new branch of American literature was thriving and attracting the world's attention.

With Chicano literature's and Chicano studies' rise, Mexican Americans as a community could reflect on their own social and economic direction, examine their interactions with the larger culture, tighten the bonds of community, and reevaluate their common values and goals—the traditional by-products of the literary enterprise. Chicano literature advanced a progressive vision, cultural pride, and a community-building spirit, all values of the Chicano movement and Chicano Renaissance. This literature fostered a strong sense of community and a common culture. It tended to foreground issues relating to the revitalization of culture as more pressing than mere assimilation into the U.S. mainstream, a crucial point of influence encouraged by Rivera and Anaya. That judgment, ranking community and cultural development above assimilation, engendered specific expectations for Chicano literature's role in the cultural reinvigoration that followed and also signaled an opening for a new relationship to the U.S. mainstream. Today, Chicano literature is a successful enterprise read and studied internationally.

In the forefront of establishing this new literary identity, Tomás Rivera and Rudolfo Anaya were writers and public intellectuals committed to keeping literary and cultural momentum moving forward. In addition to their novels, they wrote essays on education, civil liberties, land issues, and the literary influences on their own and others' works. They toured the American Southwest promoting Chicano literature, often appearing with Rolando Hinojosa, the Texas writer of the *Klail City Death Trip* series. In their work as cultural ambassadors on the national stage, they sought recognition of their culture, served on advisory panels, and directed attention to emerging authors. At decade's end, however, it was Anaya who emerged with a growing national and international following.

With a vision for Chicano literature and the engaged Chicano life that he pursued as a writer, teacher, and supporter of the community, Anaya was a gifted storyteller, educator, and keen cultural observer. He produced a classic modern novel, *Bless Me, Ultima,* as his first publication and set high standards for subsequent literature, some of which I discussed in earlier chapters on mestizo identity, land, and the Chicano voice. Recognizing the New World's ancient peoples as cultural ancestors and Mexican Americans as cultural citizens, he asked for recognition of the hemisphere as the proper frame for understanding mestizo identity and culture and argued that anything else would disempower Mexican Americans.

Rivera spoke through his writing and his administrative work in higher education. With a commitment to telling the migrant story, he sought "to document the migrant worker para siempre [forever]" and celebrate Mexican American "spiritual strength" as well as the community's work on behalf of social justice and cultural development (Bruce-Novoa 1980, 150–51). Documenting lives surviving "under the worst of conditions," he urged his community to build upon strength, especially affirming cultural ties to the United States and the Americas. Believing in education's value and literature's contribution to cultural understanding, he indicted public education and the Catholic Church for not supporting his community to make a difference when help was needed most (150). He tried to remedy these lapses by focusing his own work intently on the hard choices that Mexican Americans faced to reinvigorate their community—choices that they actually *did* face when they inaugurated the Chicano movement and Chicano Renaissance. He opposed all that blocked his community from improving its social, cultural, and economic life.

The first generation of Chicano literature through the 1970s produced writers still read and important today. In addition to Anaya and Rivera, this group includes Oscar Zeta Acosta, Lorna Dee Cervantes, Luis Omar Salinas, and Estela Portillo Trambley—all writers who focused on the four dimensions of the Chicano voice presented in the last chapter. They were giving recognition to mestizo identity, exploration of mestizo (hybrid) culture, a sense of mestizo culture's hemispheric staging, and a commitment to self-determination.[1] Also, initiating discussions of racial discrimination, community empowerment, and cultural reinvigoration, writers in this period sought to gain perspective on Mexican American life and values. Through robust literary engagement, they generally succeeded at these tasks. This first generation of Chicano writers, many of whom still write for a large readership, has since become the Chicano "canon" of authors taught in high school and college classrooms.

In the 1980s and 1990s, a second wave of Chicano writers, many of whom were baby boomers attending universities and colleges, addressed the moral and ethical issues discussed in mainstream culture—questions relating to religious faith, strengthening a sense of ethnic identity in a diverse society, racial discrimination, women's culture, feminism, immigration, and so on.[2] Many established national and international reputations equal to first-wave writers—most notably, Gloria E. Anzaldúa, Ana Castillo, Denise Chávez, Sandra Cisneros, Demetria Martínez, Gary Soto, Luis Alberto Urrea, and Helena María Viramontes. These writers adopted the cultural voice of the first generation, and most of these highly prolific writers also became part of the canon of writers being taught in college classrooms.

A third wave of young writers, dating from 2000, continues into the present and includes many third-generation Mexican Americans, some with only a few published titles. These writers focus on ties to Mexican and Latin American culture that they are in danger of losing through U.S. acculturation and assimilation.[3] Some of these writers—Adelina Anthony, Reyna Grande, Laurie Ann Guerrero, Domingo Martínez, Maceo Montoya, Daniel A. Olivas, Melinda Palacio, Patricia Santana, Carla Trujillo, Alfredo Véa Jr., and Mario Alberto Zambrano—are finding new directions for Chicano literature focused on border culture, gender roles, the Mexican past, issues of Mexican American identity, and community cohesiveness. They address many of the same issues of the first wave, except now they are *refinding* such topics as still relevant to their U.S. lives.

All of these writers adopted the Chicano "voice," which I discussed in chapter 6, and demonstrated that Chicano literature continues to function as the chronicler, in Rivera's words, of Mexican American "spiritual strength." As the Chicano movement founders hoped for, these writers continue to explore Chicano traditions, mestizo identity, and hybrid culture with an underlying commitment to work toward social justice. There is historical irony in the fact that all of this cultural development—the proliferation of Chicano and Latino literature, articles on the culture, specialized magazines, and films—has happened so quickly. Through the early 1960s, there was *no* Chicano literature and no Chicano studies programs in U.S. schools and colleges, not in California, and not in New Mexico or Texas. And then in the short span from 1967 through the early 1970s, there was the rise of Chicano literature *and* Chicano studies programs.

In 1968, Ralph Guzman, a political science professor, started the first Chicano studies program at California State College, Los Angeles. And in April 1969, students at the University of California, Santa Barbara, drafted *El Plan de Santa Barbara,* a 155-page document calling for the institution of Chicano studies programs across American higher education. These programs were frequently a mix of degree requirements, spot-on social critiques, cultural aspirations, and left-leaning manifestos that called for decisive and often sweeping social action. Other programs quickly followed, although few were as ambitious as *El Plan de Santa Barbara* called for (Acuña 2011, 59).

These higher education initiatives and the three waves of Chicano writers remain part of a productive dialogue, a special relationship, between Chicano literature and Chicano studies. With the launch of Chicano literature in the early 1970s, many young Chicano writers were already attending colleges offering Chicano studies courses. In the early 1970s, responding to *El Plan de Santa Barbara* and pressure from students, university and college faculty offered more courses focused around Mexican American literature, history, and sociology. By the mid-1970s, especially in the Midwest and Southwest, such offerings were reframed as "Chicano studies" and were becoming a formal part of American higher education. Focusing on literature, history, art, and sociology, this new initiative had the same impulse found in Chicano literature to fulfil a kind of watchdog function by standing guard over the Mexican American experience.

Without trained specialists in the new field, creative writers, immersed in their culture and articulate about history and art, taught in the new programs. Rudolfo Anaya, Tomás Rivera, Helena María

Viramontes, Lorna Dee Cervantes, and, later, Denise Chávez, and many others wrote best-selling works while teaching Chicano studies in English or Chicano studies programs. It became commonplace for famous writers to be the new discipline's professors. To this day, Chicano literature and Chicano studies overlap with active mutual influence—writers taking up key teaching and administrative posts in higher education while Chicano professors move in and out of the professional writing world.

Amid 1970s social unrest, Chicano studies promoted cultural pride and championed Mexican American civil rights. Paralleling the activities of the 1960s African American civil rights movement, the Chicano movement sponsored farm labor strikes (following upon farm labor movements in the 1930s), nationwide grape and lettuce boycotts, school walkouts (or "blowouts") in east Los Angeles at Garfield and Lincoln High Schools, among others, and *La Raza Unida*'s popular political challenge as an alternative to the Democratic Party in Texas (Acuña 2011, 27). It was also during this period in April 1969 that students formed the Movimiento Estudiantil Chicano de Aztlán (MEChA) (Acuña 2011, 166), a group of student activists who on occasion have been accused of being too partisan in support of Mexican American students. They have continued to be effective in serving and promoting the student community through the present. The early 1970s reinvigoration of Mexican American culture has little precedent in American history for a dramatic reemergence of a people, one measure of that success being the four hundred programs in higher education nationally that specialize in Chicano, Mexican American, or Latino studies (see the directory of the National Association for Chicana and Chicano Studies at www.naccs.org; Acuña 2011).

Eventually staffed with writers, historians, sociologists, and political scientists, Chicano studies programs currently analyze the Mexican American experience and also changing perspectives on U.S. national culture in the Americas, often with a critique of traditional American studies. These programs have always had a double focus on the United States in the context of the Americas pertinent to understanding Mexican American culture. Such programs explore this evolving community, especially assimilation into American culture in relation to enduring ties to Mexican culture. For over forty-five years, such approaches to inter-disciplinary studies have provided resources to train and inspire effective citizens and future Mexican American leaders and professionals.

Those defining the early Chicano studies curricula were both inside and outside of the academy. Poet and political organizer Rodolfo "Corky" Gonzales, the poet Alurista, the poet Lorna Dee Cervantes, artist Ester Hernandez, and playwright and film director Luis Valdez were "outside" and wrote, painted, directed, and in other ways contributed to what Chicanos knew about their culture. Others "inside" of the academy—for example, Ralph Guzmán and Rodolfo F. Acuña (the author also of *Occupied America*)—brought historical and cultural critiques to Chicano studies. By the later 1970s, creative writers and scholars trained in Spanish, Romance languages, history, and English were the developers of Chicano studies programs at Cal-State, Northridge, the University of California, Los Angeles, the University of Texas, the University of Minnesota, and others (Acuña 2011, 57). Their focus was on alternative course offerings meant to supplement standard requirements in U.S. history, literary studies, sociology, anthropology, and art in a formal, academic context—all of which created a new college major.

Consider again the remarkable sequence of this history: a migrant labor movement (reflecting labor struggles since the 1930s) begins in the early 1960s in Delano, California, and then mushrooms into a national wave of protests and boycotts. Then in the early 1970s, a cultural renaissance begins in literature with Tomás Rivera's . . . *y no se lo tragó la tierra*, Rudolfo Anaya's *Bless Me, Ultima*, Estela Portillo Trambley's *Rain of Scorpions*, in theatre with Luis Valdez's El Teatro Campesino, and in every other dimension of culture and the humanities. In the 1970s in American universities and colleges, Chicano culture framed as Chicano studies got recognized on a par with other programs and offerings. The Chicano Renaissance had positive repercussions all through the 1980s and 1990s in literature and the arts, with success in economic development in some Chicano communities but a persistent poor record of reform in public primary and secondary education.

The four areas of focus in Chicano studies reflect the cultural commitments of writers and scholars during this period. First is the metaphor of cultural "healing," a reference to making people "healthy" (personally but also as a community) and also a perspective on how writers and artists try to bridge or possibly close the gap between Mexican and American culture. Second is the reassessment of gender roles, particularly in regard to women's identity, and a progressive approach to defining gender in relation to cultural politics. Third is the reclamation of the Americas' indigenous and colonial past, the attempt to reestablish cultural and historical connections between the Spanish colonial period and the present day. Fourth is the need to critique and update the theoretical foundations of Chicano studies to keep it relevant and impactful, the way in which Chicano studies has kept itself focused and necessary for the Mexican American community.

Touching on issues of ongoing importance in the Chicano community, the metaphor of "healing" is in one sense about personal, communal, and social health concerns and traditional folk remedies—actual people needing treatment for diseases and health issues. This healing tradition combines, as Robert T. Trotter II and Juan Antonio Chavira say in *Curanderismo: Mexican American Folk Healing*, "Judeo-Christian religious beliefs, symbols, and rituals; early Arabic medicine and health practices (combined with Greek humoral medicine, revived during the Spanish Renaissance). This traditional healing also involved medieval and later European witchcraft; Native American herbal lore and health practices; modern beliefs about spiritualism and psychic phenomena; and scientific medicine" (1997, 25). While overlapping at times with Western allopathic medicine, curanderismo (Mexican American natural healing) differs from Western practices by focusing intently on a person's body-environment interaction and the social context of illness, as opposed to the Western tradition of treating the body in a cultural vacuum. In New Mexico, doctors even refer patients to curanderas who are licensed by the state as midwives.

Healing also has overtones of the need to remedy the disruptions to indigenous cultures during the Spanish conquest. The Spanish made the Americas "ill" with their upsetting of communal and cultural traditions in the Americas, and curanderismo (indigenous healing) also has broad cultural implications going beyond treating disease. As a "healing" practice, it has a counterinstitutional appeal connected with its indigenous, mestizo perspectives and origins. Comprised of healing strategies originating in the Americas' ancient cultures, this practice implicitly comments on the hemisphere's history. One of its undercurrents says that many spiritual and psychological afflictions result from the social and cultural fragmentation brought about by the residue of colonial oppression in the Americas—what I called earlier "postcolonial stress disorder." As Ultima's "remedies" show in *Bless Me, Ultima,* curanderismo often competes with Western medicine and the Catholic Church as a spiritual guide. The curandera acts as the agent of a suppressed culture who treats the personal and communal "ailments" that are, in part, the legacy of colonial oppression. With its indigenous orientation and somewhat subversive status, curanderismo is a trace of rebellion against the colonial past and remains at some level subversive of European culture's authority. Spanish and Portuguese cultures in the Americas have colonized but have never entirely defeated indigenous peoples.

Anaya shows curanderismo to exist within a broad cultural spectrum that has strongly influenced Chicano literature. From the landmark *Bless Me, Ultima* to the recent Sonny Baca novels (*Zia Summer, Rio Grande Fall, Shaman Winter,* and *Jemez Spring*), Anaya defines "healing" in "Shaman of Words" as a "journey of reintegration" illuminated by the writer who acts on behalf of an entire community (1999a, 25). The writer-as-curandero's task is to reunite the fragments of culture insofar as "healing" reintegrates the Chicano community's "[colonized] soul" through the social, economic, and spiritual advances that restore the "order and harmony" that the community lost in 1521 (the year of the Spanish conquest of the Aztecs) and 1848 (when the United States annexed northern Mexico). Even these dates have a monumental, iconic status, bearing the weight of so much cultural and historical reinterpretation, as well as actual political and social import. Anaya in particular has understood the importance of "healing" a culture, restoring a once-lost balance in one of Chicano literature's and culture's defining narratives.

Similar tensions play out in Chicano studies' second theme, the reassessment of gender roles in society, one of Chicano studies' most innovative developments. Often framing this area of inquiry within a hemispheric context, Chicana feminists such as Debra Castillo in *Talking Back: Toward a Latin American Feminist Literary Criticism* recognize an existing trans–Latin American feminist community that includes Mexicans, Chicanas, and other Latin American women—a hemispheric community that these writers want to thrive. Sonia Saldívar-Hull's *Feminism on the Border: Chicana Gender Politics and Literature* and Anna Marie Sandoval's *Toward a Latina Feminism of the Americas* champion the overarching cultural frame comprised of women uniting across the Americas. The cultural conversation of such a community could lead to "political commitment and community connection," benefits that would sponsor an increasingly stronger female sense of community in the hemisphere (Sandoval 2008, xvi).

This direction for Chicana activism tends to bypass U.S. mainstream feminism, the movement of middle-class, largely white women that started in the 1970s. In "The Tools in the Toolbox: Representing Work in Chicana Writing," Chicana feminist scholar Tey Diana Rebolledo supports not so much a utopian view of what women could achieve if "liberated" (as early "Anglo" feminism often emphasized) but what mestizo women have *already achieved* in domestic work and child care. "Ironing, cooking, cleaning house, and taking care of children" are all tasks that "maintain life and support the family, but have not been considered *real* work." Rebolledo examines the work of Denise Chávez, Pat Mora, Helena María Viramontes, and others to show that "contemporary Chicana writers have represented women's work [i.e., what they already do] as challenging and heroic." Through such attitudes about the nature of women's "work and its meaning," Chicana writers enter the "realm of [self] understanding and valuing themselves" (1999, 42).

B. J. Manriquez points out the dangers in Chicana feminism of treating literary texts as transparent *social* documents, sociological in orientation rather than aesthetic. This is a danger for a community that has pressing social needs and a sense of urgency to find answers. She argues for reading literature in its own context and recognizing its ties, at the same time, to "ideology, context, and literary interpretation" (1999, 53). The task should be to see how Chicana fiction functions in an aesthetic realm to advance ideology, which in turn advances *social* causes—how mere words and their aesthetic effects contribute to social and economic progress on behalf of Mexican Americans.

These often side-stepped questions can be difficult to resolve. Kristin Carter-Sanborn raises such questions in "Tongue-Tied: Chicana

Feminist Textual Politics and the Future of Chicano/Chicana Studies," asking why those who identify themselves as Chicanas at times feel compelled, as Cherríe Moraga and Ana Castillo have been, to deny literature's impact outside of cultural politics and *real* social concerns. Carter-Sanborn shows that some of Castillo's later fiction reigns in the fictional play of meaning in order to be more direct and unambiguous about having a "message" (1999, 77). Carter-Sanborn's questions also prompt the awareness that the construction of aesthetic effects *is* cultural work and necessarily operates in a medium of power and knowledge. Institutions of power and knowledge, in turn, operate in service to social values and goals—hence the connection between aesthetics, politics, and ideology. Chicana writers address these issues in a variety of ways and write fiction that has cultural *and* political significance.

The third theme is the reclamation of the Americas' indigenous and colonial past, that is, a recognition of the power of Spanish colonialism still being felt in Mexican and Mexican American culture—what Aníbal Quijano calls the "coloniality of power" (2000, 533). The horizon of that context is the past of the Americas from which Mexican American culture continues to draw much of its identity. Such inquiry focuses on the history of the Americas' ancient peoples through the period of contact and Spanish conquest culture. The aim in this area is the recognition of a lost past that is still having an impact in the Americas, one often hidden or covered over by layers of colonial culture—issues that *Mestizos Come Home!* is directed toward unmasking.

María Herrera-Sobek's work typifies this important and often neglected area of Chicano studies. Her book *The Mexican Corrido: A Feminist Analysis,* her collection (with David R. Maciel) *Culture across Borders: Mexican Immigration and Popular Culture,* and her three-volume set *Celebrating Latino Folklore: An Encyclopedia of Cultural Traditions* demonstrate her broad commitment to understanding Chicano literature and culture in the context of the Americas. In her article "Gaspar Pérez de Villagrá's Memorial: Aristotelian Rhetoric and the Discourse of Justification in a Colonial Genre," she focuses on a text by Pérez de Villagrá exposing the "unbounded power [that] many conquistadors wielded in their respective provinces to the detriment of the Native American population" (1999, 97). Her discussion, focused on the genre of New World "memorials," letters sent from the New World to the Spanish king, brings together indigenous history, culture, and European literary influences in the analysis of a revealing moment in New Spain's culture and history that is still impacting Mexican Americans.

The fourth area of Chicano studies is the critique of Chicano studies itself, the need to revise Chicano studies in response to theoretical developments, relevant cultural issues, and social change. Methodological skepticism in service to a distressed and threatened community has historically been Chicano studies' strong suit. Take, for example, the ongoing critique of Chicano studies from community activist Tomás Atencio, who at Chicano studies' inception regretted that the activities of the Chicano movement (union organizing, boycotting stores, school walkouts, and social protests in the 1960s) resulted in the mere founding of a "university discipline" such as Chicano studies—a critique that those in the academy would be less likely to advance. He believed that Chicanos should have been more ambitious about cultural change given that Mexican Americans had been left behind by industrial society's educational wing. And then "when we [were] at the threshold of a postindustrial world, the university [offered] us the ideological drippings of its industrial legacy" in the form of a college *major* (Atencio 2009, 16). He asks, "Why should we Chicanos want access to the waning industrial society?" "Should we not prepare ourselves [instead]," he goes on, "for a direct transition from a preindustrial to a postindustrial age?" (17).

Atencio also highlights the tension between curatorship and critique. Much of what has happened in Chicano studies has been about preserving Mexican American cultural practices and traditions, especially the conventional wisdom that Atencio calls "el oro del barrio" ("communal gold"). "El oro del barrio" is the total set of "values, wisdom, and applied knowledge that assured both meaning and survival to the Mexican American community within the dominant U.S. industrial society" (9). This knowledge is often "subjugated," dismissed by mainstream culture as inconsequential and not worthy of being represented outside of folkloric traditions in small communities. El oro del barrio can be found in the distinctive mixes of Tejano, Californio, Nuevo

Mexicano, and other Mexican American cultures. Mexican American culture has traditionally revered los antepasados, the ancestors, as the ones who created el oro del barrio and with such contributions made the present life possible and sustainable.

It is fitting that one preoccupation of Chicano studies has been the el oro del barrio thread connecting the social, communal, and cultural past and present so that the practices of the ancestors—from folklore and the family to natural healing and indigenous religions—are not lost in American commercial mass culture. From this perspective, support for maintaining ties to the past is a major responsibility of the Chicano community, whether through instituting Chicano studies, speaking Spanish, or sustaining community organizations.

In opposition to cultural curatorship is the activity of critique, scrutiny of underlying theoretical and cultural assumptions. Consider Rafael Pérez-Torres's theoretical challenge in "Whither Aztlán?" to the Chicano curatorship function when he questions the usefulness of the established terms "Chicano" and "Chicana" and prefers the inclusive concept of "mestizaje," a term that highlights "the ambiguity and productive antagonisms with which Chicano studies deals when it abjures a reliance upon the ontological category 'Chicano/a.'" Questioning the older term's ontological status, Pérez-Torres and others in American cultural studies have worked at the edges of Chicano studies to reset its boundaries, asking what it means ideologically to be a "Chicano" or "Chicana," and to what degree the dominant culture dictates and controls these terms and their significance. He asks, does Chicano studies advance the liberating goals it was created for, and to what extent has it become a nonthreatening and even accommodating "other" to the dominant discourse (1999, 111)?

Pérez-Torres's theoretical critique counters the settled nature of el oro del barrio. His preference for keeping Chicano studies under theoretical scrutiny, as an ongoing strategy of political and cultural reorientation and critique, encourages Chicano studies to "reach out more actively to those intellectual, political, and academic projects which will help it raise ever more difficult—and ever more important—questions in its continued quest for inclusivity and liberation" (113). Michael Soldatenko notes that this tension between curatorship and critique has always been part of Chicano studies, what he calls the rift between "perspectivist Chicano Studies," grounded in Mexican American cultural and social life, and theoretically oriented approaches.[4]

Take the example of two important works in Chicano studies on border culture—Américo Paredes's *"With His Pistol in His Hand": A Border Ballad and Its Hero* and José David Saldívar's *Border Matters: Remapping American Cultural Studies*. Both works treat influential traditions of U.S.-Mexican border culture such as the corrido (ballad), the novel, cuentos (stories), healing, and the "jest." As Tomás Rivera commented in 1980, Paredes's early work was catalytic in demonstrating that "it was possible to talk about a Chicano as a complete figure" and that a possible scholarly understanding could emerge from a focus on hybrid fields of culture contained in Mexican American traditions (Bruce-Novoa 1980, 150). Once that box of culture was opened, scholars and writers, potentially everyone, could celebrate the social and cultural traditions of U.S.-Mexican border culture and analyze their significance. Rivera's point is that it took Paredes to open the box.

Now add to this picture José David Saldívar's *Border Matters: Remapping American Cultural Studies*, a work directly challenging to traditional assumptions expressed in American culture and American studies. Saldívar critiques institutional practices and tendencies that create monolithic views of the U.S. national culture as mapped unto a traditional national identity, the tradition saying that there is one encompassing way to be "American." Once in place, that comfortable picture of a seamless U.S. national culture will attempt to encompass the entirety of the American experience and subsidiary developments like Mexican American culture, which can then be dismissed as not relevant to the national culture's interests. Whereas Paredes argues for giving scholarly attention to Mexican American cultural traditions, Saldívar exposes "the specific calculus of the U.S.-Mexico border-crossing condition" that creates a much less unified and far more complex cultural picture than American Studies has been willing to recognize (1997, 197). Saldívar attempts to expose the mechanism of "local processes and global forces, such as Euro-imperialism, colonialism, patriarchy, and economic and political hegemonies" as these forces do the work of producing "shifting and shifty versions of border culture" (35).

Under such scrutiny, the picture of a seamless national culture dissolves into a contest of different cultural forces and social interests taking place on the border. Such methodological skepticism honors the achievements of Paredes's generation of Mexican American scholars, but it also aims to disrupt settled notions of Mexican American culture, American culture, and even Chicano traditions to challenge the reign of powerful classes and elitist ideologies. To effect this critique means critiquing the traditional notion of national identity to expose "the terrors of border crossing and diaspora," the unsavory, lethal reality masked by values and effects associated with "manifest destiny and the cultures of U.S. imperialism." With such goals in mind, Saldívar's *Border Matters* moves toward a remapping of American cultural forces ever in motion and sends a reminder to "those made anxious by diaspora's borders that millions of new (im)migrants" are settling in the United States as we speak and continue to operate according to the "calculus of the U.S.-Mexico border-crossing condition" (197).

The cultural shift depicted here, starting with the recognition of a neglected community (Paredes) and moving toward a significant "remapping of American cultural studies" (Saldívar), is a change intended to enhance understanding of the complex Mexican American presence in the United States. Paredes and Saldívar each mark different entry points into U.S. cultural history and in the contest of competing cultural and ideological forces. Both honor the existence of el oro del barrio, but Saldívar frames cultural production in terms of the ideological commitments that produce culture and the appearance of cultural continuity to begin with. He wants to recognize many different versions of el oro del barrio as they interact and compete at the border where cultures meet, his goal being to remove the misdirections that hide the conflicting values and mechanisms of cultural conflict.

Cultural critique in this view is a deeply skeptical practice that, as Pérez-Torres notes in "Whither Aztlán?," "interrogates productively the relation between knowledge and power, to investigate why certain forms of knowledge are made to appear natural while others are relegated to the realm of the exotic" (1999, 104). This practice of critique marks a tension running throughout Chicano studies, as Soldatenko notes, (1) to replicate and transmit traditions and (2) to critique those traditions as they mask the present moment's politics and ideological concerns. The first impulse is archival and conservative. The second is analytical and transformative. Approaches to Chicano studies tend to emphasize one side or the other (sometimes both), and the cultural, philosophical, *and* political issues articulated on each side provide a rubric for framing and interpreting the diversity of work that comes under the heading of Chicano and Chicana studies.

When Chicano studies emerged in the late 1960s as one of the fronts of the Mexican American civil rights movement, it was a main interpreter of these conflicts, highlighting the hybrid, hyphenated nature of its work. But in the early twenty-first century, the very notion of Chicano studies can be viewed as an inquiry with its own potentially conflicted motives—perpetuating itself as a university discipline (a major), with built-in conservative tendencies in light of having territory to protect versus the critique of cultural production done in the name of the Mexican American community's socioeconomic positioning in U.S. culture.

These four directions of Chicano studies do not represent *all* that is going on in Chicano studies, or what *should* be going on in Chicano studies, all of which is too diverse to fit neatly into any one scheme. The tendency in each direction given is to replicate the tension between curatorship and (theoretical) critique as an ongoing focus. There is also a tendency for each thematic area or critical direction to proclaim itself as the encompassing perspective, the one approach to Chicano studies dominating *all* of the others. Chicano studies' brief history and its diversity of approaches suggest that no one direction of this larger undertaking is likely to assimilate everything Chicano studies does.

Fairly recently, Miguel Montiel, Tomás Atencio, and E. A. Mares advanced a provocative vision for how Chicano studies may accommo-date both the curator and critique dimensions of its work. They exam-ine the traditional notion of resolana to discover new possibilities for framing inquiry and knowledge. An archaic Spanish word (from "resol," meaning reflection of the sun), "resolana" is a reference to "the sunny side of buildings where villagers [*resolaneros*] gather to talk while iso-lated from the elements" (2009, 4). An ancient cultural practice that one can still observe in northern New Mexico, where villagers have gathered for generations to solve the day's problems, resolana contrasts to Chicano cultural studies housed behind walls, fences, and hallways in the academy. The resolana practice is a folk tradition native to New Mexico that emphasizes community "dialogue and reflection" and the sharing of knowledge in a protected communal environment (6). Montiel, Atencio, and Mares's work on resolana is not "theoretical" in the terms associated with the "remapping" of American cultural studies, and their discussion of resolana moves the practice of cultural criticism *outside* of the academy and into the community.

Resolana goes beyond personal dialogue with reflection and focusing on bringing together different kinds of knowledge that in the past have been treated to be incompatible. As a practice, resolana potentially unites (1) traditional knowledge and wisdom, (2) new knowledge produced by digital and online technology, and (3) critique as a mode of analysis that probes the underlying values and connections in social and cultural practices (7). Montiel, Atencio, and Mares especially value the potential in resolana to recognize traditional knowledge that has been suppressed or has not been valued *alongside* new knowledge produced by technology, modern science, and theoretical speculation. Believing that diverse areas of knowledge can coexist—at some level, have always coexisted—these authors develop a contemporary version of resolana in response to the fragmentation of postmodern, digital culture, and lost connections in the modern world among vital communal activities. They comment that especially "learning has become separated from practice." Once that happens—when knowledge does not serve the community that produced it—information is easily reduced to being a commodity and will become transferrable on the commercial market of ideas to the highest bidder and eventually only to the affluent (32).

They believe that the resolana practice can be implemented in contemporary digital culture as a force to strengthen the pursuit of knowledge but also democracy. They emphasize that the tradition of resolana accommodates diverse areas of knowledge with the aim of putting knowledge in service to its community—the indigenous emphasis on taking action that I discussed in the introduction and chapter 2. The "subjugated" knowledge that resolana "uncovers [in el oro de barrio] can be integrated with the knowledge and human skills necessary to adapt and transform the institutions of the postindustrial age" (4). Much like the perspective of ecofemism in Vandana Shiva's work, where there is an argument for elevating traditional knowledge to be the *equal partner* of modern forms of critique and theoretical speculation (1998, viii), resolana is above all a means for reintroducing community participation into the production and reproduction of knowledge. Resolana does this by recapturing and enhancing "(a) the wisdom traditional societies bring to bear in their adaptation to the industrial age; (b) resolana in action in community dialogues; and (c) network theory with its dispassionate view of cultural linkages as a basis for community cohesion, the democratic exchange of ideas, and the concerns for a global community" (Montiel et al. 2009, 5). The picture emerges of inquirers dialoguing in community and engaging with social issues as they always have, but now they are connecting with each other *and* beyond themselves globally through digital information networks.

Resolana presents a possible future for Chicano studies not as a prescription for themes or issues to investigate but, as Raul Yzaguirre describes, as "both a place and a process, a noun and a verb," an opportunity for situating inquiry and discovery in an interim space in the community no longer confined to higher education to reach new levels of impact and communal connection (Montiel et al. 2009, vii). Resolana could potentially close the gap between what people *used* to know as part of living in traditional communities *and* technological and theoretical knowledge as what people *may* know now in the current age and in the future.

Atencio narrates the story of learning from his Tío Eliseo about the superiority of planting native chili seeds over ones produced at a state university, since "only the native seeds," as Tío Eliseo explained, "can adapt to climatic changes" (Montiel et al. 2009, 22). Forty years later, Atencio discovers that Tío Eliseo was right about impending drought and also about the native seeds' superior adaptability. In this example, knowledge generated by modern technology coexists with traditional community-based knowledge and wisdom. Montiel, Atencio, and Mares then conclude that it is misguided and wasteful when those in search of knowledge come to believe that technology and theoretical sophistication *always* trump traditional knowledge and should automatically prevail over folk *wisdom*. As Atencio's example shows, technology may compete with traditional knowledge and on occasion will be found inferior to the high-quality wisdom that has been handed down over generations as el oro del barrio.

The resolana reframing of tradition can be helpfully contrasted with the major manifesto about tradition's value, T. S. Eliot's "Tradition and the Individual Talent." Like Montiel, Atencio, and Mares, Eliot saw tradition as the necessary platform needed to sponsor innovation and true creativity. He famously remarked that only when someone knows what already exists from the past can that person create something genuinely "new" in the present (1920, 59). Proposing that having a sense of tradition is essential to providing the conditions for creativity and change, he also saw that tradition will always be an incomplete starting place in that it must be continually refound as people recapture and internalize only certain parts of tradition for themselves. When one reaches a certain level of maturity as a knower (52), that person's mind will act as a "catalyst" for inventing new ways of bridging past and present with genuinely new forms of knowledge (54). In this view, tradition enables the discovery of what is genuinely new, and it is there not to keep the past artificially alive but to enable innovation and change to occur productively in the present.

Similarly, Montiel, Atencio, and Mares celebrate el oro del barrio as their version of "tradition," the best of what the past has to offer. Through el oro del barrio, the past survives and lives into the present. By being relevant but not always directly useful, el oro del barrio supports new forms and ideas as ways of solving new problems.

There are critical paradoxes to note in the contrast of tradition and el oro del barrio and how they are used to create new knowledge. In Eliot's view, the "historical sense" gained by understanding tradition shows what is still present and alive from the past. The acquisition of tradition "cannot be inherited" and must be continually reacquired through inquiry and reflection, an effort that can fail as well as succeed. His idea is that once a person has that "historical sense" in place, the components of tradition can be displayed together as having a "simultaneous existence." The parts of tradition that make up the "historical sense" will be available in "a simultaneous [and timeless] order," which he imagined to be a display in a virtual museum space of the mind—an exclusive vision available for the poet's *personal* scrutiny and cognition (1920, 49). Achieving that abstract manifestation of tradition projected in a timeless space on a panoramic screen is a critical step for producing new knowledge, a step that Eliot consistently describes as a stage of attainment for the *individual* knowledge seeker or artist.

By contrast, Montiel, Atencio, and Mares look not to a timeless order created for one person to scrutinize in a continuous panoramic view but to the real-time interaction of people sharing ideas and insights. In resolana, resolaneros, teachers, and students meet and talk to discover solutions to problems. Their production of knowledge is a by-product of their interaction and their work to strengthen community. Whereas Eliot sees new knowledge as a single person's vision and achievement, Montiel, Atencio, and Mares focus on community participation and the cooperative, interactive exchange of knowledge that will advance what is known and will further build and sustain community.

The resolana idea of community interaction and participation is starkly different from Eliot's idea of a single person inspecting cultural monuments projected as a single order—imagery suggesting a person having a conversation in a crowd (resolana) versus a lone visitor walking through an art museum (Eliot). Given the famous difficulty in the digital age of sustaining learning communities and the decline of face-to-face, real-time learning encounters, Montiel, Atencio, and Mares are here bringing a fresh perspective on the role that communities play in pursuing and producing new knowledge.

It is the *communal,* real-time aspect of knowing that separates resolana most directly from the abstract, cognitive encounters projected as an ideal order in Eliot's scheme. The real-time work of resolana takes place when people meet, network, and have a dialogue about questions and discoveries. Not a casual meeting, but a deliberately *open* encounter, resolana is a strategic receptivity to different kinds of knowing in an evolving frame of reference, through online and real-time participation, connecting actual students, teachers, and interested others. This process brings together different ways of knowing by connecting traditional knowledge, global awareness, and critique. Promoting an open approach to learning, a metaphor for new and expansive ways to produce knowledge, resolana is a possible future for Chicano and Mexican American studies. This vision is also a reminder that Chicano studies is emerging as a dynamic communal presence along with an open set of attitudes about learning and participating in digital and other modes of interaction.

The resolana approach echoes Adrienne Rich's idea of a "woman-centered university." Rich brings the community into the university with an "indistinct line [drawn] between 'university' and 'community' instead of the familiar [version of the academy as a] city-on-a-hill frowning down on its neighbors" in the community (1979, 152).[5] As with resolana, Rich's emphasis falls on communication and the collective production of knowledge *for* the community. To implement such an approach would require advances in learning to be communicated in the open channels of lively prose instead of articles written for insiders and specialists.[6] Both Rich's "woman-centered university" and resolana seek to position the pursuit of knowledge in service to the community that produced that knowledge.

As of this writing, the current generation of Chicano and Mexican American scholars in U.S. higher education still works with a strong sense of their antepasados (ancestors) and tradition. Many of these new scholars are still creative writers, but many are also trained in Chicano studies, cultural studies, and various modes of literary and cultural criticism. They have made their mark by consolidating the cultural and academic gains of the past to redirect Chicano studies, or its heir, into the future.

In the next few years, Chicano and Mexican American studies programs and Chicano literature will inevitably confront difficult times. Reduced funding to state universities and colleges, where many such programs reside, will be cut further, and deans and provosts will be canceling offerings not thought to be part of the educational core. The move to the political right in many state legislatures around the country will also encourage attempts to drop ethnic studies from state-sponsored curricula. All of these fiscal pressures will require Chicano and Latino scholars to be resourceful, resilient, and imaginative, in the manner that resolana fosters, as they move to protect and develop their programs.

Mexican American culture is already altering the dynamic, basic mix of America's national culture, how people define themselves as "Americans," what Americans look like, how they act, and how they see the world. This browning of America, evident in literature and the arts but also commercially in TV ads in Spanish, Latino music, movies, and popular magazines (*Poder Hispanic, Latina, People in Español,* etc.), is showing that indigenous, mestizo cultures in the Americas are gaining ground over the Western European dominance that has defined culture in this hemisphere since Spanish colonialism's advent. The inauguration of Chicano literature and Chicano studies has helped Mexican Americans to understand the cultural and historical context of their lives in the United States and in the Americas. The continuing presence and impact of Chicano literature and Chicano studies, especially as influenced by the possibilities of resolana, which can be taken as a metaphor for a new phase of openness in methodology and content, signal potentially exciting and innovative changes.

It is inevitable that Chicano and Mexican American studies in the future will be shaped by the fact that Latinos are expected to become the majority community in America by 2050, if not before. This momentous shift, regarding developments in every form of political, cultural, and social power, is still to be fully explored in the Mexican American community and, until recently, has been a distant thought in the American national consciousness. Recently, that distant thought has come forward as voiced by those who focus on immigration policy and the objections to Latino cultural and social influences.

The interest in resolana as a model for learning and discovery in the digital age suggests that Chicano literature and Chicano studies can be a many-roomed house for inquiry and innovation. The whole point of launching Chicano literature and Chicano studies to begin with was to move Mexican Americans closer to feeling at home in the United States. Resolana *is* an image of people at home in community, in dialogue with each other, and to that extent the contemporary relevance of resolana is an indication that Mexican Americans are on the right track as they try to write and learn their way home in the United States.

CONCLUSION
A Better Future for America

The six areas of cultural and social change presented in this book make the case, or the opening arguments for a case, for seeing the Mexican American community as helping to create a better future for America. Mexican Americans are asking the country to be the multicultural, multiethnic community that it has always sought to be. Their positive contributions are evident in each of the six areas of change discussed in this book. While the mood of the national culture changes with election seasons and the economy, and the United States tends to alter its attitudes toward the Mexican American community on a regular basis, these six areas of change will help to bring about a more tolerant America that embraces and celebrates cultural difference. This will be an America that continually renews its commitment to democracy and social justice for everyone—a better version of itself.

The six areas of cultural change treated in this book—mestizo identity, land, popular culture, the body, voice, and Chicano literature and Chicano studies—represent recent decisive moments in Mexican American culture and history. They are not the most famous historical moments, but they are still critical and deeply impactful encounters. Many people alive now have lived through those changes. They have family members who crossed into the United States from Mexico in the last century, or they themselves took part in the Chicano movement or the Chicano Renaissance. They may have been community organizers, street protestors, artists, or student activists. They may also have a personal recollection of the history of the Chicano movement as unfinished business—and perhaps also a sense of incompleteness about the history of the Americas. One of the arguments of *Mestizos Come Home!* is that American culture—mestizos and nonmestizos alike—needs to fill in that history by *remembering* what Mexican Americans have achieved as part of mestizo history in the Americas. They need to fill in the hemisphere's historical gaps about a racial past, as Galeano urges, that goes unacknowledged and unresolved (1992a). The consequences of cultural and historical forgetfulness are too dire, and the issue of what is remembered and can be retold—historical memory—is one of this book's most pressing concerns.

If we were playing twenty questions about historical precedents in the Americas in regard to racial identities, the social order, and oppressive cultural practices, many answers would be traced back to the Spanish colonial era. A concentrated account, a miniature version, of the whole colonial era and the Americas' history more broadly (including the arrival of the Spanish, slavery, and the advent of mestizaje), casta history is also the source for the invention of the brown body, the mestizo cultures of Latin America, the modern marginalization of brown-skin people, and much that has happened over nearly five hundred years of postcolonial culture. Casta history cannot encompass *everything* in this hemisphere, but it can answer many questions—hence the necessary place of the casta chapter in this book about Mexican American culture in the late twentieth and early twenty-first centuries.

As late as the middle twentieth century, there was little awareness of the issues discussed in these pages. Mexican Americans suffered under racial discrimination and were exploited as cheap labor. They lacked a social critique for their American lives, and they faced social marginalization, limited access to civil liberties, and had no path forward for economic success. In the 1960s, Mexican Americans responded with community organizing, the creation of labor unions, and the six initiatives, among others, chronicled in these chapters. Not merely shifts in cultural or social fashion, these were the far-reaching changes that happened as part of acculturation as long-standing residents, recent Mexican arrivals, and the children of recent immigrants learned to live in a dramatically changing world.

The 1969 Denver Youth Conference, which I discussed in this book's introduction, marked a conspicuous moment of new thinking about identity and what it means to be a citizen of the Americas. The writers, artists, educators, and community leaders in Denver urged the initiatives that became the Chicano Renaissance, including the many changes chronicled in this book. The values and goals that they fostered in the 1970s produced a new communal "voice," a fresh grasp of Mexican American cultural values, and new engagement with mainstream American culture. That cultural voice was embodied in Chicano literature, Chicano studies, and popular culture, all of which are still projecting Mexican American culture and its story to the world. The Mexican American community began reclaiming mestizo history in the Americas and discovering how to make cultural and social adjustments to lead successful U.S. lives. Such a broadly based response to discrimination and injustice has rarely developed so quickly and with such effective results.

Mexican Americans encountered a culture dense with Spanish place names, family names, communal traditions, festive holidays, and multiple layers of Spanish culture and European tradition, a culture all the while harboring a racial legacy that everyone lives but many do not, or cannot, acknowledge. In this book's analysis of cultural change are six ways of promoting strong families, children's welfare, hard work, a spiritual orientation, and communal cohesion—all changes that have challenged the U.S. status quo. After almost five hundred years of postconquest history, too many mestizos across the Americas, even in the United States, are still waiting to *belong* to the place that they already come from. When they can come home as a community that is a mixture of indigenous peoples, Europeans, Africans, Asians, and others, Mexican Americans will be contributing to the economy, the culture, and future prospects in ways that have yet to be imagined.

With this book's six initiatives, Mexican Americans are addressing those hard realities of the national culture that are long overdue for public engagement. They are fostering new citizenship responsibilities and a greater awareness of Latin America, a deeper commitment to globalization, civil rights, the need to restore indigenous sovereignty, the fight against racism, and a greater focus on the plight of the underclass. Those in U.S. mainstream culture may pass new immigration laws, deport the undocumented, prohibit the teaching of Chicano literature and culture, ban Chicano books in public schools, but Mexican Americans, already deeply invested in American culture, *are* coming home a little more every day and every moment as they make and claim different parts of the American experience as their own. All of this is already happening.

The fact that history is written and censored by the victors reflects the social *forgetting* of the domination of mestizos in this hemisphere. Cultural and historical forgetfulness references the legacy of marginalizing mestizos and people of color. As mestizos assume the reins of cultural and economic power over the next twenty years, the ratio of what is forgotten to what is remembered will change dramatically. We can wager that when people reclaim the culture of the Americas, work past cultural amnesia, as Mexican American writers and artists are attempting to do, they will see that culture in the Americas has happened against a backdrop of Spanish and European colonial domination that is still impacting the social order and often without attracting great attention. Cultural amnesia exists when those who benefit from racial hierarchies and those whom they dominate cannot assess their mutual complicity in maintaining racial and social inequities. Each side is culpable and complicit, and there are too many ways to reinforce racial thinking and too few strategies for critiquing and dismantling it. Combatting cultural amnesia by staying "obsessed with remembering, with remembering the past of America," as Galeano urges, we begin to take possession of "that [forgotten past] of Latin America" so as not to let memory slip away ever again (1992b, 176).

Helping to celebrate mestizo identity and culture in the United States and in the Americas, Mexican Americans are dedicated to overcoming the widespread regional amnesia about mestizos instead of remaining "condemned" to cultural forgetting (1992b, 176). Postcolonial amnesia will not plague this hemisphere forever, and the lingering trauma associated with the conquest—woven into the hemisphere's culture at the deepest levels—will in time become simply culture as acts of remembering and recovery succeed. The brown body that bears the traces of that past will be recognized as a colonial invention, and the time will come when mestizos, indigenous people, African Americans, and Asian Americans will be free from colonialism's residual power.

The Mexican American community and what it is accomplishing are positioned to reinvigorate the national culture. The tradition of building the nation's identity on an amalgamation of different communities is an ongoing strength of the American experiment, even when it is not followed consistently. When the country does not readily achieve that goal, the United States still benefits from aspiring to diversity and celebrating the liberty of its citizens. I am arguing that the Mexican American potential to contribute to U.S. culture will eventually overtake the preoccupation with immigration policy and border security. It will be a welcome day when there is recognition of the cultural treasures, traditions, and values, el oro del barrio, that Mexican Americans *bring* to the United States.

MESTIZO IDENTITY AND RACE

This book's examination of mestizo identity and cultural change in six areas is also a strike against cultural amnesia. Its discussions are of two kinds—the exploration of race and mestizo identity and the discussion of culture that celebrates Mexican American innovations and achievements. Critiquing identity and race is a critical first step to counter misguided tendencies in the modern era to pronounce the United States and the Americas as free of racial tensions and problems. The sociologist Samuel P. Huntington writes that "one of the greatest achievements . . . of America is the extent to which it has eliminated the racial and ethnic components that historically were central to its identity and has become a multiethnic, multiracial society in which individuals are to be judged on their merits" (2004, xvii). Few mestizos or native people in the Americas would affirm this conclusion. While *Mestizos Come Home!* celebrates mestizo culture and is optimistic about critiquing racial practices, the United States and the Americas are still fettered, as this book's analyses overwhelmingly show, by racial hierarchies and will spend yet more time in the bitter water before getting to the sweet—more time undoing the constraints of the colonial legacy before finally achieving greater social justice.

This book's attention to mestizo identity and race across the Americas shows that progress in racial awareness has advanced slowly since the middle nineteenth century. Historical bright spots exist in the Caribbean, Mexico, Brazil, Peru, and the United States where there have been bold analyses of mestizo identity and race. Mexican American writers and artists have built upon that body of thought about mestizo identity from these regions. But the "coloniality of power," the residue of Spanish colonialism woven into the fabric of this hemisphere's history and culture, still exists, frequently derailing attempts to focus on racial injustices and realities.

Current genetic research and ancient DNA studies support the spirit of the Mexican American foregrounding of ethnic diversity. Revealing a complex genetic and cultural reality, human genome researchers have found genetic diversity, not purity, to be the global norm. As geneticist Howard M. Cann notes, "human genome diversity studies have clearly shown that the large part of genetic variability is due to differences *among* individuals within populations rather than to differences *between* populations." Such findings chip away at traditional beliefs about a people's genetic uniqueness, certainly the ethnic purity, of any racial group—a finding that effectively cancels human nature as the basis for "the concept of 'race'" (Cann 1998, 443). With genetic diversity recognized as the norm of being human the world over, genetic science has undercut traditional accounts, certainly origin stories, of people always living in the same place as proof of their uncorrupted racial descent. It is now clear that the Mexican American foregrounding of mestizo identity anticipated the genetic fact of ethnically mixed people around the world before genetic science could confirm that state of affairs.

Mexican Americans promote racial diversity most effectively by continuing to be themselves, *to exist* as the Americas' mixed-race community, the historical and cultural heirs of the New World's ancient peoples and European colonizers. The fact of their existence and their claiming of a both/and "border" identity challenges the notion of racial purity and promotes a diverse, inclusive view of humanity. Exposing the concept of race as deeply flawed and defying the notion that identity can ever be reduced to such divisive terms are landmark achievements in the modern era, an advance in our understanding of the ideological underpinnings of race and what it means to be human.

Brown skin is indeed iconic, but not because of inherent properties or genetics. Instead, colonizers have assigned attributes to brown skin *as if* they were a reality of nature. Claims to racial or ethnic purity only serve specific, political ends and do not reflect a "truth" to be taken as the human body's nature or reality. This recognition points to the iconic status of being a mestizo in the Americas, as Vasconcelos said would happen, as *the* hemispheric citizen precisely because mestizos have consistently challenged strict categories of racial identity by violating them through their continuing existence. Every aspect of being "brown" in the Americas speaks not about race but about the hemisphere's history and culture. As mixed people with the history of the Americas written on our brown faces and bodies, we are the human, visible signs, the ongoing cumulative record of what has transpired in the Americas.

Lest we fear that mestizos, in being liberated from an historical burden, will now become the new privileged class, we must remember that the designation of being Americas' citizens potentially includes everyone as members of Vasconcelos's "cosmic race." *Everyone* in this hemisphere who chooses to acknowledge a complex personal history can in some sense claim the status of being a mestizo. The self-disclosing nature of mestizo identity undercuts the notion of an exclusive class or racial group, any group, and calls into question all racial platforms and hierarchies. "Brown" will not become the new "white," and racism will surely end, or we can hope that it does, when all recognize that social strategies and political manipulation, not nature or God, create the hierarchies that traditionally go under the name of race.

MESTIZO CULTURE

Mestizos Come Home! foregrounds Rodolfo Gonzales's association of the reality of ethnic identity and the complexity of mestizo culture. Working from the assumption that ethnic identity is both an unconscious *and* conscious choice, at times an assumed but at other times a deliberate investment in a cultural origin, Gonzales describes the human drama of people making and claiming the cultural traditions that they live by. These designations represent cultural constructions that at different times coalesce, some displacing others, as all move forward in new hybrid forms that people can choose to affirm or reject. For Gonzales, mestizo culture is a repository of values and practices with diversity and change at its core. The term "Chicano" brings together all of these cultural associations that have developed previously. Not only an outgrowth of the Spanish legacy, but, insofar as hybridity disrupts and reverses hierarchies, the term "Chicano" continues to challenge assumptions about being white as a line of development superior to other ethnic identities.

The way that Gonzales, Anzaldúa, and Anaya apply "Chicano" as a concept to understand contemporary Mexican American culture gives a glimpse of the reality of hybrid culture as applied to Mexican American lives. Mexican American writers not only bring ideas about mestizo identity and hybrid culture onto the Americas' broad stage, but in doing so they join the larger Latin American conversation about community, place, identity, and culture, some of which I discussed in relation to Latin American writers in chapter 2. The Mexican American racial critique and celebration of mestizo culture are part of this hemisphere's cultural legacy and give a sense of how future citizens of the Americas will critique, accept, and, on occasion, when they deem our ideas as harmful or irrelevant, reject the values of *our* time.

We also saw that Mexican Americans contribute to contemporary discussions of the cultural frame surrounding land and land use. During the 1960s, there was "no other activity of the Chicano Movement," Rudolfo Anaya writes, that "was as important" as the recognition of indigenous ties to the American Southwest as a Mexican American homeland that embodied their sense of place (Anaya and Lomeli 1991, 232). The concerns about land use unite Mexican American writers and American cultural geographers in believing that national social ills understood as the loss of shared communal values are hastened by land's commodification and the resulting loss of land-based traditions. They believe that this problem can be addressed with the renewal and affirmation of social and cultural ties to land.

Mexican American writers and land activists are helping to shape this important conversation about land and the U.S. communities of the future—ultimately raising issues that include, as Chicana philosopher Laura Pulido comments, "social injustice, growing inequality, and a looming environmental crisis." The crisis rests on the decision of companies and corporations to reduce land to the status of a commodity sold on the open market, thus ignoring land's complex ties to culture and all of life on the planet. Pulido cautions that land problems are "the greatest threats facing the global community as we enter the twenty-first century" (1996, 210). By engaging in and advancing this vital debate, Mexican Americans are making the United States a stronger community.

In contemporary popular culture, Mexican Americans have attempted to make microadjustments in the tension between Mexican traditions and current social life. The inaugurators of the U.S. (as opposed to the Mexican) Day of the Dead, Cinco de Mayo, and lowrider car culture have tried to negotiate the Mexican American community's recognized need for tradition and ethnic identity with demands arising from economic issues and current social accommodations. These cultural practices reference the U.S. hemispheric cultural and social context wherein a history unfolds that shows the traces of social and economic exploitation and, in the case of el dia de los muertos, death on an unprecedented scale in colonial New Spain in the seventeenth century. We must never forget that close to 25 *million* indigenous people died in New Spain at the hands of the Spanish by the middle of the seventeenth century. This neglected history reveals social and cultural forces that have shaped the modern conception of race in a way that impacts the United States every day.

An intimate part of this racial history is the Western regard for the reality and the fortunes of the human body, the long arm of connection for many of the concerns of this book. The Spanish in the colonial era designated normative social bodies as blanco ("white") and Spanish, and they designated all mixed people in New Spain as belonging to the casta system with the predetermined positions of its social order. Remnants of that order have persisted for nearly five hundred years, as can be seen in daily life and the critiques advanced by Tomás Rivera, Rudolfo Anaya, Gloria Anzaldúa, Denise Chávez, Sandra Cisneros, and Demetria Martínez, along with Mexican American artists John Valadez, Alma López, Alex Donis, Luis Jiménez, and others.

Mexican Americans are attempting to change the culture's fundamental view of the body en route to reclaiming and revaluing mestizo lives. These writers and artists understand that the focus on the body and its care are the most direct ways to expose the effects of poverty, violence, poor health, and abuse. They choose to depict the body at risk, pushed beyond its limits when plagued by disease, malnutrition, violence, dislocation, and social marginalization. Focusing on the ways in which the colonized body still exists in the present, they are intending to recover a sense of humanity that has been lost in the Americas through racial typing, social marginalization, and economic exploitation. Brown bodies in colonial New Spain and in the Americas since the conquest have for too long been the unseen bodies that do work for others—emptying trash cans, cleaning houses, taking care of children, and mowing yards. Mexican American writers and artists bring to light an awareness of brown bodies that, marginalized and made invisible, live in the shadows in poverty along with the bodies of people incarcerated, "deformed," or "disabled."

Samuel Huntington identifies America's "Puritan legacy" as "the American essence," and in Anglo-Protestant America, where the body, its needs, and its appetites are always made to look suspect, brown bodies have historically been rendered invisible or lifeless. They are also expected to conform to and imitate what is "civilized" and "godly" according to the normative standards of white culture (2004, 65). Trying to refind and reanimate those lost bodies, these writers and artists, many of them women, have focused on recovering bodily knowledge in Mexican American literature, art, and philosophy amid the debris of modern culture where lost bodies, most often the bodies of the poor and the marginalized, have been discarded like so much refuse. These writers and artists explore the Anglo-Protestant cultural frame where the brown body, not part of the Western master plan, is hidden and its fate always uncertain.

What they recover, or on occasion *reinvent*, as needed, is the Mesoamerican model of the body, in which "the body," as Ana Castillo notes, "is never separate from the spirit or mind" (1994, 156). Implicitly countering and reversing the role that marginalized bodies play in communities and people's lives, Mexican American writers and artists advocate for Mesoamerican practices to promote a robust and healthy life, recentering the body as the vital locus of emotional and mental processes that constitute being human.

This project to recover and critique the brown body as a cultural construction is far reaching, and Cisneros, Chávez, and Martínez pursue this goal with great inventiveness. They show that reclaiming the body is an undertaking that involves reintegrating the political and spiritual dimensions of our lives with bodily interests in regard to health, values, and emotions—the total package of being human. When the body's importance is denied, it is far easier to justify physical and political neglect, violence, torture, rape, and hidden abuse—practices vividly in evidence in societies where the body is made invisible and routinely performs the manual labor that others refuse to acknowledge. Recovering the body is a profoundly humanizing act that entails acknowledging the effects of political, historical, and social forces and the goals that community is striving to accomplish regardless of what it professes.

Mexican American writers critique the body's isolation in American life where it is confined to a realm seemingly free and "personal" but ultimately inconsequential. In America, Puritan culture achieves the dream of negating and punishing the body all at once, proving Huntington's claim that "the Puritan legacy [is] . . . the American essence" (Huntington 2004, 65). Puritanical culture in the United States has succeeded too well, and the human body in America is excluded from spheres of importance and counts for too little in the exercise of common judgment and authority. French cultural critic Jean Baudrillard gauges the American, Anglo-Protestant appreciation of the body as always moving toward "an ensuing effect of under-nourishment," by which he means that the body in the United States, particularly the brown body, is excluded from public spheres except as special cases in limited roles. The body in the United States "takes on a transparent form, a lightness near to complete disappearance" in that the body and its interests are little evident and missing when corporations make decisions about waste disposal in the neighborhoods of the poor and allow the dumping of industrial wastes where children play and live or when local governments fail to support children's health or the quality of education (2010, 28). Environmental scientist Elizabeth Hoover and her colleagues, discussing the recurrent pattern in America of storing industrial wastes near the neighborhoods of the poor and dis-enfranchised, describe the transparence and invisibility of the brown body when they detail how "indigenous American communities" must consistently "face disproportionate health burdens and environmental health risks [from industrial waste products] compared with the average North American population" (2012, 1645).

In line with Mexican American attempts to recover and reinsert the brown body in spheres of social importance regarding health, the well-being of children, and the poor, Baudrillard suggests that in America bodies foregrounded *as bodies*—brown bodies, the bodies of the homeless, people with disabilities and health impairments, people with physical "deformities," and incarcerated people—are kept hidden to create an American display of prosperity and the specter of mass well-being, the platitude that says that everyone is "okay" (2010, 28). This marginalizing of the body in American public life coincides with the overexposure of bodies in sports, beauty pageants, entertainment, and pornography—cultural realms deliberately chosen as places to hide the political significance of marginalization and putting at risk the bodies of the poor. In these public arenas, bodies are paraded under the bright lights of entertainment and commercial distraction, with excesses of adulation, while brown bodies that do not fit the master plan remain invisible and vulnerable to industrial and environmental damage that is always doing its harm away from TV cameras and separate from public acknowledgment or attention.

In complex, bureaucratic cultures, even in historically Puritanical cultures like the United States, the body *needs* to matter and to be protected for the culture to be sustainable. Without reclaiming the body, without taking possession of issues of health in the public sphere, without the willingness to understand what the body's fortunes can convey about social value, without the full acknowledgment and assent to look at the needs of the poor and disempowered whose bodies are constantly at risk, America "suffers." By this, Baudrillard means that such "suffering" comes from a needless "desertification" in American culture resulting from the reckless waste of human resources when the bodies of whole communities are poisoned by toxic water systems, when industrial wastes and contaminates are allowed to enter the food supply, and when children are socially marginalized and their health is sacrificed and destroyed (28). Without reclaiming mestizo and other bodies of color and committing to care for them in public and private life, with the tremendous political and social implications of that recovery, there can be little progress toward social justice for anyone.

An America that acknowledges the human body would be an America with a renewed sense of community, better public health programs, stronger environmental justice, and a clear national purpose. It would be an America that has overcome severe Puritanical, blinding constraints, the cultural "desertification" that results from ignoring and denying what is implied politically, socially, and culturally in caring for bodies labeled brown, white, red, yellow, young, and old. Mexican American writers and artists are addressing what connects individual lives with the national sense of who we are and what we want to achieve as a community. Even if these writers and artists are only partially successful in this quest to reclaim the human body for U.S. culture, they are inaugurating a critical conversation that once started cannot be stopped about what binds people together as a community, how certain people are socially marginalized and forgotten, and why education and health, as John Dewey advances in *The Public and Its Problems*, should be our foremost national priorities.

A BETTER FUTURE FOR AMERICA

The bold reclamation of the mestizo body for American culture, along with the recognition of mestizo identity, the homeland, and popular culture have contributed to the rise of a Chicano "voice" in Mexican American culture, a voice getting louder every day and expressing a reinvigorated sense of cultural identity and values. That communal voice continues to grow stronger in the Mexican American community through the work of writers, artists, and educators who are pointing the direction back to the body and its needs. These voices signal that the crossing of a cultural divide took place in the 1960s and 1970s when Mexican Americans began to champion civil rights, and their progress since is recorded in the fate of human bodies in every chapter of this book.

Mexican American writers, artists, and public intellectuals initially opened the way for the national culture to explore Mexican American communal and personal life. The traditional belief that culture heals (la cultura cura) and the effective alignment of social, communal, and individual values and issues strengthen the Mexican American engagement with the national culture. Going forward with a reinvigorated cultural

tradition in the making, Mexican Americans are examining their interactions with mainstream culture and are reevaluating common values
and goals on everyone's behalf.

In the early 1970s, new Chicano studies' programs began exploring
evolving aspects of Mexican American identity and community, assimilation into American life, and understanding the cultural past in Mexico
and Mesoamerica. Chicano studies programs today still have that responsibility of exploring and understanding the community and advancing
its interests. That responsibility will evolve as Chicano and Mexican
American studies programs reshape themselves as Latinos become
America's majority community at midcentury, even as laws like Arizona's
ban on ethnic studies attempt to thwart the potential of such programs to
educate widely for creative and locally effective social-activist strategies.

The Mexican American folk tradition of resolana, of community
members gathering by a warm wall on a sunny day, with the joint aim
of participatory, dialogic problem solving and discovery, is an important
metaphor for the reinvigoration of community. This traditional practice
from rural New Mexico is an effective model for valuing folk ways and
traditional wisdom alongside new knowledge, critiques, and emerging
technologies. The lesson of resolana not only encourages community
participation in education and communal decision making but validates
"the wisdom [that] traditional societies bring to bear in their adaptation
to the industrial age" (Montiel et al. 2009, 5). The resolana approach to
knowledge and decision making should be seen as a move toward a new
openness about connecting traditional perspectives with emerging cultural and technological knowledge. Future Latino forms of engagement
both in online and real-life encounters will facilitate these old/new con-
versations in ways that have not been fully anticipated but which will
benefit all of American culture.

I mentioned earlier that Samuel P. Huntington, possibly the major
voice of American sociology since World War II and also one of the
architects of the postwar international east-west global order, describes
in detail his view of the six Mexican American initiatives discussed
in this book. He addresses much of what I have discussed and more,
except that he sees the Mexican American community as pursuing a
course that ultimately will weaken and degrade America. He sees no

potential in the Mexican American community for cultural renewal or reinvigoration, no celebration of mestizos coming home and contributing to the national culture's health, economy, and character.

He does acknowledge the distinctiveness of Mexican American identity but suggests that Mexican Americans, not choosing to venture beyond themselves and their own interests, will remain culturally isolated in the United States, separate and without assimilation. He grants that Mexican Americans may feel connected to land in the United States, to the American Southwest region that used to be Mexico, but in this he spots a "serious potential for conflict" wherein the "Southwest could become America's Quebec." He forecasts that Mexican Americans will choose to reclaim land that was once theirs and will try to secede from the United States (2004, 230). He hears the distinctive "voice" of the Mexican American community, particularly its use of Spanish, but in this voice he finds a disheartening trend if bilingualism "becomes institutionalized in the Mexican American community." He predicts that bilingualism will be "reinforced by the continuing inflow of new immigrants speaking only Spanish," suggesting that the use of Spanish, too, will divide America (232). He acknowledges the robust Mexican American engagement with culture, literature, film, music, and art but forecasts that Latinos will surely undervalue the "Anglo-Protestant" dimension of the U.S. national community that he believes is responsible for America's accomplishments and prosperity.

Huntington's sobering reflections directly counter the broad horizons described and analyzed in this book, suggesting observations possibly made about two entirely different worlds. He allows no room for reconsidering what Mexican Americans have already achieved to come home to American culture and sees only invading brown bodies and greedy takers running loose across the country. He projects a frightening, dystopian vision of Mexican Americans growing into a giant community, eventually coming into political power, controlling, and finally destroying the Anglo-Protestant sense of identity that anchors the United States to its unique past and its once-bright future.

At the very least, Huntington and others have allowed their fear of change to cloud their vision and judgment in these matters. *Mestizos Come Home!* argues that there are vital, ongoing connections to traditional "American" values in almost everything that Mexican Americans do, stand for, and care about, especially in their respect for family, religion, hard work, home, and community. Famous for their assent to these traditional values supporting family and community, Mexican Americans would have great trouble and some genuine sense of alarm at the prospect of seeing themselves, or any of their concerns, inserted into a dystopian vision of a near-term Latino catastrophe.

Rather, in the six initiatives described in this book Mexican Americans are striving to live according to the values that support their interests *and* those of the national community. From 1848 onward, their greatest resources have been their cultural energy, their work ethic, their willingness to innovate, and their unshakable belief in a brighter U.S. future—the very aspirations traditionally associated with America as a Western icon of open and free community. History teaches that the American story is about immigration (even for traditional native peoples), struggle, denial, betrayal, persistence, and, on occasion, communal success. Each area of Mexican American achievement chronicled in this book tells this story of an unshakable commitment and continual belief in the United States as Mexican Americans create better lives for themselves and the national culture. There is no one way to tell that story, no master narrative with the authority to say that there is only one legitimate road to travel that journey home.

We can also be certain that America's founders never intended coming home and becoming a part of American culture to work only for Anglo-Protestants or for any group seeking to stand apart from and limit possibilities for others. On the contrary, the *Federalist Papers* shows repeatedly that the founders foresaw and actively feared such exclusionary initiatives. James Madison focused on the danger to democracy posed by a future tyranny of "factions." He imagined elite groups and communities that, at some moment in the future, would become wealthy and too powerful. Those groups would come to believe that America was theirs alone, and they would become a threat to others' rights. In "The Federalist No. 10," Madison describes such factions as "united and actuated by some common impulse of passion, or of interest, averse to the rights of other citizens, or to the permanent and aggregate interests of the community" (2009, 48). In the rise of such elite, powerful groups, he saw the antidemocratic tendencies that could change and damage American democracy. He noted the "propensity of mankind to fall into mutual animosities that where no substantial occasion presents itself, the most frivolous and fanciful distinctions have been sufficient to kindle their unfriendly passions and excite their most violent conflicts" (49).

Madison foresaw the existence of social groups and clans that could seize upon "the most frivolous and fanciful distinctions" and then use those distinctions as a basis for inciting "violent conflicts." In this regard, one need only think of Huntington's panic over the possible secession of the American Southwest from the United States in a dark fantasy future when that land becomes overrun with dark Latino bodies. Such dystopian fantasies and the overpromotion of "Anglo-Protestants" as the *real* America go hand in hand and are exactly the developments that Madison feared when he pointed toward the danger of power accruing to "factions" and the destructive competition that they can foster. Huntington's groundless concerns remind us that some, even great minds, can allow their conception of the United States to become too small in comparison to the grand architecture envisioned by the founders.

The founders had famous blind spots in the areas of race and gender, which have been well documented, but there is also no mistaking the nobility and good sense of their aspiration for America to remain receptive to all who seek its shores. They actively explored ways to keep America open and vital, to protect America from exclusionary and nondemocratic attitudes, and to make allowances for cultural change and progress, what Barry Lopez calls "the [continual] Rediscovery of North America" (1992). *The Federalist Papers* expresses a passionate defense of democracy that trumps the Puritanical vision and the Anglo-Protestant tradition.

Mexican American culture has taken a broad view through its many voices of supporting the rights of women, differently gendered people, and ethnic minorities to chart their own course. In Rivera's. . . . *y no se lo tragó la tierra* , Helena Maria Viramonte's *Under the Feet of Jesus*, Anaya's *Randy Lopez Goes Home*, Carla Trujillo's *What Night Brings*, and Denise Chávez's *The King and Queen of Comezón,* the theme says that the Mexican American community is building its own better future with ever-stronger ties to mainstream America. The call to action and the journey home in this book are versions of the traditional promise of renewal—the tradition of a people coming to the United States to find a new beginning and further enlarging and enriching the American experience.

A specific message of this journey is the mandate to reset the cultural compass toward the future of the United States but also toward the whole of the Americas as the proper perspective for U.S. cultural and demographic developments in a global age. The presence of Mexican Americans is living proof that in the middle of U.S. culture, Americans have begun to live in a globalized world. This reorientation *from* an east-west view fostered by a narrow band of British and Dutch settlements on the Eastern Seaboard, and *toward* a north-south orientation prompted by the need to see more of the Americas and the region's cultures over greater spans of time, is the appropriate perspective in the age of globalization and is not a sign of America's weakness or downfall. A sign of national health, sustainability, and a belief in the future, this perspective breaks through all constraints against seeing the United States as a part of the Western hemisphere and not merely as the isolated nation in the north.

In choosing to come home to the United States, and then choosing America all over again in the Chicano Renaissance, and continually resetting the markers of that promise for a new beginning, Mexican Americans are the latest incarnation of this compact for renewal and an investment in the future. The founders valued an openness to possibility that goes deeper in American culture and is far more inclusive than the Anglo-Protestant "Creed" or the social prestige of being Anglo Protestant can possibly express. The founders saw the American experiment as grand architecture that includes countless "creeds," many versions of el oro del barrio, a large conception that easily accommodates Mexican Americans coming home.

Mestizos coming home is also about the cultural relationships and practices that have been evolving, in many cases, for as long as people have been in the Americas. These stories about mestizaje and liberation—about everything discussed in this book—for five hundred years could not be told fully. These once-forbidden mestizo stories about identity, land, bodies, race, gender, social exclusion, popular culture, and voice (the true histories and accounts of what has happened in the Americas) are now being told in the ways that I have described. These are stories about the conquest's legacy and the racial barriers that still divide people against each other and against themselves. These are stories about liberation, social change, and communal health for which there were previously no tellers and no hearers.

There are also stories to be told about the lifting of social barriers and the exposure and canceling of racial and gender practices that for so long have shaped New World cultures. Coming home in this deliberate and calculated way, Mexican Americans are creating for themselves a moment of freedom, a kind of historical turning room, in which the telling of *new* stories becomes possible. Telling stories about race and mestizo peoples is critical to make way for the as-yet untold stories, the unwritten stories, that will be told about culture in the Americas and about those who come after us.

At a similar turning point in Anaya's *Shaman Winter,* Spanish soldiers were mobilizing to enter New Mexico, and a new epoch was opening in the Americas. Here Anaya identifies his version of the greatest threat to life in this hemisphere. His villain, an evil figure called the Raven (an anagram for "never"—as in the radical canceling of memory), embodies the destructive threat of amnesia, forgetfulness about the Americas' cultural past. Anaya cites the untold stories of the ancestors and the possibility of losing parts of the Americas' past before those stories can be saved and retold to others. *Shaman Winter*'s "Calendar of Dreams," the fabled instrument for the recording and telling of everyone's story, is his mythical anecdote for amnesia and forgetfulness. This passage echoes Eduardo Galeano's similar warning about cultural amnesia as the devastating enemy of the Americas' cultural and social renewal. It is also Cherríe L. Moraga's message when she refers to the United States as "a country built on the shaky ground of a duplicitous and strategic amnesia" in regard to gender and women's lives (2011, 27). Anaya, Galeano, and Moraga fear the loss of connectedness to the past and the ancestors and to all that those proud women and men struggled to achieve in this hemisphere. They particularly fear losing the ability, and perhaps even the desire, to tell stories about the vital and enduring dimensions of life in the Americas.

The cultural challenge of being a mestizo in this difficult age should not be taken as a sign of living under a curse, under what Junot Díaz calls the "Curse and the Doom of the New World" (2007, 1)—that is, the fallen condition of all who live the legacy of postcolonial culture. It must not be forgotten that since 1848 many Mexican Americans have been in their ancestral home, exactly where they belong, and since the 1960s Mexican Americans have been coming home *again* by affirming their past and their present identifies afresh. They have taken stock of communal resources and have recounted what they bring to America's cultures, enacting what philosopher of education Jane Roland Martin calls cultural bookkeeping, a reorientation and accounting of accumulated cultural assets and liabilities. They have accomplished this profound cultural update, this taking stock of cultural accounts, in the six ways that I have discussed in this book. Their understanding has moved them past many of the barriers that created cultural amnesia and invisibility to begin with.

We are right to celebrate mestizos coming home to who they are and reclaiming their heritage in the United States and in the Americas. They are seeking truth and reconciliation, and their testimonios (this book's six initiatives) are critical accounts of the past and of everyone's future in the United States and in this hemisphere. For all who live in the Americas and recognize the importance of seizing this cultural moment when it is available, that moment is *now* when, as Anaya comments in *Shaman Winter*, "the human dream" can still be "born again" (1999b, 139). Anaya, Galeano, and Moraga each convey their own apprehension that such moments of opportunity eventually fade. Refusing to be bystanders or passive readers of our own narratives, we must be thoughtful authors of change, directing our own dreams, and writing and rewriting our own stories. Mexican Americans are coming home by authoring their stories in the ways that I have described, and in so doing they (we) are revisioning the unfolding stories of all Americans. Their continuing struggle in these quests to find social justice is a sign that the six initiatives of this book are milestones in the journey homeward to find their new American lives.

Notes

PREFACE

1. See Joy DeGruy (2006) for a description similar to "post-colonial stress disorder."

CHAPTER 1

1. For comprehensive, earlier scholarly treatments of the casta painting tradition, see Isidro Moreno Navarro, *Los cuadros del mestizaje Americano: Studio antropológico del mestizaje* (1973), and María Concepción García Sáiz, *La américa española en la época de Carlos III* (1985). See also the special issue "La pintura de castas" in *Artes de México* 2, 8 (1998).

2. María Herrera-Sobek proposes that the Spanish were depicting casta people in largely harmonious settings and circumstances as a "direct response" to the "attacks emanating from Europe via the Black Legend master narrative"— accounts of how the Spanish abused slaves and colonial subjects in the New World (2015, 86). She argues that the Spanish were doing public relations with the paintings to show the general happy state of their colonial slaves and subjects. My question to her regards how to understand the many casta paintings that do not fit this pattern in that they show rampant discord and misbehavior among racially mixed people.

3. María Herrera-Sobek cautions that "the artistic renderings of the men, women, and children depicted on canvas do not explicitly or implicitly state whether the black Africans appearing in the numerous and varied settings are actually slaves or free people" (2015, 85), suggesting that interpretation of the paintings often rests on this indeterminate factor.

4. A common selection of racial categories is as follows: mestizo (a person with Spanish and indigenous parents), castizo (mestizo and Spanish), Español (the recovered, "mended" version of being "Spanish" when a castizo and a Spaniard had a child), mulatto (Spanish and black), and so on. Other common terms making up the sixteen are morisco (mulato and Spanish), chino (morisco and Spanish), salta atrás (chino and indigenous), lobo (salta atrás and mulata), cribero (lobo and china), albarazado (cribero and mulata), canbufo (albarazado and black), sanbaigo (canbufo and indigenous), calpamulato (sanbaigo and loba), tente en el aire (calpamulato and canbufa), no te entiendo (tente en el aire and mulato), and torna atrás (no te entiendo and indigenous).

5. Jacques Lafaye argues that there were no less than sixty-six casta categories among mestizo people in the sixteenth century (1998, 81).

CHAPTER 2

1. For those of us who are mestizos, there is a historical irony in this novel's suggestion that mestizaje in the Americas, for good or ill, begins on a drunken date.

2. As Juan E. De Castro points out in *Mestizo Nations*, the actual cognates in Portuguese for the Spanish "mestizo"—"mestiço" or "mestiçagem"—are not generally used in Brazil (2002, xv).

3. For important discussions of Martí, see also Roberto Fernández Retamar, "Nuestra América y Occidente" and *José Martí: Ensayos sobre arte y literatura*, and Jean Franco, *An Introduction to Spanish American Literature*.

4. Ateneo de México writers were Antonio Caso, Alfonso Reyes, Pedro Henriquez Ureña, José Vasconcelos, among others, who addressed the plight of Mexicans in relation to Mexican identity, Mexicanidad, and promoted a debate over what was characteristic and unique about Mexican culture and identity.

5. There is also the claim that Vasconcelos and the supporters of his approach to mestizaje were trying to absorb native people into a less indigenous-identified version of Mexican nationhood as a way of transitioning them into a mainstream identity. See Richard Graham, ed., *The Idea of Race in Latin America, 1870–1940*, and Marilyn Grace Miller, *The Rise and Fall of the Cosmic Race: The Cult of Mestizaje in Latin America*. Most commentators agree that this was not Vasconcelos's motive. I tend to agree with Rafael Pérez-Torres's position, which says that whatever the reality of Mexican cultural politics during this period, "Chicana mestizaje [should be seen] as a race [tilted] *toward* the Indian" and not toward mainstream identification (2006; 16).

6. Border theory and border studies constitute a sizable subfield of Chicano studies and ethnic studies. See Rudolfo A. Anaya, "Aztlán: A Homeland without Boundaries," Gloria Anzaldúa, *Borderlands/La Frontera: The New Mestiza*, Héctor Calderón and José David Saldívar, eds., *Criticism in the Borderlands: Studies in Chicano Literature, Culture, and Ideology*, Emily D. Hicks, *Border Writing: The Multidimensional Text*, David R. Maciel and María Herrera-Sobek, eds., *Culture across Borders: Mexican Immigration and Popular Culture*, José David Saldívar, *Border Matters: Remapping American Cultural Studies*, and Carlos G Vélez-Ibáñez, *Border Visions: Mexican Cultures of the Southwest United States*.

7. For the broad American Indian view of "blood" and "mixed blood" issues, see Geary Hobson, ed., *The Remembered Earth: An Anthology of Contemporary Native-American Literature* (1–11), and Alan R. Velie, "Indian Identity in the Nineties." Both of these critics of American Indian literature and culture reflect the reality of but also an impatience with "blood-quantum" issues.

After explaining the "blood-quantum" system, Hobson writes, "However, I feel that in the final analysis the most important concern is not whether one is 'more' Indian than his fellow-Indian; it is much more imperative that both recognize their common heritage, no matter to what differing degree, and that they strive to join together for the betterment of Native Americans—as well as other—one-eighth bloods as well as full-bloods, 'unenrolled' as well as 'enrolled'" (1993, 9). Velie makes a similar comment when he says "genetic heritage, or Indian 'blood' as it is popularly called, is becoming increasingly less important in determining Indian identity." He goes on to quote the American indigenous fiction writer Gerald Vizenor in saying that the "notion of an arithmetic reduction of blood as a historical document is . . . detestable and detrimental to mental health" (1998, 192).

8. In *Seven Interpretive Essays on Peruvian Reality* Mariátegui advances, in the Vasconcelos vein, that "the future of Latin America depends on the fate of mestizaje." But unlike Vasconcelos, Mariátegui believes that "the *mestizaje* extolled by Vasconcelos [should not be seen as] precisely the mixture of Spanish, Indian, and African which has already taken place on the continent," which happened under colonialism. Instead, he saw the need for "a [further] purifying fusion and refusion [of mestizaje culture], from which the cosmic race will emerge centuries later" (1971, 278). He was arguing that a new mestizo vision would first need to find its indigenous roots and then take time, perhaps many years, to remove colonial influence and evolve after liberty is restored so as to take whatever form the new cultural identity may become.

Such cultural work, on which a nation's fate and future depend, must be accomplished over time by mestizos—as Mariátegui also claims—as they tell their own story and establish their own foundation for nationhood. In this view, following upon Haya de la Torre's emphasis on the creation of a mestizo cultural voice, I will later detail the rise of a Mexican American cultural *voice* in chapter 6.

9. Such thinking about being a mestizo in the Americas finds expression in the late twentieth century in Chicano literary and critical texts that foreground the hybrid, multicultural nature of being a mestizo. Homi K. Bhabha proposes that the recognition of cultural "hybridity" as underlying the Mexican American understanding of race and culture is not a simple joining of disparate values or cultural elements, like comparing a casta painting with a noncasta eighteenth-century portrait. Rather, the theoretical goal of hybridity is that it "overcomes the given grounds of opposition and opens up a space of translation," a new proposition that marks the moment when significant change can happen. In creating that "place of hybridity . . . where the construction of a political object that is new, *neither the one nor the other*," happens, hybridity is generating an explanatory alternative that undermines and subverts the authority of what it analyzed (1994, 37).

10. Keep in mind that I have not abandoned my earlier comment about the underlying colonial perspective of Gonzales's view of mestizo identity and culture. Anzaldúa is the Chicana writer most sensitive to the implications of defining mestizo identity and culture within a colonial model, and her comment about having a "tolerance for contradictions" is her way of removing Mexican Americans from an oppositional (colonial) relationship with mainstream culture.

11. There is also an extensive body of contemporary literary and cultural theory that investigates mestizo identity, U.S.-Mexico border issues, and Chicano avant-garde culture, and I will take up that discussion in chapter 7 when I analyze Chicano literature and Chicano studies.

12. As founder of APRA (Alianza Popular Revolucionaria Americana), modern Peru's dominant political party, Haya de la Torre advocated recognizing indigenous cultures everywhere. Whereas Martí argued from the criollo (transplanted Spanish) perspective, seeking to *appreciate* and *understand* indigenous peoples, Haya de la Torre argued that indigenous cultures cannot be comprehended in Western terms. Indigenous thinking "cannot be adjusted to the known European ideological molds" without distorting its nature and worldview (1986, 38). A living, vibrant culture must comprehend itself in its own terms to recover its past and origins, and that process of cultural discovery needs to happen in relation to other mestizo cultures in the Americas. A people must find its own cultural voice for inquiry and discovery, and this process of discovery on behalf of one's own culture is empowering. Only when such historical coordinates underpin a national narrative, only when indigenous people have learned to speak about themselves in terms of what Haya de la Torre termed the national coordinates of "time" and "space," specific historical placement, will the world of the Americas "fit into a logical scheme of history, one that would enable [indigenous people]" to forge their own destiny (1986, 39).

13. See Miguel Montiel, Tomás Atencio, and E. A. Mares (2009) for a discussion of the early days of Chicano studies.

14. Also writing in Mariátegui's period is Ciro Alegría, the Peruvian journalist and novelist who wrote about indigenous people and who believed, as Mariátegui did, that social engagement required a cultural foundation. In 1930, Alegría joined the APRISTA union and movement, the brainchild of Haya de la Torre, and dedicated himself to social reform and action. Alegría went to prison several times for political offenses and then exiled himself before returning from the United States to Peru in 1948. He was later elected to the Peruvian Chamber of Deputies in 1963 and brought into office his vision of being a poet and political philosopher.

15. Aníbal Quijano (1928–), a contemporary Peruvian sociologist, has had a similar significant impact on the contemporary understanding of race in the Americas. Like Mariátegui, he takes a broad view of the mestizo community over

several hundred years. A comprehensive and systematic thinker in his understanding of race, labor, and the distribution of power to classes and categories of people in the New World, he nonetheless resists intellectual platitudes and premature closure in his thought, any final "truth," and revises his work constantly in light of new discoveries about the Spanish colonial impact on race and power in the Americas. This openness about mestizos and the nature of liberation in the Americas can be seen as "the freedom to choose between various cultural orientations, and, above all, the freedom to produce, criticize, change, and exchange culture and society" (2007, 178).

Many of his contributions to the understanding of race in the Americas come under the concept of "the coloniality of power" (2000, 533), by which he means the advent of the Spanish in the Americas and the social and racial legacy, still having an impact, that they left behind. He focuses on the culture and society that Spain put in place to maintain power over indigenous people and on how those institutions set in motion social and economic processes that have continued to shape life in the Americas into the present. The Spanish invention of racial categories—black, white, mestizo, and so on—and a system of labor permanently separating conquerors from the conquered created a colonial culture and worldview that is still having an effect and doing harm (534). He consistently raises questions about critical topics that everyone knows about but which no one (for whatever reason) has been willing to articulate in such bold terms. Like Vasconcelos in his ability to reapproach what everyone else has taken for granted, he asks, why there are so few mestizos among the power elite? Why are mestizos performing most of the manual and low-wage labor? Why are they the marginalized in society to begin with? (Quijano 1976, 1983, 1989, 1993, 2002, 2007).

16. Mario T. García's *Mexican Americans* analyzes the rise of the League of United Latin American Citizens (LULAC), educational politics in San Antonio, and the contributions of historical critics Carlos E. Castañeda, George I. Sánchez, and Arthur L. Campa as shapers of Mexican American identity. He analyzes the historical forces shaping Mexican American culture and identity. Building on García's work, George J. Sánchez's *Becoming Mexican American: Ethnicity, Culture, and Identity in Chicano Los Angeles, 1900–1945* examines religion, music, political culture, and community organization in Los Angeles to assess the intersecting cultural strands that shape Mexican American identity in the first half of the twentieth century. García's and Sánchez's pioneering works investigate different forms of community and legitimize the study of Mexican American identity, culture, and community as areas of interest for mainstream historical and cultural inquiry.

17. See Menchaca's *Recovering History, Constructing Race*, a work that transitions from historical studies of culture to more complex modes of historical and cultural analysis. Menchaca notes that many approaches to Chicano art

and culture omit African American contributions to mestizo culture and identity. She treats "Mexican American people's Indian, White, *and* Black racial history" in the American Southwest and shows mestizo identity to be shaped by the *intersection* of historical and cultural events and circumstances (2001, 1; italics added). Starting with the Spanish colonial concepts of race and how "racial status hierarchies are often structured upon the ability of one racial group to deny those who are racially different access to owning land," she sees ownership and access to land as important determinants of communal power and cultural identity (1). The Mexican American focus on land, which I will return to in chapter 3, is a persistent concern of Mexican Americans in light of the mainstream U.S. tendency to reduce land's significance to its market value without considering its traditional cultural significance tied to mestizo identity.

She then analyzes land ownership patterns of indigenous cultures in California to determine when key land relationships were still intact and culturally relevant to maintaining indigenous traditions and establishing a personal and communal sense of identity. She shows how indigenous communities celebrate their ties to land and how land relationships bear on every aspect of communal identity in California and Texas. Undertaking this exploration of mestizo identity as it can be understood in relation to land ownership, she is doing ethnographic interpretation in the discussion of her husband's Chumash and African ancestry. This many-sided, dynamic approach to historical understanding of indigenous and African heritages in relation to land ownership anticipates Kimberlé Crenshaw and those who focus on cultural and social intersections in the late 1980s and beyond. The attention that Menchaca gives to mestizo culture and its impact on racial identity sets the stage for other sophisticated studies of mestizo identity and race that will follow.

18. During this period, there are also new sociological approaches to understanding mestizo identity. One example is *Chicana/o Identity in a Changing U.S. Society: ¿Quién Soy? Quiénes Somos?* in which two social psychologists, Aída Hurtado and Patricia Gurin, examine the "subjective definitions [that] individuals have about the different social groups that they identify with" (2004, xviii-xix). They analyze the way that Mexican Americans describe their own ethnicity and race and how those descriptions reflect discrete areas of their experience. They research how Mexican Americans and Latinos view identity as part of a "transcultural," hemispheric perspective on the Americas and argue that this broad perspective benefits mainstream, non-Latino culture where people are living with unspoken and perhaps undiscovered "transcultural" perspectives of their own. Viewing mestizo identity within the context of "transculturation" across the Americas (117), largely the forces and influences discussed in *Mestizos Come Home!,* Hurtado and Gurin note that mainstream culture is acquiring "Spanish language ability and Mexican [and Latin

American] cultural knowledge that [will] allow them to navigate between different cultural worlds" (127). In the focus on mestizo identity, the Latino community is bringing new cultural skills into the mainstream community that will enhance the country's receptivity to Mexican American culture.

The importance that Hurtado and Gurin place on an emerging transculturation in the United States notes the rise of a common culture and sense of community, ideas that also arise in Laura E. Gómez's *Manifest Destinies: The Making of the Mexican American Race*. Gómez studies the renegotiation of racial categories in the U.S. colonization of northern Mexico and history in the late nineteenth and early twentieth centuries, especially during the time when Mexican Americans were *and* were not regarded as legally white.

The "mongrel" status of Mexican Americans as a multiracial people has on occasion led to questions concerning their on-again, off-again whiteness. Shifting definitions of whiteness have left Mexican Americans with little sense of their racial status at any one moment. Mexican Americans have often occupied "a position in the American racial hierarchy that was between white and nonwhite . . . 'off-white'" (2007, 83–84). This history of being white, nonwhite, and off-white has created awkward and painful periods of social rejection for the Mexican American community.

CHAPTER 3

I owe the suggestion for this chapter's title to Alicia Gaspar de Alba, "There's No Place Like Aztlán: Embodied Aesthetics in Chicana Art."

1. See Chris Wilson, *The Myth of Santa Fe* (1997). For a valuable overview of land problems in New Mexico, see Briggs and Van Ness, *Land, Water, and Culture* (1987).

2. An insightful discussion of Ritch's books, which I am generally following here, is Gutiérrez, "Aztlán, Montezuma, and New Mexico" (1989).

3. It is the overriding thesis of Gutiérrez's "Azlán, Montezuma, and New Mexico" that the drive to associate the territory of New Mexico with Aztlán was politically and commercially motivated.

4. The focus of "El Plan Espiritual de Aztlán" on Mexican American life and land, new and liberating, advanced that "EDUCATION must be relative to our people, i.e., history; culture, bilingual education, contributions, etc. Community control [is needed] of our schools, our teachers, our administrators, our counselors, and our programs" (1991, 3). Following this call to action, in March 1968, one thousand students walked out of Lincoln and Garfield High Schools (among others) in East Los Angeles, and a bloody "blow-out" confrontation followed in a seven-month standoff between the Chicano community, the police, and the Los Angeles Unified School District Board of Education (Rosales 1996, 184–85). Such protests and the concern for educational reform

274 NOTES TO PAGES 101–9

in "El Plan Espiritual de Aztlán " argued for the institution of bilingual education and student-oriented curricula in Latino schools across the country. Such protests also led to the startup of Chicano studies programs in colleges and universities nationally and even worldwide, an initiative advanced in detail in *El Plan de Santa Barbara* (Chicano Coordinating Council 1969).

Key to "El Plan Espiritual de Aztlán" was economic development to serve the Mexican American community. A Mexican American "economic program" could "drive the exploiter [white investors] out of our community" and bring about "a welding together of our people's combined resources to control their own production through cooperative effort." The community had to be willing to "make its own decisions" on "the taxation of goods" and "the profit of our sweat" (1991, 4). If needed, "Chicano defense units"—Brown Berets—could enforce economic and other transformative measures essential for advancing the Mexican American cause (2). An armed paramilitary unit had weak support as an initiative over time, but it was originally based on 1960s optimism about social protest, inspired by successes such as that of César Chávez (though nonviolent) in organizing the National Farm Workers Association and the United Farm Workers in Delano.

5. In 1979, Joseph Sommers wrote that the Aztlán idea was nothing more than a "harkening back in sadness and nostalgia for a forgotten, idealized, and unobtainable past," an empty cultural abstraction (Sommers and Ybarra 1979, 38). Others worried that the Aztlán movement was just another appropriation of Native culture for non-Native cultural capital and gain. But within the Mexican American community, the effect of the Aztlán claim was electric and helped to bring about a renaissance in Chicano culture, art, and social life. Aztlán was a constructed "place," if not a real location, and the early debunkers of Aztlán seemed to miss this larger picture and the significance of claiming a Mexican American homeland in the United States as a validating act in itself.

6. For a variety of perspectives on the multicultural approach to education and identity, see Giroux, *Border Crossings*, Anyon, "Social Class and the Hidden Curriculum of Work," Apple, *Ideology and Curriculum*, and Sleeter, *Empowerment through Multicultural Education*.

7. I fully understand that educational theorists and actual teachers are not *intending* to distance their students from racial issues by taking the broad view of ethnic cultures and races. David Hursh, for example, in "Multicultural Social Studies," seems to be arguing the opposite of multiculturalism as I describe it when he says the aim of multiculturalism is "to recognize, draw out, and analyze with students, the diversity of their own lives and society. . . . The school becomes a public arena where teachers, students, and others use history, political science, and other social sciences to make sense of their lives" (1997, 119). These are laudable aims, clearly. It is not evident to me that

multiculturalism as it has been theorized and advanced can actually accomplish such aims. While multiculturalism is the beginning of a good idea, it needs to be thought out far enough to recognize that the "view from nowhere" is not tenable or even desirable.

CHAPTER 5

1. Plato associated the mind, by contrast, almost completely with the highest cultural aspirations, creative endeavors, and rational thought, attributes that are "the highest, the best, the noblest, [and] the closest to God" (Bordo 2003, 5). The mind's lofty ambitions contrast to the lowly bodily pleasures cast as an "animal, as appetite, [a] deceiver, a [kind of] prison of the soul and confounder of [the mind's] projects" (3). The mind reaches for an elevated realm, the "best" of the human adventure, while the body squanders such opportunities owing to its base appetites of hunger, sexuality, and creature comfort. Trapped in a mortal, bodily shell with a dim future, as Judith Butler notes, "the mind occasionally seeks to flee its embodiment altogether" to commune with nature and God directly (1990, 17). This happens in Western scenarios of ecstatic experience, purported out-of-body events, and stories of people learning to fly to transcend their otherwise limited bodily lives. When transcendence is the goal, the Western body is almost always depicted as the "albatross," the regrettable necessity, around the neck of being human (Bordo 2003, 5).

2. There is cause for optimism in that the thick, cross-indexed nature of culture allows for the possibility of change in living traditions. The persistence and vitality in the La Llorona/La Malinche traditions show them to be works still being written that may yet be altered. "It's past time for [La Llorona/La Malinche] to cut her hair, put on her Nikes and tied-dyed-shirt, and get the life she's earned," writes Candelaria optimistically. If such cultural reorientation succeeds, a reconstituted and radically redirected La Llorona/La Malinche could "lead the radicals in organizing the quincentennial protests marking La Conquista de Méjico in 2021" (Candelaria 1997, 94).

Going in this creative direction alters La Llorona/La Malinche stories and strategically reframes them within the context of a larger, evolving cultural response to women's bodies in Mexican and Mexican American culture. In Gloria Anzaldúa's reinterpretation of this complex material, she proclaims that "la gente Chicana tiene tres madres" ("the Chicano people have three mothers"): "All three are mediators: *Guadalupe* [is] the virgin mother who has not abandoned us, *la Chingada (Malinche)* [is] the raped mother whom we have abandoned, and *la Llorona* [is] the mother who seeks her lost children and is a combination of the other two" (Anzaldúa 1987, 30). This approach recasts La Llorona/La Malinche as a broad cultural response to women that can be altered, not a misogynistic, inevitable conclusion about women corrupted by bodily pleasure. With this kind of cultural reframing, Chicana writers and scholars can reinterpret the past and undo the condemnation of women that these traditions promote.

3. This is a remarkable cultural transformation wherein La Malinche's body (always with ties to La Llorona) is recast in poetry to suggest an entirely new set of cultural coordinates framed and understood in different gender terms. On the order of recasting Eve's story in the Garden of Eden, this alternative interpretation of La Malinche rejects the idea that the actions of one young woman caused native people to succumb to Spanish rule. Even if Malintzín Tenepal did everything attributed to her, these poets are saying that it strains credulity to posit that a woman's reckless use of her body lost the Mesoamerican world for the Aztecs and others to the Spanish. In effect, the condemnation that Iracema suffered as a destructive indigenous woman (see chapter 2) is here redeemed as a new view of women and the female body in the Americas.

4. For discussion of her biography and health, see www.anb.org/articles/16/16–03593.html.

5. While seemingly the opposite of the Western body, the Mesoamerican body follows its own set of rules, surprising in their precision, in how it relates to the world. The contemporary curandera, indigenous folk healer, Elena Avila (with Joy Parker) lists specific Aztec protocols for keeping the body healthy physically, emotionally, and mentally, protocols that not only restrict the way the mestizo body behaves but reveals its rule-bound relationship to the environment and the world. She shows that Aztec health practices operate under the assumption that the *body*'s health is the prime standard for judging a person's general health, spiritual engagement, mental health, and even one's productive relationship with the social and physical world (1999, 34).

Central to human health is the notion of "balance," the guiding principle for healthy living. Whereas the Western idea of "balance" is often a loose set of beliefs about not concentrating too many interests in one corner of experience (hence "balanced"), Mesoamerican balance is a precise expectation, a formula, for how bodies can productively interact with other bodies and the environment. Underpinning balance and all values related to health is the goal to "to live in harmony with the universe," which is "made up of an immense net of energy channels that meet and combine at different points." The Aztecs believed (and still believe) that "if everything is in balance, what they refer to as supreme equilibrium exists," which is the optimal positioning of a person to "[benefit from] the universal energies, [which] . . . are also important in the human realm" to maintain a healthy body and a successful life (Avila and Parker 1999, 34).

This Aztec approach to staying healthy takes the form of mathematical formulas for acknowledging the relationship of the body's interior and exterior worlds, the self and the environment, in a way beneficial for health. In the

Aztec logarithm for effective living, the body interacts with the environment according to four percentages—52 percent, 26 percent, 13 percent, and 9 percent. The Aztecs believed, for example, that 52 percent of one's time should go to the body's proper respiration (since breathing is a reflex, I take this to mean respiratory/cardio health). Twenty-six percent is needed for the body's rest and sleep. Thirteen percent is required for proper hydration, and 9 percent goes to proper nutrition. Adjusting one's behavior to achieve these percentages enhances the body's interactions in its overlapping human and environmental relationships (Avila and Parker 1999, 34).

As a curandera with advanced training in Aztec healing practices, Avila champions this formula for balance as a best practice for healthy living. She also applies it to other areas of health, assigning 52 percent of a person's focus to personal health and that of family and community. Twenty-six percent goes toward maintaining creative and productive approaches to culture and traditions. Thirteen percent is allotted to the acquisition of wisdom and the development of perception, and 9 percent remains for the maintenance of conscience. These numbers, taken from the *body's* interactions with the environment, keep the body at the center of well-being and happiness in relation to the environment and the world (1999, 34).

6. What I have written here about Robert's male mask and Liz's openness is intentionally reminiscent of W. B. Yeats description of two portraits, one of a Venetian gentleman and the other of President Wilson: His thought is that the Venetian gentleman lives in his whole body, and a change in his thought would alter his posture. President Wilson lives only in his eyes, while the rest of his body is effectively dead (1999, 127–28).

7. The circumstances for creating this work are fascinating. From 1995 to 1996, Alex Donis produced a series of prints at Self Help Graphics (a community center) in east Los Angeles. Donis put texts over images of Catholic saints to give these figures psychological and sexual responses to their circumstances as saints. The project was canceled owing to the attention around the poster *I Lied*. www.latinoartcommunity.org.

8. He made this comment in 1999 on a PBS TV show that I hosted called *The Power of Ideas*.

9. Camille Flores-Turney quotes Jiménez on the importance of "coming to terms with the Indian and mestizo legacy in Mexico" (1997, 29), and E. Carmen Ramos points out that at least from the 1960s onward Jiménez started giving "keen attention to skin color" in his work and saw it as a critical feature in the depiction of mestizos (2012, 10).

10. He even received criticism from early Mexican viewers of *Fiesta Jarabe* for making "the male dancer" too "dark-skinned" and "too Indian" in appearance (Flores-Turney 1997, 32).

11. I wish to thank Pres. David L. Boren and Mrs. Molly Shi Boren for making possible this visionary and powerful display of Jiménez's work on the University of Oklahoma campus.

CHAPTER 6

Quotations from Tomás Rivera's "And the Earth Did Not Devour Him" (© 2015 Arte Público Press, University of Houston) are reprinted by permission of the publisher.

1. I quote some of the critical commentary about this novel to underline the fact that *Tierra* is that interesting case of a major text that is still a challenge for readers. Traditional commentary about Rivera's novel suggests appreciation of its achievement but with few details or analyses. An early commentator, John C. Akers writes in "Fragmentation in the Chicano Novel: Literary Technique and Cultural Identity" that Rivera's "use of fragmentation does not signal chaos or disintegration in Chicano literature." "To the contrary," he argues: "its development is a reflection of a consciously chosen path to bring readers to a deeper experience of the unique cultural identity of the Chicano" (1986, 124). Fragmentation in *Tierra* and other Chicano novels is "a progressive detailing of deception through an episodic unfolding of life," and this is a far as his analysis goes (133).

   Another general approach, with autobiographical overtones, involves seeing *Tierra's* chapters as corresponding to months of the year. In "The Search for Being, Identity and Form in the Work of Tómas Rivera," Juan Olivares says that "twelve stories and thirteen vignettes" in this novel function to "portray the life of migrant workers, each story representing a month of the lost year" of Rivera's own life that this novel is presumably recounting (1985, 68). For this twelve-month scheme to work, the first and last chapters must be omitted to get the months right. Olivares notes that Rolando Hinojosa, the Chicano novelist and Rivera's close friend, attests that in the original *Tierra* manuscript he saw that "the twelve stories had months for titles" (79n7). But the fact remains that this correspondence of months to chapters provides little understanding of *Tierra* as a narrative, no analysis of chapters, no explanation of their order or interrelationship, no sense of a progression, and so on. And yet this novel's success with two generations of readers tells us that there *is* a dynamic pattern energizing *Tierra's* chapters, which my interpretation accounts for and readers consistently respond to it.

2. An irony of the era from 1950 to 1960, as Douglas S. Massey and Julia Gelatt discuss, is that it was "a time when virtually all Mexicans working in the United States *were* documented, either as legal guest workers or permanent residents" (2010, 338; italics added). The later absence of a guest-worker program brought about the problem with the undocumented that people decry today.

CHAPTER 7

1. The following is not an exhaustive list, but it shows the writers who are most frequently associated with and discussed in relation to this period: Oscar Zeta Acosta (fiction), Rudolfo Anaya (fiction, poetry, drama, and essay), Lorna Dee Cervantes (poetry), Rodolfo "Corky" Gonzales (poetry), Rolando Hinojosa (fiction), Tomás Rivera (fiction, essay, and poetry), Luis Omar Salinas (poetry), Estela Portillo Trambley (drama and fiction), Luis Valdez (drama), Tino Villanueva (poetry), and John Rechy (fiction).

2. Again, this list is not meant to be exhaustive but to cover the figures most often associated with this generation of Mexican American writers: Gloria E. Anzaldúa (poetry and essay), Norma Elia Cantú (memoir and fiction), Ana Castillo (fiction, poetry, essay), Denise Chávez (fiction), Sandra Cisneros (fiction and poetry), Terri de la Peña (fiction), Alicia Gaspar de Alba (fiction and essay), Dagoberto Gilb (fiction), Ernest Anthony Mares (poetry), Demetria Martínez (poetry and fiction), Cherríe Moraga (drama, fiction, and essay), Sheila Ortiz Taylor (fiction), Alberto Ríos (poetry and fiction), Benjamin Alire Sáenz (poetry and fiction), Gary Soto (poetry and fiction), Luis Alberto Urrea (fiction and poetry), Alma Luz Villanueva (poetry), and Helena María Viramontes (fiction).

3. Of the three lists I have provided, this one is the most volatile in light of the fluid nature of contemporary writing and writing careers, and only a few of many possibilities are mentioned here: Adelina Anthony (fiction), Joseph Delgado (poetry), María Amparo Escandón (fiction), Rodney Gomez (poetry), Reyna Grande (fiction), Rigoberto González (fiction), Laurie Ann Guerrero (poetry), David Tomás Martínez (poetry), Domingo Martínez (memoir), Michael Nava (fiction), Maceo Montoya (poetry), Daniel A. Olivas (fiction), Melinda Palacio (fiction and poetry), Toni Margarita Plummer (fiction), Patricia Santana (fiction), Sergio Troncoso (fiction), Carla Trujillo (fiction), Alfredo Véa Jr.(fiction), Richard Yañez (fiction), and Mario Alberto Zambrano (fiction).

4. For the history of *critique*, see Robert Con Davis-Undiano and Ronald Schleifer, *Criticism and Culture: The Role of Critique in Modern Literary Theory*.

5. As Rich comments in "Toward A Woman-Centered University," this model for education would be receptive to many different kinds of knowledge—"folk medicine, the psychology, architecture, economics, and diet of prisons; union history, the economics of the small farmer," traditional knowledge and new knowledge derived from technology and theory (1979, 152–53). She recommends that "as a research institution, [the university] should organize its resources around problems specific to its community" (152). This conception of a university would establish "a sympathetic and concerned relation with all

of these groups [that make up its local community and] would involve members of the university in solving an extremely rich cluster of problems (153). She concludes by saying that "the nature of such research (and its usefulness) might be improved if it were conceived as research *for*, rather than *on*, human beings" (153).

6. For discussion of scholarly writing in the essay format, see my "Back to the Essay: *World Literature Today* in the Twenty-First Century" and "No Scholar Left Behind in the Future of Scholarly Writing."

Works Cited

Abrams, M. H. 2009. *A Glossary of Literary Terms.* Boston: Wadsworth Cengage Learning.

Acosta, Oscar Zeta. 1972. *The Autobiography of a Brown Buffalo.* New York: Vintage Books.

———. 1973. *The Revolt of the Cockroach People.* New York: Vintage Books.

Acuña, Rodolfo. 2000. *Occupied America: A History of Chicanos.* New York: Longman.

———. 2011. *The Making of Chicana/o Studies: In the Trenches of Academe.* New Brunswick, N.J.: Rutgers University Press.

Ahluwalia, Pal, Bill Ashcroft, and Roger Knight, eds. 1999. *White and Deadly: Sugar and Colonialism.* Hauppauge: Nova Science Publishers.

Ahmed, Sara, Claudia Castañeda, Anne-Marie Fortier, and Mimi Sheller. 2003. *Uprootings/Regroundings: Questions of Home and Migration.* Oxford: Berg.

Akers, John C. 1986. "Fragmentation in the Chicano Novel: Literary Technique and Cultural Identity." In *International Studies in Honor of Tomás Rivera,* edited by Julián Olivares, 121–35. Houston: Arté Publico Press.

Aldama, Arturo J. 2001. *Disrupting Savagism: Intersecting Chicana/o, Mexican Immigrant, and Native American Struggles for Self-Representation.* Durham, N.C.: Duke University Press.

Aldama, Arturo J., and Naomi H. Quiñonez, eds. 2002. *Decolonial Voices: Chicana and Chicano Cultural Studies in the 21st Century.* Bloomington: Indiana University Press.

Alencar, José de. 2000. *Iracema.* Translated by Clifford E. Landers. New York: Oxford University Press.

Almaguer, Tomás. 1994. *Racial Fault Lines: The Historical Origins of White Supremacy in California.* Berkeley: University of California Press.

Alonso O'Crouley, Pedro. 1972. *A Description of the Kingdom of New Spain, 1774.* Translated and edited by Seán Galvin. San Francisco: John Howell Books.

Alurista. 1991. "Myth, Identity and Struggle in Three Chicano Novels: Aztlán . . . Anaya, Méndez, and Acosta." In *Aztlán: Essays on the Chicano Homeland,* edited by Rudolfo A. Anaya and Francisco Lomelí, 219–29. Albuquerque: University of New Mexico Press.

Anaya, Rudolfo A. 1972. *Bless Me, Ultima.* Berkeley, Calif.: TQS Publications.

————. 1988. *Heart of Aztlán: A Novel.* Albuquerque: University of New Mexico Press.

————. 1990. "Rudolfo A. Anaya: An Autobiography, 1937–." In *Rudolfo A. Anaya: Focus on Criticism,* edited by César A. González-T., 359–88. La Jolla, Calif.: Lalo Press.

————. 1991. "Aztlán: A Homeland without Boundaries." In *Aztlán: Essays on the Chicano Homeland,* edited by Rudolfo A. Anaya and Francisco Lomelí, 230–41. Albuquerque: University of New Mexico Press.

————. 1992. "Rudolfo Anaya." In *Interviews with Writers of the Post-Colonial World,* edited by Feroza Jussawalla and Reed Way Dasenbrock, 244–55. Jackson: University Press of Mississippi.

————. 1995a. *The Anaya Reader.* New York: Warner Books.

————. 1995b. *Zia Summer.* New York: Warner Books.

————. 1996. *Rio Grande Fall.* New York: Warner Books.

————. 1999a. "Shaman of Words." *Genre* 32 (1 and 2) (Spring–Summer, 1999): 15–26. Special issue edited by Rudolfo Anaya and Robert Con Davis-Undiano.

————. 1999b. *Shaman Winter.* New York: Warner Books.

————. 2005. *Jemez Spring.* Albuquerque: University of New Mexico Press.

————. 2009. *The Essays.* Norman: University of Oklahoma Press.

Anaya, Rudolfo A., and Francisco Lomeli, eds. 1991. *Aztlán: Essays on the Chicano Homeland.* Albuquerque: University of New Mexico Press.

Antonsich, M. 2010. "Searching Belonging—An Analytical Framework." *Geography Compass* 4 (6): 644–59.

Anyon, Jean. 1980. "Social Class and the Hidden Curriculum of Work." *Journal of Education* 162: 67–92.

Anzaldúa, Gloria. 1987. *Borderlands/La Frontera: The New Mestiza.* San Francisco: aunt lute books.

Apple, Michael M. 1979. *Ideology and Curriculum.* London: Routledge and Kegan Paul.

Arroyo, Sergio Raúl. 2004. "In Praise of the Mesoamerican Body." *Artes de México* 69: 75–77.

Arteaga, Alfred, ed. 1994. *An Other Tongue: Nation and Ethnicity in the Linguistic Borderlands.* Durham, N.C.: Duke University Press.

————. 1997. *Chicano Poetics: Heterotexts and Hybridities.* Cambridge: Cambridge University Press.

Atencio, Tomás. 2009. "El Oro del Barrio in the Cyber Age: Leapfrogging the Industrial Revolution." In *Resolana: Emerging Chicano Dialogues On Community and Globalization,* by Miguel Montiel; Tomás Atencio; E. A. Mares, 9–68. Tucson: University of Arizona Press.

Austin, Alfredo López. 2004. "The Mesoamerican Conception of the Body." *Artes de Mexico* 69: 77–84.

Avila, Elena, and Joy Parker. 1999. *Woman Who Glows in the Dark: A Curandera Reveals Traditional Aztec Secrets of Physical and Spiritual Health*. New York: Jeremy Press, Tarcher/Putnam.

Bachelard, Gaston. 1964. *The Poetics of Space*. Boston: Beacon Press.

Bailey, Gauvin Alexander. 2005. *Art of Colonial Latin America*. London: Phaidon Press.

Baudrillard, Jean. 2010. *America*. Translated by Chris Turner. London: Verso.

Beck, Peggy. 1980. "The Low Riders: Folk Art and Emergent Nationalism." *Native Arts/West* 4: 25–27.

Bender, Steven W. 2003. *Greasers and Gringos: Latinos, Law, and the American Imagination*. New York: New York University Press.

Benhabib, Seyla. 1986. *Critique, Norm, and Utopia: A Study of the Foundations of Critical Theory*. New York: Columbia University Press.

Bhabha, Homi K. 1994. *The Location of Culture*. London: Routledge.

Blumenbach, Johann. 1969. *On the Natural Varieties of Mankind*. Translated by Thomas Bendyshe. New York: Bergman. Originally published 1865.

Bordo, Susan. 2003. *Unbearable Weight: Feminism, Western Culture, and the Body*. Berkeley: University of California Press. Originally published 1993.

Bost, Suzanne. 2010. *Encarnación: Illness and Body Politics in Chicana Feminist Literature*. New York: Fordham University Press.

Bourdieu, Pierre. 1990. *The Logic of Practice*. Translated by Richard Nice. Stanford, Calif.: Stanford University Press.

Brandes, Stanley. 1997. "Sugar, Colonialism, and Death: On the Origins of Mexico's Day of the Dead." *Comparative Studies in Society and History* 39 (2): 270–99.

———. 1998a. "The Day of the Dead, Halloween, and the Quest for Mexican National Identity." *Journal of American Folklore* 111 (442): 359–80.

———. 1998b. "Iconography in Mexico's Day of the Dead: Origins and Meaning." *Ethnohistory* 45 (2): 181–218.

Brenson, Michael. 1997. "Movement's Knowledge." In *Luis Jiménez: Working Class Heroes: Images from the Popular Culture*, 11–20. Kansas City: Mid-America Arts Alliance.

Briggs, Charles L., and John R. Van Ness. 1987. Introduction to *Land, Water, and Culture: New Perspectives on Hispanic Land Grants*, 3–13. Albuquerque: University of New Mexico Press.

Bright, Brenda. 1985. "Remappings: Los Angeles Low Riders." In *Looking High and Low: Art and Cultural Identity*, edited by Brenda Bright and Lisa Blakewell, 89–123. Tucson: University of Arizona Press.

———. 1998. "'Heart Like a Car': Hispano/Chicano Culture in Northern New Mexico." *American Ethnologist* 25 (4): 583–609.

Brimelow. Peter. 1996. *Alien Nation: Common Sense about America's Immigration Disaster*. New York: Harper Perennial.

Brinton, Daniel Garrison. 1891. *The American Race: A Linguistic Classification and Ethnographic Description of the Native Tribes of North and South America.* New York: N. D. C. Hodges.

Bruce-Novoa, Juan. 1975. "The Space of Chicano Literature." *De Colores* 1: 22–42.

———. 1980. *Chicano Authors: Inquiry by Interview.* Austin: University of Texas Press.

———. 1982. *Chicano Poetry: A Response to Chaos.* Austin: University of Texas Press.

Burciaga, José Antonio. 1993. *Drink Cultura: Chicanismo.* Santa Barbara, Calif.: Joshua Odell Editions.

Burke, Kenneth. 1966. *Language As Symbolic Action.* Berkeley: University of California Press.

Butler, Judith. 1990. *Gender Trouble: Feminism and the Subversion of Identity.* New York: Routledge.

———. 1993. *Bodies That Matter: On the Discursive Limits of "Sex."* New York: Routledge.

Cahill, David. 1994. "Colour by Numbers: Racial and Ethnic Categories in the Viceroyalty of Peru, 1532–1824." *Journal of Latin American Studies* 26 (2): 325–46.

Calderón, Héctor, and José David Saldívar, eds. 1991. *Criticism in the Borderlands: Studies in Chicano Literature, Culture, and Ideology.* Durham, N.C.: Duke University Press.

Calvo, Luz. 2004. "Art Comes for the Archbishop: The Semiotics of Contemporary Chicana Feminism and the World of Alma López." *Meridians* 5 (1): 201–24.

Candelaria, Cordelia. 1997. "Letting La Llorona Go, or, Re/reading History's 'Tender Mercies.'" In *Literatura Chicana: 1965–1995,* edited by Manuel de Jesús Hernández-Gutiérrez and David William Foster, 93–97. New York: Garland Publishing.

Cann, Howard M. 1998. "Diversite genomique humaine." *Comptes Rendus de l'Academie des Sciences Series III Sciences de la Vie* 321 (6): 443–46.

Carrera, Magali M. 2003. *Imagining Identity in New Spain: Race, Lineage, and the Colonial Body in Portraiture and Casta Paintings.* Austin: University of Texas Press.

Carter-Sanborn, Kristin. 1999. "Tongue-Tied: Chicana Feminist Textual Politics and the Future of Chicano/Chicana Studies." *Genre* 32 (1 and 2): 73–84. Special issue edited by Rudolfo Anaya and Robert Con Davis-Undiano.

Castañeda, Jorge G. 1995. *The Mexican Shock: Its Meaning for the U.S.* New York: New Press.

Castillo, Ana. 1990. *Sapogonia: An Antiromance in 3/8 Meter.* Tempe, Ariz.: Bilingual Press/Editorial Bilingüe.

———. 1994. *Massacre of the Dreamers: Essays on Xicanisma.* Albuquerque: University of New Mexico Press.

Castillo, Debra. 1992. *Talking Back: Toward A Latin-American Feminist Literary Criticism.* Ithaca, N.Y.: Cornell University Press.

Chappell, Ben. 2012. *Lowrider Space: Aesthetics and Politics of Mexican American Custom Cars.* Austin: University of Texas Press.

Chávez, Denise. 1991. *Last of the Menu Girls.* Houston: Arte Publico Press.

Chávez, Ernesto. 2002. "¡Mi Raza Primero!" (My People First!): Nationalism, Identity, and Insurgency in the Chicano Movement in Los Angeles, 1966–1978. Berkeley: University of California Press.

Chávez, John R. 1991. "Aztlán, Cibola, and Frontier New Spain." In *Aztlán: Essays on the Chicano Homeland,* edited by Rudolf A. Anaya and Francisco Lomeli, 49–71. Albuquerque: University of New Mexico Press.

Chavez, Linda. 1991. *Out of the Barrio: Toward a New Politics of Hispanic Assimilation.* New York: Basic Books.

Chicano Coordinating Council on Higher Education. 1969. *El Plan de Santa Bárbara.* Oakland, Calif.: La Cause Publications.

Cisneros, Sandra. 1987. *My Wicked, Wicked Ways.* Berkeley, Calif.: Third Woman Press.

———. 1992. "Sandra Cisneros." In *Interviews with Writers of the Post-Colonial World,* edited by Feroza Jussawalla and Reed Way Dasenbrock, 286–306. Jackson: University Press of Mississippi.

———. 1994. *Loose Woman.* New York: Knopf.

———. 1996. "Guadalupe the Sex Goddess." In *Goddess of the Americas: La Diosa de las Américas,* edited by Ana Castillo, 46–51. New York: Riverhead.

Code, Lorraine. 1991. *What Can She Know? Feminist Theory and the Construction of Knowledge.* Ithaca, N.Y.: Cornell University Press.

Concannon, Kevin, Francisco A. Lomelí, and Marc Priewe, eds. 2009. *Imagined Transnationalism: U.S./Latino/a Literature, Culture, and Identity.* New York: Palgrave/Macmillan.

Cook, Sherbourne F., and Woodrow Borah. 1979. *Essays in Population History: Mexico and California.* Berkeley: University of California Press.

Cope, R. Douglas. 1994. *The Limits of Racial Domination: Plebeian Society in Colonial Mexico City, 1660–1720.* Madison: University of Wisconsin Press.

Corpi, Lucha. 1993. "Marina." In *Infinite Divisions: An Anthology of Chicana Literature,* edited by Tey Diana Rebolledo and Eliana S. Rivero, 196–97. Tucson: University of Arizona Press.

Cota-Cárdenas, Margarita. 1993. "Malinche a Cortez y Vice Versa/La Malinche to Cortez and Vice Versa." In *Infinite Divisions: An Anthology of Chicana Literature,* edited by Tey Diana Rebolledo and Eliana S. Rivero, 200–202. Tucson: University of Arizona Press.

Cruz, Cindy. 2001. "Toward an Epistemology of a Brown Body." *International Journal of Qualitative Studies in Education* 14 (5): 660–69.

Dávila, Arlene. 2001. *Latinos Inc.: The Marketing and Making of a People.* Berkeley: University of California Press.

Davis-Undiano, Robert Con. 2000. "Back to the Essay: *World Literature Today* in the Twenty-First Century." *World Literature Today* 74 (1): 5–9.

———. 2005. "No Scholar Left Behind in the Future of Scholarly Writing." *LIT: Literature Interpretation Theory* 16 (4): 359–70.

———. 2016. "Rudolfo Anaya." In *Oxford Bibliographies in American Literature,* edited by Jackson Bryer, Richard Kopley, and Paul Lauter. New York: Oxford University Press.

Davis-Undiano, Robert Con, and Ronald Schleifer. 1991. *Criticism and Culture: The Role of Critique in Modern Literary Theory.* Essex: Longman.

Dawson, Alexander S. 2004. *Indian and Nation in Revolutionary Mexico.* Tucson: University of Arizona Press.

De Castro, Juan E. 2002. *Mestizo Nations: Culture, Race, and Conformity in Latin American Literature.* Tucson: University of Arizona Press.

DeGruy, Joy. 2006. *Post Traumatic Slave Syndrome.* Portland, Ore.: Joy DeGruy Publications.

Deleuze, Gilles, and Félix Guattari. 1977. *Anti-Oedipus: Capitalism and Schizophrenia,* vol. 1. Translated by Robert Hurley, Mark Seem, and Helen Lane. New York: Viking.

Delgado Bernal, Dolores. 2002. "Critical Race Theory, Latino Critical Theory, and Critical Race-Gendered Epistemologies: Recognizing Students of Color as Holders and Creators of Knowledge." *Qualitative Inquiry* 8 (1): 105–26.

Delgado, Richard, and Jean Stefancic. 2012. *Critical Race Theory: An Introduction.* New York: New York University Press.

de Montellano, Ortiz. 1989. "The Body, Ethics, and Cosmos: Aztec Physiology." In *The Imagination of Matter: Religion and Ecology in Mesoamerican Tradition,* edited by Davíd Carrasco, 191–209. Oxford: BAR International Series 515.

Dewey, John. 1927. *The Public and Its Problems.* New York: H. Holt.

Díaz, Junot. 2007. *The Brief Wondrous Life of Oscar Wao.* New York: Riverhead Books.

Dowling, Julie A. 2014. *Mexican Americans and the Question of Race.* Austin: University of Texas Press.

Du Bois, W. E. B. 1903. *The Souls of Black Folk.* Chicago: A. C. McClurg.

Duncan, Arne. 2012. "Minority Students Face Harsher Discipline, Fewer Options, New Federal Data Shows." *Huffington Post,* March 16.

Dunn, Richard S. 2000. *Sugar and Slaves: The Rise of the Planter Class in the English West Indies.* Williamsburg, Va.: Early American History and Culture.

Ebright, Malcolm. 1987. "New Mexican Land Grants: The Legal Background." In *Land, Water, and Culture: New Perspectives on Hispanic Land Grants,* edited by Charles L. Briggs and John R. Van Ness, 15–64. Albuquerque: University of New Mexico Press.

Eliot, T. S. 1920. "Tradition and the Individual Talent." In *The Sacred Wood: Essays on Poetry and Criticism*, 47–59. London: Methuen.

Elizondo, Virgilio. 2000. *The Future Is Mestizo: Life Where Cultures Meet*. Introduction by David Carrasco. Rev. ed. Boulder: University of Colorado Press.

"El Plan Espiritual de Aztlán." 1991. In *Aztlán: Essays on the Chicano Homeland*, edited by Rudolfo A. Anaya and Francisco Lomeli, 1–5. Albuquerque: University of New Mexico Press.

Esteva-Fabregat, Claudio. 1994. *Mestizaje in Ibero-America*. Tucson: University of Arizona Press.

Fanon, Frantz. 2004. *The Wretched of the Earth*. Translated by Richard Philcox. New York: Grove Press.

Fenster, T. 2004. *The Global City and the Holy City: Narratives of Planning, Knowledge, and Diversity*. New York: Pearson/Prentice Hall.

Fernández, Francisco Lizcano. 2005. "Composición Étnica de las Tres Áreas Culturales del Continente Americano al Comienzo del Siglo XXI." *Convergencia* 38: 185–232; table on p. 218.

Flores, William V., and Rina Benmayor, eds. 1997. *Latino Cultural Citizenship: Claiming Identity, Space, and Rights*. Boston: Beacon Press.

Flores-Turney, Camille. 1997. *Howl: The Artwork of Luis Jiménez*. Santa Fe: New Mexico Magazine.

Foley, Neil. 1997. *The White Scourge: Mexicans, Blacks, and Poor Whites in Texas Cotton Culture*. Berkeley: University of California Press.

———. 2014. *Mexicans in the Making of America*. Cambridge, Mass.: Harvard University Press.

Franco, Jean. 1969. *An Introduction to Spanish American Literature*. Cambridge: Cambridge University Press.

Fry, Richard. 2009. "The Changing Pathways of Hispanic Youths into Adulthood." Pew Hispanic Center. October 7, 1–27. www.pewhispanic.org/www.pewhispanic.org, accessed July 26, 2016.

———. 2010. "Hispanics, High School Dropouts and the GED." Pew Hispanic Center. May 13, 1–19. www.pewhispanic.org/, accessed July 26, 2016.

———. 2011. "Hispanic College Enrollment Spikes, Narrowing Gaps with Other Groups." Pew Hispanic Center. August 25, 1–25. www.pewhispanic.org/, accessed July 26, 2016

Fry, Richard, and Mark Hugo Lopez. 2012. "Hispanic Student Enrollments Reach New Highs in 2011. Pew Hispanic Center. August 20, 1–26. www.pewhispanic.org/, accessed July 26, 2016.

Fry, Richard, and Paul Taylor. 2013. "Hispanic High School Graduates Pass Whites in Rate of College Enrollment." Pew Hispanic Center. May 9, 1–12. www.pewhispanic.org/, accessed July 26, 2016.

Galeano, Eduardo. 1992a. *The Book of Embraces.* Translated by Cedric Belfrage. New York: W. W. Norton.

———. 1992b. *We Say No: Chronicles, 1963–1991.* Translated by Mark Fried. New York: W. W. Norton.

García, Mario T. 1989. *Mexican Americans: Leadership, Ideology, & Identity, 1930–1960.* New Haven, Conn.: Yale University Press.

García, Reyes. 1998. "Notes on (Home) Land Ethics: Ideas, Values, and the Land." In *Chicano Culture, Ecology, Politics: Subversive Kin,* edited by Devon G. Peña, 79–118. Tucson: University of Arizona Press.

García Muniz, Humberto. 2010. *Sugar and Power in the Caribbean.* San Juan: La Editorial Universidad de Puerto Rico.

García Sáiz, María Concepción. 1985. *La américa española en la época de Carlos III.* Exch. Cat. Seville: Archivo General De Indias, Ministerio de Cultura.

———. 1989. *The Castes: A Genre of Mexican Painting.* Edited by Mario de la Torre and Claudio Landucci. Np: Olivetti.

Gaspar de Alba, Alicia. 1993. "Malichista, a Myth Revisted." In *Infinite Divisions: An Anthology of Chicana Literature,* edited by Tey Diana Rebolledo and Eliana S. Rivero, 212–13. Tucson: University of Arizona Press.

Gaspar de Alba, Alicia, and Alma López. 2004. "There's No Place Like Aztlán: Embodied Aesthetics in Chicana Art." *New Centennial Review* 4 (2): 103–40.

———, eds. 2011. *Our Lady of Controversy: Alma López's Irreverent Apparition.* Austin: University of Texas Press.

Giroux, Henry A. 1992. *Border Crossings: Cultural Workers and the Politics of Education.* New York: Routledge.

Gómez, Laura E. 2007. *Manifest Destinies: The Making of the Mexican American Race.* New York: New York University Press.

Gómez-Peña, Guillermo. 2005. *Ethno-techno: Writings on Performance, Activism, and Pedagogy.* New York: Routledge.

Gonzales, Rodolfo. 1997. "I Am Joaquin." In *Literatura Chicana, 1965–1995: An Anthology in Spanish, English and Caló,* edited by Manuel De Jesús Hernáandez-Gutiérrez and David William Foster, 207–22. New York: Garland Publishing. Originally published 1967.

Gonzales-Berry, Erlinda. 1993. "Malinche Past: Selection from Paletitas de guayaba." In *Infinite Divisions: An Anthology of Chicana Literature,* edited by Tey Diana Rebolledo and Eliana S. Riverso, 207–12. Tucson: University of Arizona Press.

Gonzalez-Barrera, Ana, and Mark Hugo Lopez. 2013. "A Demographic Portrait of Mexican-Origin Hispanics in the United States." Pew Hispanic Center. 1–7. www.pewhispanic.org/, accessed July 26, 2016.

Gould, Stephen Jay. 1981. *The Mismeasure of Man.* New York: Norton.

Graham, Richard, ed. 1990. *The Idea of Race in Latin America, 1870–1940.* Austin: University of Texas Press.

Gratton, Brian, and Myron Gutmann. 2000. "Hispanics in the US, 1850–1990 Estimates of Population Size and National Origin." *Historical Methods* 33 (3): 137–53. www.tandfonline.com/loi/vhim20#.V5RSFmgrLIU, accessed July 24, 2016.

Griffin, John. 1995. *A Shared Space: Folklife in the Arizona-Sonora Borderlands.* Logan: Utah State University Press.

Griswold Del Castillo, Richard. 1990. *The Treaty of Guadalupe Hidalgo: A Legacy of Conflict.* Norman: University of Oklahoma Press.

Grosfoguel, Ramón. 2002. "Colonial Difference, Geopolitics of Knowledge, and Global Coloniality in the Modern/Colonial Capitalist World-System." *Review* 25 (3): 203–24.

———. 2006. "World-Systems Analysis in the Context of Transmodernity, Border Thinking, and Global Coloniality." *Review* 29 (2): 167–87.

———. 2012. "Les dilemmes de etudes ethniques aux États-Unis." *IdeAs* 2. https:// ideas.revues.org/, accessed July 24, 2016.

Guissani, Luigi. 2001. *The Risk of Education: Discovering Our Ultimate Destiny.* New York: Crossroad Publishing.

Gutiérrez, Ramón A. 1991. "Aztlán, Montezuma, and New Mexico: The Political Uses of American Indian Mythology." In *Aztlán: Essays on the Chicano Homeland,* edited by Rudolfo A. Anaya and Francisco Lomeli, 172–90. Albuquerque: University of New Mexico Press.

Gutiérrez-Jones, Carl. 1995. *Rethinking the Borderlands: Between Chicano Culture and Legal Discourse.* Berkeley: University of California Press.

Hage, G. 1997. "At Home in the Entrails of the West: Multiculturalism, 'Ethnic Food' and Migrant Home Building." In *Home/World Space, Community, and Marginality in Sydney's West,* edited by H. Grace, G. Hage, L. Johnson, J. Langsworth, and M. Symonds, 1–47. Western Sydney: Pluto Press.

Haney López, Ian. 1996. *White by Law: The Legal Construction of Race.* New York: New York University Press.

Hannerz, U. 2002. "Where Are We and Who We Want to Be." In *The Post National Self: Belonging and Identity,* 217–32. Minneapolis: University of Minnesota Press.

Hassig, Ross. 1994. *Mexico and the Spanish Conquest.* London: Longman.

Haya de la Torre, Víctor Raúl. 1956. *Trienta Años de Aprismo.* Mexico City: Fonde de Cultura Econónmica.

———. 1973. *Aprismo. The Ideas and Doctrines of Víctor Raúl Haya de la Torre.* Translated by Robert J. Alexander. Kent, Ohio: Kent State University Press.

———. 1986. *Espacio-Tiempo-Historico.* Lima: Serie Ideologia Aprista.

Hayes-Bautista, David E. 2012. *El Cinco de Mayo: An American Tradition.* Berkeley: University of California Press.

Heredia, Juanita. 2009. *Transnational Latina Narratives in the Twenty-First Century: The Politics of Gender, Race, and Migrations.* New York: Palgrave/ MacMillan.

Herrera-Sobek, María. 1990. *The Mexican Corrido: A Feminist Analysis.* Bloomington: Indiana University Press.

——. 1999. "Gaspar Pérez de Villagrá's Memorial: Aristotelian Rhetoric and the Discourse of Justification in a Colonial Genre." *Genre* 32 (1 and 2): 85–98. Special issue edited by Rudolfo Anaya and Robert Con Davis-Undiano.

——. 2012. *Celebrating Latino Folklore: An Encyclopedia of Cultural Traditions.* Santa Barbara, Calif.: ABC-CLIO.

——. 2015. "Casta Paintings and the Black Legend: Ideology and Representation of Black Africans in New Spain (1700–1790)." In *Slavery as a Global and Regional Phenomenon*, edited by Eric Hilgendorf, Jan-Christoph Marschelke, and Karin Sekora, 85–100. Heidelberg: Universitatsverlag Winter.

Hickey, Dave. 1997. "Luis Jiménez and the Incarnation of Democracy." In *Luis Jiménez: Working Class Heroes: Images from the Popular Culture*, 21–27. Kansas City: Mid-America Arts Alliance.

Hicks, Emily D. 1991. *Border Writing: The Multidimensional Text.* Minneapolis: University of Minnesota Press.

Hobson, Geary, ed. 1993. *The Remembered Earth: An Anthology of Contemporary Native-American Literature.* Albuquerque: University of New Mexico Press.

Hoover, Elizabeth, Katsi Cook, Ron Plain, Kathy Sanchez, Vi Waghiyi, Pamela Miller, Renee Dufault, Caitlin Sislin, and Davis O. Carpenter. 2012. "Indigenous Peoples of North America: Environmental Exposures and Reproductive Justice." *Environmental Health Perspectives* 120 (2): 1645–49.

Howard, Phillip A. 2015. *Black Labor, White Sugar: Caribbean Braceros and Their Struggle for Power in the Cuban Sugar Industry.* Baton Rouge: Louisiana State University Press.

Huerta, Benito. 1997. "Working Class Heroes." In *Luis Jiménez: Working Class Heroes: Images from the Popular Culture*, 7–10. Kansas City: Mid-America Arts Alliance.

Huntington, Samuel P. 2004. *Who Are We? The Challenges to America's National Identity.* New York: Simon and Schuster.

Hursh, David. 1997. "Multicultural Social Studies: Schools as Places for Examining and Challenging Inequality." In *The Social Studies Curriculum: Purposes, Problems, and Possibilities*, edited by E. Wayne Ross, 107–19. Albany: State University of New York Press.

Hurtado, Aida, and Patricia Gurin. 2004. *Chicana/o Identity in a Changing U.S. Society: ¿Quién Soy? ¿Quiénes Somos?* Tucson: University of Arizona Press.

Hyams, Melissa. 2003. "Adolescent Latina Bodyspaces: Making Homegirls, Homebodies, and Homeplaces." *Antipode* 35 (3): 536–58.

Iceland, John. 2003. "Why Poverty Remains High: The Role of Income Growth, Economic Inequality, and Changes in Family Structure." *Demography* 40 (3): 499–519.

Inda, Jonathan Xavier. 2000. "Performativity, Materiality, and the Racial Body." *Latino Studies Journal* 11 (3): 74–99.

Jiménez, Tomás. 2010. *Replenished Ethnicity: Mexican Americans, Immigration, and Identity.* Berkeley: University of California Press.

Jussawalla, Feroza, and Reed Way Dasenbrock, eds. 1992. *Interviews with Writers of the Post-Colonial World.* Jackson: University Press of Mississippi.

Katzew, Ilona. 2004. *Casta Painting: Images of Race in Eighteenth-Century Mexico.* New Haven, Conn.: Yale University Press.

Katzew, Ilona, and Susan Deans-Smith, eds. 2009. *Race and Classification: The Case of Mexican America.* Stanford, Calif.: Stanford University Press.

King, Rosemary A. 2004. *Border Confluences: Borderland Narratives from the Mexican War to the Present.* Tucson: University of Arizona Press.

Knight, Alan. 1990. "Race, Revolution, and *Indigenismo:* Mexico, 1910–1940." In *The Idea of Race in Latin America, 1870–1940*, edited by Richard Graham, 71–113. Austin: University of Texas Press.

Kochhar, Rakesh. 2012. "The Demographics of the Jobs Recovery." Pew Hispanic Center. 1–40. www.pewhispanic.org/, accessed July 26, 2016.

Kochhar, Rakesh, Ana Gonzalez-Barrera, and Daniel Dockterman. 2009. "Through Boom and Bust: Minorities, Immigrants and Homeownership." Pew Hispanic Center. 1–42. www.pewhispanic.org/, accessed July 26, 2016.

Lafaye, Jacques. 1998. "Mexican Casta Painting: Caste Society in New Spain." *Artes de México* 2 (8): 81–83.

Lastra, Yolanda. 1992. "The Present-Day Indigenous Languages of Mexico: An Overview." *International Journal of the Sociology of Language* 96: 35–43.

Latorre, Guisela. 2008. "Icons of Love and Devotion: Alma López's Art." *Feminist Studies* 34 (1/2): 131–51.

Lefebvre, Henri. 1991. *The Production of Space.* Translated by Donald Nicholson-Smith. Oxford: Blackwell. Originally published as *La Production de 'espace*, 1974.

Lemire, Elise. 2002. *"Miscegenation": Making Race in America.* Philadelphia: University of Pennsylvania Press.

Lipset, Seymour Martin. 1996. *American Exceptionalism: A Double-Edged Sword.* New York: W. W. Norton.

Livingston, Gretchen. 2000. "Hispanics, Health Insurance and Health Care Access." Pew Hispanic Center. 1–5. www.pewhispanic.org/, accessed July 26, 2016.

Lomelí, Francisco. 1993. *Handbook of Hispanic Cultures in the United States: Literature and Art.* Houston: Arte Publico Press.

Lopez, Barry. 1992. *The Rediscovery of North America.* New York: Vintage.

Lopez, Mark Hugo, Gretchen Livingston, and Rakesh Kochhar. 2009. "Hispanics and the Economic Downturn: Housing Woes and Remittance Cuts." Pew Hispanic Center. 1–43. www.pewhispanic.org/, accessed July 26, 2016.

Loza, Steven. 1993. *Barrio Rhythm: Mexican American Music in Los Angeles.* Urbana: University of Illinois Press.

Lugones, María. 2007. "Heterosexualism and the Colonial/Modern Gender System." *Hypatia* 22 (1): 186–209.

Maciel, David R., and María Herrera-Sobek, eds. 1998. *Culture across Borders: Mexican Immigration and Popular Culture.* Tucson: University of Arizona Press.

Maciel, David R., Isidro D. Ortiz, and María Herrera-Sobek, eds. 2000. *Chicano Renaissance: Contemporary Cultural Trends.* Tucson: University of Arizona Press.

Madison, James. 2009. "The Federalist No. 10, The Same Subject (The Utility of the Union as a Safeguard Against Domestic Faction and Insurrection) Continued." In *The Federalist Papers.* Edited and introduction by Ian Shapiro, 47–53. New Haven, Conn.: Yale University Press.

Madsen, Deborah L. 2000. *Understanding Contemporary Chicana Literature.* Columbia: University of South Carolina Press.

Manriquez, B. J. 1999. "Doing Rhetorical Analysis—*Sapagonia:* The Rhetoric of Irony." *Genre* 32 (1–2): 53–72. Special issue edited by Rudolfo Anaya and Robert Con Davis-Undiano.

Marchi, Regina M. 2008. "Race and the News: Coverage of Martin Luther King Day and Dia de los Muertos in Two California Dailies." *Journalism Studies* 9 (6): 925–44.

———. 2009. *Day of the Dead in the USA: The Migration and Transformation of a Cultural Phenomenon.* New Brunswick, N.J.: Rutgers University Press.

———. 2013. "Hybridity and Authenticity in US Day of the Dead Celebrations." *Journal of American Folklore* 126 (501): 272–301.

Marcos, Sylvia. 2009. "Mesoamerican Women's Indigenous Spirituality: Decolonizing Religious Beliefs." *Journal of Feminist Studies in Religion* 25 (2): 25–45.

———. 2013. "Beyond Binary Categories: Mesoamerican Religious Sexuality." In *Religion and Sexuality in Cross Cultural Perspective,* edited by Stephen Ellingson and M. Christian Green, 111–35. New York: Routledge.

Mares, E. A. 2004.*With the Eyes of A Raptor.* San Antonio, Tex.: Wings Press.

Mariátegui, José Carlos. 1971. *Seven Interpretive Essays on Peruvian Reality.* Translated by Marjory Urquidi. Austin: University of Texas Press.

Marsh, George Perkins. 2003. *Man and Nature.* Seattle: University of Washington Press. Originally published 1864.

Martí, José. 1982. "Aboriginal American Authors." In *On Art and Literature: Critical Writings,* edited by Philip S. Foner, translated by Elinor Randall, 201–4. New York: Monthly Review Press.

———. 1998. "Our America." In *The Health Anthology of American Literature,* 746–53. Vol. 2. 3rd ed. Boston: Houghton Mifflin.

Martin, Jane Roland. 2002. *Cultural Miseducation: In Search of a Democratic Solution.* New York: Teachers College Press.

Martínez, Demetria. 1994. *Mother Tongue: A Novel.* New York: Ballantine Books.

Martínez, María Elena. 2008. *Genealogical Fictions: Limpieza de Sangre, Religion, and Gender in Colonial Mexico.* Stanford, Calif.: Stanford University Press.

Massey, Douglas S., and Julia Gelatt. 2010. "What Happened to the Wages of Mexican Immigrants? Trends and Interpretations." *Latino Studies* 8 (3): 328–54.

Matos Moctezuma, Eduardo. 1988. *The Great Temple of the Aztecs: Treasures of Tenochtitlan.* Translated by Doris Heyden. New York: Thames and Hudson.

McWilliams, Carey. 1968. *North from Mexico: The Spanish-Speaking People of the United States.* New York: Greenwood Press.

Menchaca, Martha. 2001. *Recovering History, Constructing Race: The Indian, Black, and White Roots of Mexican Americans.* Austin: University of Texas Press.

Mignolo, Walter D. 2012. *Local Histories/Global Designs: Coloniality, Subaltern Knowledges, and Border Thinking.* Princeton, N.J.: Princeton University Press.

Miller, Marilyn Grace. 2004. *The Rise and Fall of the Cosmic Race: The Cult of Mestizaje in Latin America.* Austin: University of Texas Press.

Mintz, Steven. 2016. "Viva La Raza." *Digital History.* (ID. 3347). www.digitalhistory.uh.edu/, accessed May 10, 2016.

Mitford, Jessica. 1963. *The American Way of Death.* New York: Buccaneer Books.

Molina, Natalia. 2014. *How Race Is Made in America: Immigration, Citizenship, and the Historical Power of Racial Scripts.* Berkeley: University of California Press.

Montiel, Miguel, Tomás Atencio, and E. A. Mares. 2009. *Resolana: Emerging Chicano Dialogues on Community and Globalization.* Tucson: University of Arizona Press.

Montoya, María E. 2000. "Beyond Internal Colonialism: Class, Gender, and Culture as Challenges to Chicano Identity." *Voices of a New Chicana/o History,* edited by Refugio I. Rochín and Dennis N. Valdés, 183–95. East Lansing: Michigan State University Press.

Moraga, Cherríe L. 2011. *A Xicana Codex of Changing Consciousness: Writings, 2000–2010.* Durham, N.C.: Duke University Press.

Morgan, Lewis Henry. 1964. *Ancient Society.* Cambridge, Mass.: Belknap Press of Harvard University Press. Originally published 1877.

Morrison, Toni. 1992. *Playing in the Dark: Whiteness in the Literary Imagination.* Cambridge, Mass.: Harvard University Press.

Motel, Seth, and Eileen Patten. 2012. "Characteristics of the 60 Largest Metropolitan Areas by Hispanic Population." Pew Hispanic Center. 1–21. www.pewhispanic.org/, accessed July 26, 2016.

Muñoz, Carlos, Jr. 2007. *Youth, Identity, Power: The Chicano Movement.* New York: Verso.

Navarro, Isidro Moreno. 1973. *Los cuadros del mestizaje Americano: Studio antropológico del mestizaje.* Madrid: José Porrúa Turanza.

Nostrand, Richard L. 1972. *The Hispano Homeland.* Norman: University of Oklahoma Press.

Olivares, Julián. 1985. "The Search for Being, Identity, and Form in the Works of Tomás Rivera." *Revista Chicano-Requeña* 13 (3–4): 66–80.

Olivas, Daniel A., ed. 2008. *Latinos in Lotusland: An Anthology of Contemporary Southern California Literature.* Tempe, Ariz.: Bilingual Press.

———. 2011. *The Book of Want.* Tucson: University of Arizona Press.

Omi, Michael, and Howard Winant. 1986. *Racial Formation in the United States: From the 1960s to the 1980s.* New York: Routledge and Kegan Paul.

Ortiz, Vilma, and Edward Telles. 2012. "Racial Identity and Racial Treatment of Mexican Americans." *Race and Social Problems.* 4 (1): 41–56.

Ortíz-Torres, Rubén. 2000. "Cathedrals on Wheels." In *Customized: Art Inspired by Hot Rods, Low Riders, and American Car Culture*, edited by Nora Donnelly, 37–38. New York: Abrams.

Padilla, Genaro. 1991. "Myth and Comparative Cultural Nationalism: The Ideological Uses of Aztlán." In *Aztlán: Essays on the Chicano Homeland*, edited by Rudolfo A. Anaya and Francisco Lomeli, 111–34. Albuquerque: University of New Mexico Press.

Painter, Nell Irvin. 2010. *The History of White People.* New York: W. W. Norton.

Paredes, Américo. 1971. "Mexican Legendry and the Rise of the Mestizo: A Survey." In *American Folk Legend: A Symposium*, edited by Wayland D. Hand, 97–107. Berkeley: University of California Press.

———. 1989. *"With His Pistol in His Hand": A Border Ballad and Its Hero.* Austin: University of Texas Press. Originally published 1958.

———. 1993. *Folklore and Culture on the Texas-Mexican Border.* Austin: Center for Mexican American Studies, University of Texas Press.

Parsons, James J. 1985. "'Bioregionalism' and 'Watershed Consciousness.'" *Professional Geographer* 37 (1): 1–6.

Paz, Octavio. 1985. *The Labyrinth of Solitude. The Labyrinth of Solitude and Other Writings*, 7–212. Translated by Lysander Kemp, Yara Milos, and Rachel Phillips Belash. New York: Grove Press. Originally published in 1959.

Peña, Devon G., ed. 1998. *Chicano Culture, Ecology, Politics: Subversive Kin.* Tucson: University of Arizona Press.

Pérez, Emma. 1999. *The Decolonial Imaginary: Writing Chicanas into History.* Bloomington: Indiana University Press.

Pérez, William, and Richard Douglas. 2011. *Undocumented Latino College Students: Their Socio-emotional and Academic Experience.* El Paso, Tex.: LFB Scholarly Publishing.

Pérez-Torres, Rafael. 1995. *Movements in Chicano Poetry: Against Myths, against Margins.* Cambridge: Cambridge University Press.

———. 1999. "Whither Aztlán? Considering a Millennial Chicana/o Studies." *Genre* 32 (1 and 2): 99–114. Special issue edited by Rudolfo Anaya and Robert Con Davis-Undiano.

———. 2006. *Mestizaje: Critical Uses of Race in Chicano Culture.* Minneapolis: University of Minnesota Press.

Pike, Fredrick B. 1986. *The Politics of the Miraculous in Peru: Haya de la Torre and the Spiritualist Tradition.* Lincoln: University of Nebraska Press.

Plascencia, Luis F. B. 1983. "Low Riding in the Southwest: Cultural Symbols in the Mexican Community." In *History, Culture, and Society: Chicano Studies in the 1980s,* 141–75. Ypsilanti, Mich.: Bilingual Press.

Power of Ideas. 1999. Robert Con Davis-Undiano, host. "Luis Jiménez." University of Oklahoma, DVD.

Pulido, Laura. 1996. *Environmentalism and Economic Justice: Two Chicano Cases from the Southwest.* Tucson: University of Arizona Press.

———. 1998. "Ecological Legitimacy and Cultural Essentialism: Hispano Grazing in North New Mexico." In *Chicano Culture, Ecology, Politics: Subversive Kin,* edited by Devon G. Peña, 121–40. Tucson: University of Arizona Press.

Quijano, Aníbal. 1976. "Imperialism and the Working Class in Latin America." *Latin American Perspectives* 3 (1): 15–18.

———. 1983. "Imperialism and Marginality in Latin America." *Latin American Perspectives* 10 (37–38): 76–85.

———. 1989. "Paradoxes of Modernity in Latin America." *International Journal of Politics, Culture, and Society* 3 (2): 147–77.

———. 1993. "Modernity, Identity, and Utopia in Latin America." *boundary 2* 20 (3): 140–55.

———. 2000. "Coloniality of Power, Eurocentrism, and Latin America." *Nepantla* 1 (3): 533–80.

———. 2002. "The Return of the Future and Questions about Knowledge." *Current Sociology* 50 (1): 75–87.

———. 2007. "Coloniality and Modernity/Rationality." *Cultural Studies* 21 (2–3): 168–78.

Quinn-Sánchez, Kathryn. 2015. *Identity in Latin American and Latina Literature.* Lanham, Md.: Lexington Books.

Quiñones, Juan Gómez. 1990. *Chicano Politics: Reality and Promise 1940–1990.* Albuquerque: University of New Mexico Press.

Ramos, E. Carmen. 2012. "The Latino Presence in American Art." *American Art* 26 (2): 7–13.

Rebolledo, Tey Diana. 1995. *Women Singing in the Snow: A Cultural Analysis of Chicana Literature.* Tucson: University of Arizona Press.

———. 1999. "The Tools in the Toolbox: Representing Work in Chicana Writing." *Genre* 32 (1 and 2): 41–52. Special issue edited by Rudolfo Anaya and Robert Con Davis-Undiano.

Resmovits, Joy. 2014. "Americans Schools Are Still Racist, Government Report Finds." *Huffington Post*. www.huffingtonpost.com, accessed July 24, 2016.

Retamar, Roberto Fernández. 1976. "Nuestra América y Occidente." *Casas de las Américas* 98: 36–57.

———. 1979. *José Martí: Ensayos sobre arte y literature*. Havana: Editorial Letras Cubanas.

Reyes, David, and Tom Waldman. 1998. *Land of a Thousand Dances: Chicano Rock 'n Roll from Southern California*. Albuquerque: University of New Mexico Press.

Rich, Adrienne. 1979. "Toward a Woman-Centered University." In *On Lies, Secrets, and Silence: Selected Prose, 1966–1978*, 125–55. New York: W. W. Norton.

———.1994. "Resisting Amnesia: History and Personal Life." In *Book, Bread, and Poetry: Selected Prose 1979–1985*, 136–59. New York: W. W. Norton.

Rishel, Joseph J., and Suzanne Stratton-Pruitt, eds. 2006. *The Arts in Latin America 1492–1820*. Philadelphia: Philadelphia Museum of Art.

Ritch, William G. 1885. *Aztlán: The History, Resources and Attractions of New Mexico*. Boston: D. Lothrop.

Rivera, Tómas. 1980. "Tomás Rivera." In *Chicano Authors: Inquiry by Interview*, edited by Bruce-Novoa, 137–62. Austin: University of Texas Press.

———. 1992a. "The Searchers." In *Tomás Rivera: The Complete Works*, edited by Julián Olivares, 285–91. Houston: Arte Publico Press.

———. 1992b. . . . *y no se lo tragó la tierra* / . . . *And the Earth Did Not Devour Him*. Translated by Evangelina Vigil-Piñon. Houston: Arte Publico Press. Originally published 1971.

Roberts-Camps, Traci. 2008. *Gendered Self-Consciousness in Mexican and Chicana Women Writers: The Female Body as an Instrument of Political Resistance*. Lewiston, N.Y.: Edwin Mellen Press.

Rodriguez, Richard. 1982. *Hunger of Memory: The Education of Richard Rodriguez*. New York: Bantam.

———. 1992. *Days of Obligation: An Argument with My Mexican Father*. New York: Penguin.

———. 2002. *Brown: The Last Discovery of America*. New York: Penguin.

Rodríguez, Sylvia. 1987. "Land, Water, and Ethnic Identity in Taos." In *Land, Water and Culture: New Perspective on Hispanic Land Grants*, edited by Charles L. Briggs and John R. Van Ness, 313–403. Albuquerque: University of New Mexico Press.

Rodriguez-Salgado, M. J. 1997. "Christians, Civilized, and Spanish: Multiple Identities in Sixteenth-Century Spain." *Transactions of the Royal Historical Society* 8: 233–51.

Rosaldo, Renato, and William Flores. 1997. "Identity, Conflict, and Evolving Latino Communities: Cultural Citizenship in San Jose, California." In *Latino*

Cultural Citizenship: Claiming Identity, Space, and Rights, edited by William Flores and Rina Benmayor, 57–96. Boston: Beacon.

Rosales, F. Arturo. 1996. *Chicano!: The History of the Mexican American Civil Rights Movement*. Houston: Arte Publico Press.

Saldívar, José David. 1991. *The Dialectics of Our America*. Durham. N.C.: Duke University Press.

———. 1997. *Border Matters: Remapping American Cultural Studies*. Berkeley: University of California Press.

Saldívar, Ramón. 1990. *Chicano Narrative: The Dialectics of Difference*. Madison: University of Wisconsin Press.

Saldívar-Hull, Sonia. 2000. *Feminism on the Border: Chicana Gender, Politics and Literature*. Berkeley: University of California Press.

Salinas, Lupe S. *U.S. Latinos and Criminal Injustice*. East Lansing: Michigan State University Press, 2015.

Sánchez, George J. 1993. *Becoming Mexican American: Ethnicity, Culture and Identity in Chicano Los Angeles, 1900–1945*. New York: Oxford University Press.

Sandiford, Keith A. 2010. *The Cultural Politics of Sugar: Caribbean Slavery and Narratives of Colonialism*. Cambridge: Cambridge University Press.

Sandoval, Anna Marie. 2008. *Toward a Latina Feminism of the Americas: Repression and Resistance in Chicana and Mexicana Literature*. Austin: University of Texas Press.

Sauer, Carl O. 1962. "Homestead and Community in the Middle Border." *Landscape* 20 (2): 44–47.

Schiebinger, Londa. 2004. *Nature's Body: Gender in the Making of Modern Science*. New Brunswick, N.J.: Rutgers University Press.

Seed, Patricia. 1988. *To Love, Honor, and Obey in Colonial Mexico: Conflicts Over Marriage Choice, 1574–1821*. Stanford, Calif.: Stanford University Press.

Segura, Denise A. 2001. "Challenging the Chicano Text: Toward a More Inclusive Contemporary Causa." *Signs* 26 (2): 541–50.

Sennett, Richard. 1994. *Flesh and Stone: The Body and the City in Western Civilization*. New York: W. W. Norton.

Serros, Michele. 2000. *How to Be a Chicana Role Model*. New York: Riverhead Books.

Sharma, Nitasha Tamar. 2010. *Hip Hop Desis: South Asian Americans, Blackness, and a Global Race Consciousness*. Durham, N.C.: Duke University Press.

Shildrick, Margrit. 2000. "The Body." In *Encyclopedia of Feminist Theories*, edited by Lorraine Code, 63–65. New York: Routledge.

Shiva, Vandana. 1998. "Subversive Kin: A Politics of Diversity." In *Chicano Culture, Ecology, Politics: Subversive Kin*, edited by Devon G. Peña, vii-ix. Tucson: University of Arizona Press.

Shotwell, Alexis. 2011. *Knowing Otherwise: Race, Gender, and Implicit Understanding.* University Park: Pennsylvania State University Press.

Shusterman, Richard. 2008. *Body Consciousness: A Philosophy of Mindfulness and Somaesthetics.* Cambridge: Cambridge University Press.

———. 2012. *Thinking through the Body: Essays in Somaesthetics.* New York: Cambridge University Press.

Sleeter, C., ed. 1991. *Empowerment through Multicultural Education.* Albany: State University of New York Press.

Solorzano, Daniel G., and Tara J. Yosso. 2001. "Critical Race and LatCrit Theory and Method: Counterstorytelling Chicana and Chicano Graduate School Experiences." *International Journal of Qualitative Studies in Education* 14: 471–95.

Sommers, Joseph, and Tomas Ybarra-Frausto, eds. 1979. *Modern Chicano Writers: A Collection of Critical Essays.* Englewood Cliffs, NJ: Prentice-Hall.

Storey, John. 2003. *Inventing Popular Culture: From Folklore to Globalization.* Malden, Mass.: Blackwell Publishing. Kindle Edition.

Tafolla, Carmen. 1993. "La Malinche." In *Infinite Divisions: An Anthology of Chicana Literature*, edited by Tey Diana Rebolledo and Eliana S. Rivero, 198–99. Tucson: University of Arizona Press.

Taine, Hypolyte A. 1871. *On Intelligence.* Translated by T. D. Haye. London: L. Reeve.

———. 1872. *History of English Literature.* Vol. 2. Translated by H. Van Laun. Edinburgh: Edmonton and Douglas.

Takaki, Ronald. 1993. *A Different Mirror: A History of Multicultural America.* Boston: Little, Brown.

Telles, Edward E., and Vilma Ortiz. 2008. *Generations of Exclusion: Mexican Americans, Assimilation, and Race.* New York: Russell Sage Foundation.

Thoreau, Henry David. 2004. *Walden.* London: CRW Publishing. Originally published 1854.

Trambley, Estela Portillo. 1975. *Rain of Scorpions and Other Writings.* Berkeley, Calif.: Tonatiuh International.

Trotter, Robert T., II, and Juan Antonio Chavira. 1997. *Curanderismo: Mexican American Folk Healing.* 2nd ed. Athens: University of Georgia Press.

Trueba, Enrique (Henry) T. 1999. *Latinos Unidos: From Cultural Diversity to the Politics of Solidarity.* Lanham, Md.: Rowman and Littlefield.

Tuan, Yi-Fu. 1977. *Space and Place: The Perspective of Experience.* Minneapolis: University of Minnesota Press.

U.S. Department of Education. 2010–15. *Status and Trends in the Education of Racial and Ethnic Groups.* NCES. Institute of Education Sciences. http://nces.ed.gov/pubs2010/2010015.pdf, accessed July 24, 2016.

Valencia, Reynaldo Anaya, Sonia R. García, Henry Flores, and José Roberto Juárez Jr. 2004. *Mexican Americans and the Law: ¡El pueblo unido jamás sera vencido!* Edited by Adela de la Torre. Tucson: University of Arizona Press.

Vargas, Zaragosa. 2011. *Crucible of Struggle: A History of Mexican Americans from Colonial Times to the Present Era*. New York: Oxford University Press.

Vasconcelos, José, and Manuel Gamio. 1926. "The Latin-American Basis of Mexican Civilization." In *Aspects of Mexican Civilization*, 1–102. Chicago: University of Chicago Press.

———.1961. *La Raza Cósmica: Misión de la raza iberoamericana*. Madrid: Aguilar. Originally published 1925.

Vélez, Veronica, Lindsay Perez Huber, Corina Benavides Lopez, Ariana de la Luz, and Daniel G. Solorzano. 2008. "Battling for Human Rights and Social Justice: A Latina/o Critical Race Analysis of Latina/o Student Youth Activism in the Wake of 2006 Anti-Immigrant Sentiment." *Social Justice* 35: 7–27.

Vélez-Ibáñez, Carlos G. 1996. *Border Visions: Mexican Cultures of the Southwest United States*. Tucson: University of Arizona Press.

Velie, Alan R. 1998. "Indian Identity in the Nineties." *Oklahoma City University Law Review* 23 (1–2): 189–209.

Vigil, James Diego. 1991. "Car Charros: Cruising and Lowriding in the Barrio of East Los Angeles. *Latino Studies Journal* 2 (2): 71–79.

Wade, Peter, Vivette García Deister, Michael Kent, María Fernanda Olarte Sierra, and Adriana Díaz del Castillo Hernández. 2014. "Nation and the Absent Presence of Race in Latin American Genomics." *Current Anthropology* 55 (5): 497–522.

Waters, Frank. 1975. *Mexico Mystique: The Coming Sixth World of Consciousness*. Athens: Swallow Press/Ohio University Press.

Wertheimer, Eric. 1999. *Imagined Empires: Incas, Aztecs, and the New World of American Literature, 1771–1876*. Cambridge: Cambridge University Press.

Wilde, Jean T., and William Kimmel, eds. 1962. *The Search for Being: Essays from Kierkegaard to Sartre on the Problem of Existence*. New York: Twayne Publishers.

Willinsky, John. 2000. *Learning to Divide the World: Education at Empire's End*. Minneapolis: University of Minnesota Press.

Wilshire, Diana. 1988. "The Uses of Myth, Image, and the Female Body in Re-Visioning Knowledge." In *Gender/Body/Knowledge: Feminist Reconstructions of Being and Knowing*, edited by Alison M. Jaggar and Susan R. Bordo, 92–114. New Brunswick, N.J.: Rutgers University Press.

Wilson, Chris. 1997. *The Myth of Santa Fe: Creating a Modern Regional Tradition*. Albuquerque: University of New Mexico Press.

Winant, Howard. 1994. *Racial Conditions: Politics, Theory, Comparisons*. Minneapolis: University of Minnesota Press.

———. 2004. *The New Politics of Race: Globalism, Difference, Justice*. Minneapolis: University of Minnesota Press.

Yeats, W. B. 1999. *Autobiographies. The Collected Works of W. B. Yeats III*. Edited by William H. O'Donnell and Douglass N. Archbald. New York: Scribner.

Yosso, Tara J. 2006. *Critical Race Counterstories along the Chicana/Chicano Educational Pipeline.* New York: Routledge.

Young, Robert J. C. 1995. *Colonial Desire: Hybridity in Theory, Culture, and Race.* New York: Routledge.

———. 2004. *White Mythologies: Writing History and the West.* 2nd ed. New York: Routledge.

Yuval-Davis, Nira. 2011. "Power, Intersectionality, and the Politics of Belonging." *FREIA Working Paper Series* 75: 1–16.

Index